Christiane Strohm

United States and European Union Auditor Independence Regulation

GABLER EDITION WISSENSCHAFT

Forschungsreihe
Rechnungslegung und Steuern

Herausgegeben von
Professor Dr. Christoph Watrin,
Universität Münster

Christiane Strohm

United States and European Union Auditor Independence Regulation

Implications for Regulators and Auditing Practice

With a foreword by Prof. Dr. Christoph Watrin

Deutscher Universitäts-Verlag

Bibliografische Information Der Deutschen Bibliothek
Die Deutsche Bibliothek verzeichnet diese Publikation in der Deutschen Nationalbibliografie; detaillierte bibliografische Daten sind im Internet über <http://dnb.ddb.de> abrufbar.

Dissertation Universität Münster, 2005

D6

1. Auflage März 2006

Lektorat: Ute Wrasmann / Anita Wilke

Der Deutsche Universitäts-Verlag ist ein Unternehmen von Springer Science+Business Media.
www.duv.de

Umschlaggestaltung: Regine Zimmer, Dipl.-Designerin, Frankfurt/Main
Druck und Buchbinder: Rosch-Buch, Scheßlitz
Gedruckt auf säurefreiem und chlorfrei gebleichtem Papier
Printed in Germany

ISBN 3-8350-0287-2

Foreword

In recent years, the Sarbanes-Oxley-Act has received international attention unlike few other laws. The rules presented in this act take influence on business practice and dominate the ongoing discussion on business constitution in the USA as well as in Europe. Christiane Strohm's dissertation investigates the effects of the Sarbanes-Oxley-Act and the revised 8th EU-Directive – as a response toward the US-law – on auditing.

This study is innovative for several reasons. Combining an auditor independence risk model (Mock et. al. 2005) with considerations on task complexity (Bonner 1994, 1995), the author develops an experimental approach that can be put to future use in research on regulation. In the following, the American and European regulations are investigated in three separate experiments that are conducted with participants of international background. With this, the author provides – to my knowledge – the first empirical comparative analysis of the Sarbanes Oxley Act and the revised 8th EU-Directive.

As both statutes provide representative examples for rules-based (Sarbanes-Oxley-Act) and for principles-oriented (8th EU-directive) regulation, this work deserves recognition from beyond the limited scientific community of those interested in auditing. The experimental design and the results generated by this study are of high significance for the general discussion on the advantages of either rules-based or principles-oriented regulation that characterizes the current controversial debate on corporate governance.

This study, awarded with summa cum laude, was presented at the PhD workshop of the European Audit Research Network in October 2005 in Amsterdam, Netherlands, where it raised considerable attention. The author has furthermore been accepted for the American Accounting Association Auditing Section Doctoral Consortium in January 2006 in Los Angeles, USA. For the future, I wish this work all the attention and academic recognition it deserves.

Christoph Watrin

Preface

This document was accepted as a dissertation by the Wirtschaftswissenschaftliche Fakultät of the Westfälische Wilhelms-Universität Münster in November 2005. The development of such a document is only possible with the support of many individuals who have contributed to this thesis in many different ways. To the many people who have enabled me to bring this project to fruition, my sincere thanks. Especially I want to thank the following persons:

Many thanks to my supervisors, Professor Christoph Watrin (Westfälische Wilhelms-Universität Münster, Germany) and Professor Theodore Mock (University of Southern California Los Angeles, USA and Universiteit Maastricht) who generously provided the opportunity, continuing support, guidance and space to learn.

I am also most grateful to Assistant Professor Tatiana Sandino for her suggestions on my research. Thank you to Melissa Boyle for providing valuable input. Thanks to Ralf Struffert for helpful research discussions and for keeping the faith during my stay at the University of Southern California.

I appreciate the financial support of the German Academic Exchange Service for major parts of this research.

My sincere thanks to the many individuals who participated in the experimental studies.

This document is dedicated to my parents. They constantly supported me throughout this project.

Thank you all.

Christiane Strohm

Table of Contents

List of Tables

List of Figures

List of Equations

List of Abbreviations

AICPA	American Institute of Certified Public Accountants
al.	alii *(others)*
ANOVA	Analysis of Variance
BAnz.	Bundesanzeiger
BGBl.	Bundesgesetzblatt
CEO	Chief Executive Officer
Co	Company
CPA	Certified Public Accountant
Df	degrees of freedom
e.g.	exempli gratia *(for example)*
e.V.	eingetragener Verein
EEC	European Economic Community
EU	European Union
F	F-statistic
FEE	Fédération des Experts Comptables Européens *(The European Federation of Accountants)*
H	Hypothesis
HGB	Handelsgesetzbuch *(German Commercial Code)*
i.e.	id est *(that is)*
IDW	Institut der Wirtschaftsprüfer in Deutschland e.V.
IFAC	International Federation of Accountants
IT	Information Technology
KPMG	Klynveld Peat Marwick Goerdeler
LLP	Limited Liability Partnership
MAS	Management Advisory Service(s)
P	p-value

PCAOB	Public Company Accounting Oversight Board
PwC	PriceWaterhouseCoopers
R&P	Roberts & Partner
RGBl.	Reichsgesetzblatt
RPICS	Roberts & Partner Independence Compliance System
RQ	Research Question
S&H	Streich & Holz
SDA	Scuola di Direzione Aziendale
SEC	Securities and Exchange Commission
Std. Dev.	Standards Deviations
t	t-statistic
UK	United Kingdom
URN	Uniform Resource Names
US	United States
USA	United States of America
US-GAAP	United States Generally Accepted Accounting Principles
WP	Wirtschaftsprüfung

Chapter I. Introduction

A. Motivation and Objective

The harsh criticism of the audit profession, which followed in the wake of the Enron collapse, had a major impact on regulators' activities worldwide. One result of the Enron debacle was that regulators started to address auditor independence issues as never before,[1] claiming auditors' independence was impaired for the following reasons:

1. Arthur Andersen, the audit firm of Enron, was earning more from the provision of non-audit than audit services ($27 million and $25 million, respectively) and non-audit services included assisting Enron devise accounting schemes compliant with US-GAAP, but which had the objective of keeping liabilities off the balance sheet,
2. Enron had been the managing partner's only client for some years and was the principal client of Andersen's local office, thus both the partner and the office were economically dependent on retaining Enron as a client,
3. a number of ex-Andersen staff worked for Enron and the relationship was believed to be very intimate, and
4. there were concerns about how Andersen managed its internal quality control and its partner incentive mechanisms (Fearnley and Beattie 2004: 118).

After the Enron collapse and several other accounting scandals,[2] there were demands for significant revisions in accounting practices, foremost being the rotation of audit firms, the implementation of an effective audit committee and the banning of the provision of many non-audit services by incumbent auditors.

Regulating bodies in the United States and the European Union provided two different responses: the Sarbanes-Oxley Act of the United States (2002) and the European Union proposal for a revised 8th Directive (European Commission 2004a). These regulations include more severe penalties and larger enforcement budgets to help protect financial markets from fraud and other inappropriate behavior. However, although the goals of both regulations are essentially the same, the paths taken by the American and European regulators to achieve their objectives are quite different.

[1] For a more detailed analysis of structural deficits of the US-Corporate Governance System pre Sarbanes-Oxley see Schwarz and Holland (2002).
[2] A detailed analysis of auditors' responsibility for German accounting scandals is provided by Wüstemann (2001).

Whereas the Sarbanes-Oxley Act tends to be more rules-based, the European approach tends to be principles-oriented.

The Sarbanes-Oxley Act directly addresses audit firms and auditors, whereas the European proposal issues minimum requirements for the 25 European Member States. Thus, after the European proposal becomes law, it is each Member States' responsibility to implement, at a minimum, these requirements into national law to promote harmonization in Europe. This explains to some extent why the European conceptual approach is based on principles, because it provides Member States with the possibility to address the national legal environment by adding local requirements which may either be rules-based or principles-based.

Since I am interested in the effects of solely rules-based and principles-based regulation, it is important for this research to assume that Member States will adopt only the principles-based requirements as proposed by the European Union. However, even if the Member States add local requirements, this research will provide some evidence on whether these additional requirements should be more rules-based or principles-based.

In line with this, I will provide a short summary of the regulatory actions of Germany prior to the adoption of the European proposal but after the Sarbanes-Oxley Act was issued. Many European Member States issued national regulations concerning auditor independence regulation as a response to the Sarbanes-Oxley Act and started to issue requirements as a response to the European Union proposal and other recommendations. Thus, as soon as the European proposal becomes law, many European Member States will have to adjust their national requirements to satisfy the European requirements.

The primary objective of this research is to study the effect of regulation approach, which is based on detailed rules or on broad principles, on subjects' decisions as they apply the regulation. Since auditor independence regulation is designed to help minimize auditor independence risk in practice, accurate communication is critical. Such regulation should reduce both independence in fact and independence in appearance. Impaired auditor independence in fact occurs when the auditor compromises professional decisions. When a third party reasonably concludes that auditor integrity or objectivity is compromised, auditor independence in appearance is questioned (International Federation of Accountants 2004).

However, there is little research on the approach of regulation where two different regulation approaches are involved. The main aim of this research is to contribute to the existing body of knowledge on regulation approaches in accounting by investigating the effects of rules- and principles-based auditor independence regulation on auditor independence risk. The first research question asks whether the approach to auditor independence regulation is associated with the effectiveness of the regulation in reducing risks to auditor independence in fact. This research question is studied in experiments one and two. I assess the effectiveness of the regulation approach by investigating subjects' decisions about the performance of additional non-audit services for a financial statement audit client[3].

Experiments one and two test whether there is a difference in the communication accuracy and safeguarding intention of the regulation depending on the regulatory approach used. Prior research suggests that the choice of regulation approach has an incremental effect on behavior, since the communication accuracy of the regulations may differ according to complexity (Nelson 2003).

A rules-based approach includes both specific prohibitions, such as the prevention of some non-audit services, as well as specific requirements, such as the pre-approval of non-audit services by the audit committee. Because rules are written with explicit detail, it is expected that what is required and what is prohibited will be more clearly understood, and this suggests higher communication accuracy. Alternatively, the principles-based approach requires greater interpretation of what is or is not allowed, and this suggests lower communication accuracy.

A third experimental study, to be discussed later, was designed to address questions related to stakeholders' assessments of independence risk. Specifically, experiment three investigates whether greater transparency in the way audit firms communicate the policies and procedures that they use to minimize independence risk is an effective mechanism to reduce the risk of auditor independence in appearance as assessed by stakeholders.

---

[3] The term audit client is used as a synonym for 'issuer' as defined in Section 2 (7) of the Sarbanes-Oxley Act and for 'public interest entities' as defined in Article 2 (11) in the European proposal for a revised 8th Directive.

This thesis uses the auditor independence risk model by Mock, Srivastava and Turner (2005)[4] and Task Complexity Theory (e.g., Wood 1986, Bonner 1994, Nelson 2003) as overall theoretical frameworks. Figure 1 presents an extract of these frameworks modified for this research. Auditor independence regulations, which itself differs in how requirements are specified (see the rectangle labeled Safeguard: Auditor Independence Regulation), are issued to help mitigate threats (incentives, opportunities and/or lack of integrity). Regulations concerning the opportunity to provide certain non-audit services may affect an audit firm's decision on whether to perform additional non-audit services for a financial statement audit client (see the rectangle labeled Audit Firm Decisions).

Under-compliance occurs when a regulation is not applied where it is intended to be applied (e.g., a certain service is prohibited, but the regulation is interpreted as if this service is allowed to be performed). Over-compliance occurs when a regulation is applied where it is not intended to be applied (e.g., a certain service is allowed, but the regulation is interpreted as if this service is prohibited). As for this research, I define the optimal decision making quality as the non-audit decision based on auditor independence regulation that complies exactly with the intended outcome. Thus, decision making is compromised when subjects under or over-comply with the regulation, meaning the decision deviates from the intended outcome.

Based on the quality of this decision, incentive and opportunity threats (see the rectangles labeled respectively) may lead to biased auditor decisions concerning audit work and the client's financial reporting (see the rectangle labeled respectively)[5]. For example, an audit firm may perform additional non-audit services for a financial statement audit client, although the auditor independence regulation intends to restrict these services.

Due to this multi-service engagement, incentive and opportunity threats may occur. Incentives to compromise the audit work and the client's financial reporting may derive from additional non-audit fees and may lead to impaired auditor independence (see the rectangle labeled Auditor Decisions). Furthermore, an opportunity related to additional knowledge concerning the client's business and a strong professional relationship may also affect auditor's independence.

---

[4] See Appendix 1 for the complete model.

[5] In Figure 1, integrity is assumed not to be directly affected by the audit firm decisions concerning the performance of additional non-audit services.

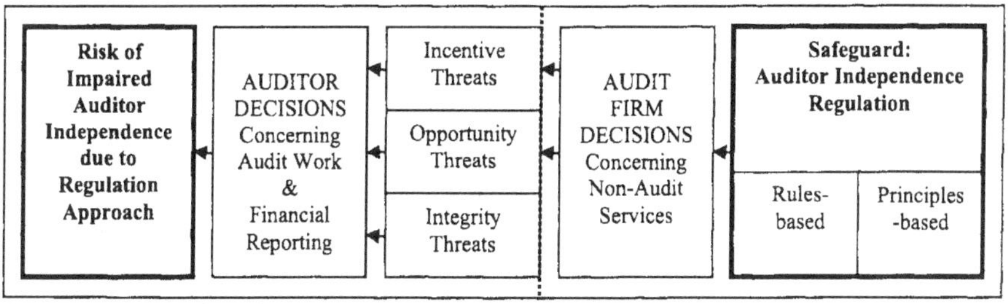

Figure 1: Auditor Independence Risk and Regulation

B. Empirical Studies

Experiment on Regulation Approach and Knowledge

Task complexity decreases with an increase in task-specific knowledge. To achieve a task, people need task-specific knowledge (Bonner 2005). Since I study the complexity of regulation, I am concerned with the decision maker's knowledge about specific regulatory requirements, including their ability to understand the content and to apply the regulation as intended. Regulatory knowledge can be present due to experience in the field, and one can assume auditors and assurance partners have more task-specific knowledge due to both training and experience than novices.

Different knowledge levels can also be generated through experimental manipulation. This means that higher level knowledge can be achieved through a special introduction into the field of the regulation and through special tools to use this knowledge given in an experimental setting. The first experiment addresses the questions of whether the approach to auditor independence regulation and the knowledge level of a person applying the regulation is associated with the effectiveness of regulation to reduce auditor independence risk. Figure 2 shows the modified auditor independence risk and task complexity models including the experimental design used.

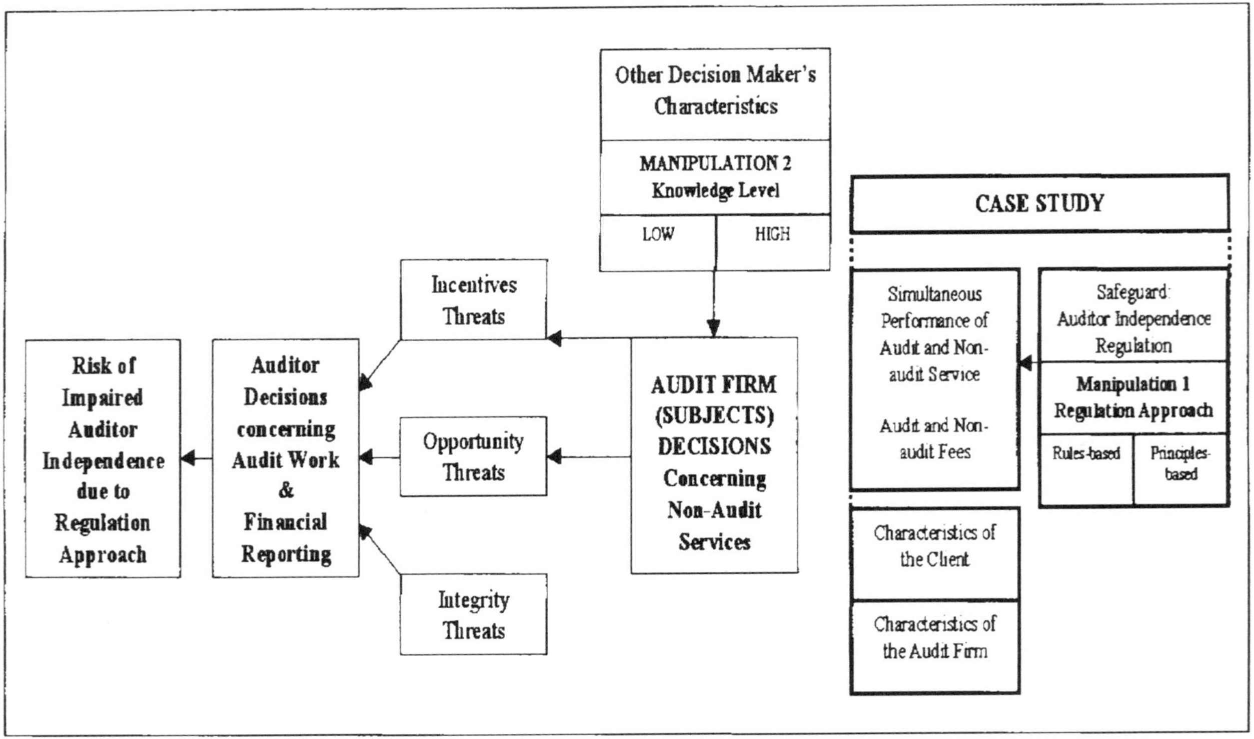

Figure 2: Auditor Independence Risk and the Experiment 1 Manipulations of Regulation Approach and Knowledge

I study the different effects of rules- versus principles-based auditor independence regulation and different knowledge levels in an experimental 2 x 2 between subjects design. In the first experiment I manipulated regulation approach and thus task complexity by taking European or Sarbanes-Oxley Act regulation which proxy for principles- or rules-based regulation respectively (see the rectangle labeled Manipulation 1) and provided knowledge at two levels (low and high) (see the rectangle labeled Manipulation 2). In the high knowledge treatment, subjects got a detailed introduction into the audit firm's own policies and procedures addressing auditor independence issues.

This information was given to provide subjects with the knowledge needed to perform the task of deciding whether the audit firm should perform additional non-audit services for a financial statement audit client. With more information the interpretation of auditor independence regulation is expected to be as intended by the regulation. Subjects of the low knowledge setting did not get any special introduction into the field of the regulation and therefore may lack the information needed to apply the regulation as intended.

The experiment was conducted using 39 undergraduate students, who were put in the position of a deciding audit firm representative. Subjects got a case study reflecting an audit firm client engagement whereas the audit firm earns audit fees and is able to earn additional non-audit fees by performing non-audit services. Furthermore, the case study details the client characteristics, such as size, number of employees, financial strength and market presence and share (see the rectangles labeled Case Study).

The experimental task was to decide whether an audit firm should provide additional non-audit services for a financial statement audit client given different regulation approaches (see the rectangle labeled Audit Firm Decisions). In addition to integrity, other decision maker's characteristics are relevant when performing this task (see the rectangle labeled Other Decision Maker's Characteristics). Subjects' decisions concerning additional non-audit services provide measures of the dependent variables. One manipulation check question was used to test the success of both manipulations.

Results indicate the communication and safeguarding effect of a regulation to not significantly affect subject decisions, depending on regulation approach. The first experiment was used to improve the research instrument and the experimental setting.

To address possible demand effects, the audit firm-client setting of the second experiment leaves the performance decision entirely to the subjects. In addition, I increased the overall task complexity by adding regulations concerning the implementation of an audit committee. Finally, I control for the decisions subjects make by asking them related questions in the main experiment.

Regression Analysis to Identify Relevant Threats

Additional statistical analysis was undertaken based on two post-experimental questions taken from experiment one. Subjects were asked to assess the significance of the listed fee threats to the risk of auditor independence. Three potential incentive threats were given: audit service fees, tax service fees and information technology service fees. This analysis facilitates examining the relationship between these threats and perceived auditor independence risk. Thus, the research question addressed ask for the most relevant threat, represented by fees, to auditor independence risk in a multi service audit firm-client engagement and whether auditor independence regulation is perceived to safeguard against perceived threats.

Regression analysis was undertaken to identify the most relevant threat, represented by fees, to auditor independence risk. I compared the subjects' decision depending on the regulation approach made in experiment one with their assessed fee threat perceptions from regression analysis to investigate whether auditor independence regulation safeguards against perceived threats. That is, I compare the results of experiment one with the results from the regression analysis based on the post-experimental questions. Results of regression analysis indicate that the tax fee is not assessed to be a threat. However, results of subjects' decision in experiment one show that subjects were unsure about the performance decision. Thus, the subjects' assessment of this fee threat and their decision making in experiment one are not completely consistent.

Experiment on Regulation Approach and Audit Firm-Client Characteristics

Audit firm-client characteristics affecting the audit firm's litigation risk and monetary incentives as a proxy for task motivation can compromise the safeguarding effect that an imprecise regulation has because incentive-consistent interpretation of a regulation is more likely (Bonner 2005). If an audit firm-client setting is characterized by an audit firm that is more dependent on client fees, the audit firm is more likely to interpret an inexact regulation in favor of performing a non-audit service to earn an additional fee.

The opposite situation is also conceivable. An audit firm's fear of litigation may outweigh the incentive to earn a fee. If so, then it is more likely that an imprecise regulation will be interpreted in favor of not performing a non-audit service. Thus, my research question asks whether the effectiveness of a regulation to reduce auditor independence risk is dependent on certain audit firm-client engagement characteristics affecting litigation risk and monetary incentives.

In experiment two, different effects of rules-based versus principles-based auditor independence regulation and different audit firm-client engagement characteristics were studied in an experimental 2 x 2 between subjects design. The research design is shown in Figure 3. I again manipulated regulation approach and thus complexity by taking Sarbanes-Oxley Act or European regulation which proxy rules- or for principles-based regulation respectively (see the rectangle labeled Manipulation 1).

Litigation risk and monetary incentives were manipulated at two levels (low and high). The high litigation risk and monetary incentives manipulation depicted a small audit firm in terms of employees, services offered and international presence, versus a large client in terms of employees, international presence, market position and management tenure which represent major audit firm and client characteristics, respectively. In addition, the relative non-audit and audit fee amounts represented a great portion of the total revenues the audit firm is earning. This manipulation captures both a weak position for the audit firm in a potential litigation situation if the regulation is applied incorrectly, as well as an engagement where monetary incentives are strong. In comparison, subjects of the low litigation risk and monetary incentives version were informed that the client is small and the audit firm is large, the same characteristics given as before (see rectangle labeled Manipulation 2).

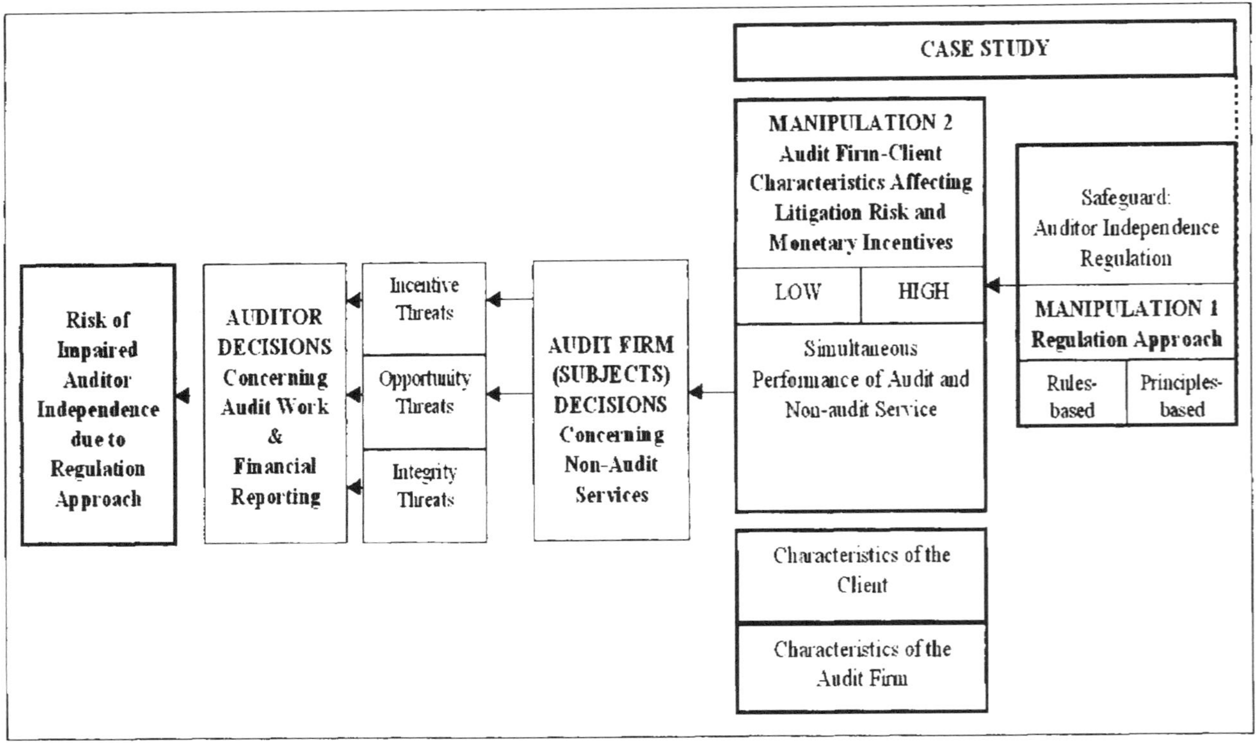

Figure 3: Auditor Independence Risk and the Experiment 2 Manipulations of Regulation Approach and Audit Firm-Client Characteristics

The audit firm-client information was incorporated into a case study in addition to other information such as the potential performance of additional non-audit services for a financial statement audit client (see the rectangle labeled Case Study). The experiment was conducted using 54 graduate students, who were put in the position of a deciding audit firm representative (see the rectangle labeled Audit Firm Decisions). The experimental task or main dependent variable studied was to decide whether an audit firm should provide additional non-audit services for a financial statement audit client.

Findings indicate that if the audit firm's risk of litigation is high, the interpretation of the regulation is compromised. The position of the audit firm in litigation is weak and the relative costs in terms of loosing an important client are higher than the monetary incentives to earn the additional fees. This may be the explanation for more conservative, safe decision making and to over-compliance of the regulation. The inverse may lead to more risky decision making and leads to under-compliance of the regulation.

Comparative Analysis of Education Differences

To study education related knowledge effects on how the regulation is interpreted and applied, I aggregated the data of the first and second experiments. Recall that undergraduate students participated in the first experiment, whereas the second experiment was conducted with accounting graduate students. The analysis was conducted using students' decisions as whether an audit firm should provide additional non-audit services for a financial statement audit client given different regulation approaches. Knowledge differences were assumed and statistically supported to be present in the two groups of students.

Education related knowledge levels did have a significant effect on how regulation is applied, that is graduate students achieved a higher level of decision making quality. More often, they tend to interpret less complex regulation as intended, but decrease in relative performance, when complexity of regulation increases.

Experiment on Transparency Effects on Perceived Auditor Independence Risk

Results of the second experiment indicated that European Union principles-based auditor independence regulation may require additional mechanisms to be put in place for effectiveness. Probably, due to the many recent audit failures, stakeholders assess auditors' independence in appearance as being highly questionable (e.g., European Federation of Accountants 2001). Thus, it is important to lower the risk of impaired auditor independence in appearance in addition to the profession's effort to lower independence in fact. However, the existing information gap between auditors and its client's stakeholders leads auditor independence in appearance to differ (Backhaus, Meffert, Bongartz and Eschweiler 2003, Mock et al. 2005). Assuming the auditor is most likely able to assess her or his level of independence in fact more precisely; this may also lead independence in appearance and fact to differ. One means of aligning auditor independence in appearance between stakeholders and auditor independence in fact and in appearance is greater transparency to serve stakeholders' needs such as is being suggested by the European Union (European Commission 2004a).

Thus, experiment three was designed to test the perceived effectiveness of a transparency report such as is being proposed by the European Union (European Commission 2004a). This report requires audit firms to publish their policies and procedures as related to auditor independence annually. For this experiment I am interested in the assessment of stakeholder representatives on the effectiveness of a transparency report. The proposed report requires audit firms to publish information about their corporate governance structure, the firm's internal quality controls, the performed quality assurance, the firm's independence practice and compliance, the audited entities, detailed fee information and the firm's continuing professional education.

The proposed transparency report is seen differently throughout the European Union. The German Chamber of Public Accountants (2004) is generally supportive towards more transparency, but questions the level of detail proposed. More supportive is the government of the United Kingdom. The United Kingdom delegation has suggested that the proposed report is an appropriate compromise between all of the stakeholders' interests. There are also costs implications; the benefits of greater transparency should outweigh those costs (United Kingdom Department of Trade and Industry 2005: 10). Finally, the European Federation of Accountants (2003: 17) believes that a transparency report provides only a meaningful mechanism if appropriate oversight is arranged. Related to this discussion I try to investigate whether a mandatory versus a voluntary and a reviewed versus a not reviewed report would better serve as an overall framework to improve an auditor's perceived level of independence risk (Houghton and Trotman 2003).

Subjects of the experiment were 91 participants in a University of Southern California conference on current regulatory developments. Two independent variables were manipulated in a 2 x 2 between subjects design. The first variable was whether the transparency report is mandatory or voluntary and the second variable was whether the transparency report was reviewed or not. Participants (accountants, auditors and financial analysts) were randomly assigned to one version.

Figure 4 shows how the transparency report is intended to affect stakeholders' perceptions of the risk of auditor independence. Furthermore, the experimental design is presented (see the rectangle labeled Transparency Report).

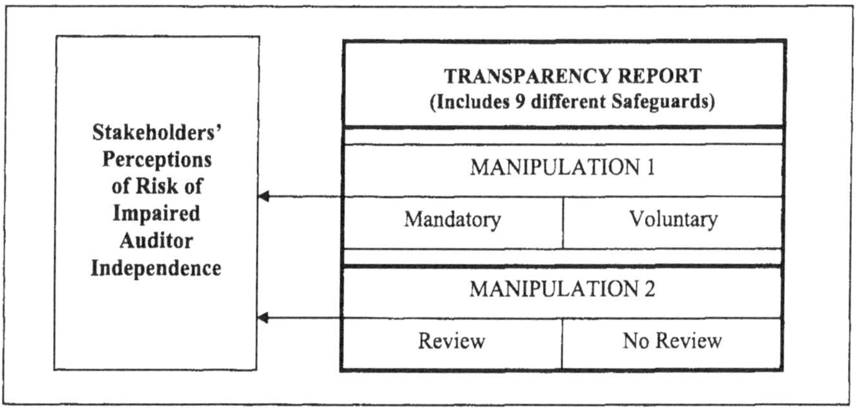

Figure 4: Stakeholders' Perceptions of Auditor Independence Risk and Transparency

Results indicate no significant difference on subject's assessments given either treatment. These outcomes may be related to the participating subjects, who were informed auditors, accountants and financial analysts. These groups of stakeholder are getting the safeguards related information throughout the professional relationship to the firm publishing a transparency report. Particularly auditors might be able to assess their level of independence (in fact) without being provided with this transparency report.

Assessment of Single Safeguards: Regression Analysis

One post experimental question addressed in experiment three asked the conference participants to indicate which of the safeguards listed in the transparency report would be more effective than the others to maintain auditor independence. Since the conference participants represent one important group of stakeholders, their assessments provide further information on which of available safeguards are perceived to be more important to align independence in appearance and in fact. Thus, I investigate which of the proposed disclosures are viewed as being relatively more important to be informed of and which are thought to contribute significantly to the maintenance of auditor independence.

The most important safeguards (policies and procedures) are perceived to be quality assurance, internal quality controls and independence practice and compliance. However, results of a performed regression analysis indicate the quality assurance, continuing professional education and internal quality control contribute the most to the assessed effectiveness of the transparency report to safeguard auditor independence. The difference between the participants' assessment and the actual contribution of the listed safeguards to maintain auditor independence shows how perceived and actual importance of safeguards may differ. Principal component analysis undertaken to investigate the reports underlying constructs and to address multicollinearity concerns indicates both direct and indirect safeguards are perceived to be important to maintain auditor independence.

C. Structure of Dissertation

Chapter 2 presents the overall theoretical framework of auditor independence as it may be impaired due to certain threats, which may be reduced by safeguards. Using the auditor independence risk model structure, I then provide a literature review followed by the main research questions in Chapter 3. After this theoretical explanation of auditor independence risk, I summarize how regulators try to reduce this risk in Chapter 4 by contrasting two competing auditor independence regulations, the United States Sarbanes-Oxley Act and the European Union proposal for a revised 8th Directive. Furthermore, Germany's auditor independence regulation is summarized to demonstrate exemplarily how a Member State responded to the Sarbanes-Oxley Act and the European Union proposal for a 8th Directive. Chapter 5 analyzes the American and European regulations by using the framework of task complexity and explaining two possible moderators' (knowledge and task motivation) of auditor independence risk, which are tested in this research. Incorporated in this theoretical framework I also develop my hypotheses. In Chapter 6, the first two experimental settings, their results and discussion are presented. Furthermore, education related knowledge effects are studied in a comparative analysis of data obtained from the two experiments. Finally, I perform additional regression analysis with data from a post-experimental question to investigate whether the regulations address perceived fee threats.

Related to my findings from experiment one and two, I then discuss in Chapter 7 consequences for European Union Regulation setting in terms of the conceptual approach and the national requirements of Germany, France and the United Kingdom and possible effects for the European capital market. Since greater transparency is one proposed means to decrease auditor independence risk in appearance, I study the effects of a mandatory versus a voluntary transparency report and of a review of the safeguards listed in the transparency report in my third experiment. Furthermore, I perform additional regression analysis to investigate which of the safeguards listed in the transparency report might be more effective than the others to maintain auditor independence. Finally, I conclude my research with implications for (European Union) regulation and state limitations and future research areas in Chapter 8.

Chapter II. Auditor Independence Risk

The purpose of this chapter is to lay the economical and theoretical explanations for auditor independence risk. Therefore, in section A I first defines the relevant terms[6] related to this research and in section B I then explain the economical changes which lead to auditor independence risk issues. In section C I extend the theoretical framework by explaining the identified threats to auditor independence and the safeguards created to reduce threats.

A. Definitions of Auditor Independence

The ex ante value of an audit to consumers of audit services (which include current and potential owners, managers and consumers of the firm's products) depends on the auditor's perceived ability to (1) discover errors or breaches in the accounting system, and (2) withstand client pressure to disclose selectively in the event a breach is discovered. In this context the level of auditor independence can be defined as the conditional probability that, given a breach has been discovered, the auditor will report the breach (DeAngelo 1981a: 115-116).

Recent scandals in the United States and the European Union have highlighted the fact that the audit is an important element in ensuring the credibility and reliability of companies' financial statements. However, significant economic damage to the capital markets and the economy may have resulted due to impaired auditor independence. In many early studies, independence is not specifically defined (Briloff 1966, Firth 1980, Gul 1989, Hartley and Ross 1972, Lavin 1976, Pany and Reckers 1983). More recent studies have defined independence as the auditor's ability to resist client pressure (Pany and Reckers 1980, Pearson and Ryan 1982, Knapp 1985) or the auditor's ability to act with integrity and objectivity (Pany and Reckers 1980, McKinley, Pany and Reckers 1985). To avoid non-specific terms such as integrity or objectivity, independence is also defined as an unbiased mental attitude in making decisions about audit work and financial reporting (Bartlett 1993). Finally, independence can be defined as freedom from those pressures and other factors that compromise, or can reasonably be expected to compromise, an auditor's ability to make unbiased audit decisions (International Standards Board 2000a).

[6] See Appendix 2 for a summary of the relevant terms and definitions.

For purposes of regulatory frameworks, independence is usually separated into two related concepts. First, independence requires independence in mind, defined as a state of mind that is unaffected by influences which compromise professional judgment and that allows an individual to act with integrity and to exercise objectivity and professional skepticism (International Federation of Accountants 2004: 17). Frameworks use the phrase "independence in mind" when referring to independence in fact, and the term "objectivity" is generally referred to as "independence" (Securities and Exchange Commission 2001, European Commission 2002). Second, independence requires independence in appearance, which is described as the avoidance of significant facts and circumstances that would cause a rational and informed third party to reasonably conclude that a firm's, or a member of the assurance team's, integrity, objectivity or professional skepticism had been compromised (International Federation of Accountants 2004: 17).

As can be seen in Figure 5, an unexpected collapse casts doubt on auditor independence. This collapse suggests the existence of risk–referred to as independence risk–that a threat may have impaired auditor independence. Independence risk is the risk that threats to auditor independence, to the extent that they are not mitigated by safeguards, compromise or can reasonably be expected to compromise, an auditor's ability to make unbiased audit decisions (Independence Standards Board 2000b). Whereas whether it is caused by impaired independence in fact or in appearance is unobserved at this point in time. If there is evidence of lack of independence due to a certain fact, independence in fact is compromised.

The appearance of an independence failure is enough to undermine confidence in audit and financial reporting. This is the suspicion (belief) that independence is impaired because independent behavior (independence in fact) is unobservable. The result of evidenced or only believed auditor failure, leads to a loss of confidence in the audit and throughout this in financial reporting, which destabilizes markets (Fearnley and Beattie 2004: 121).

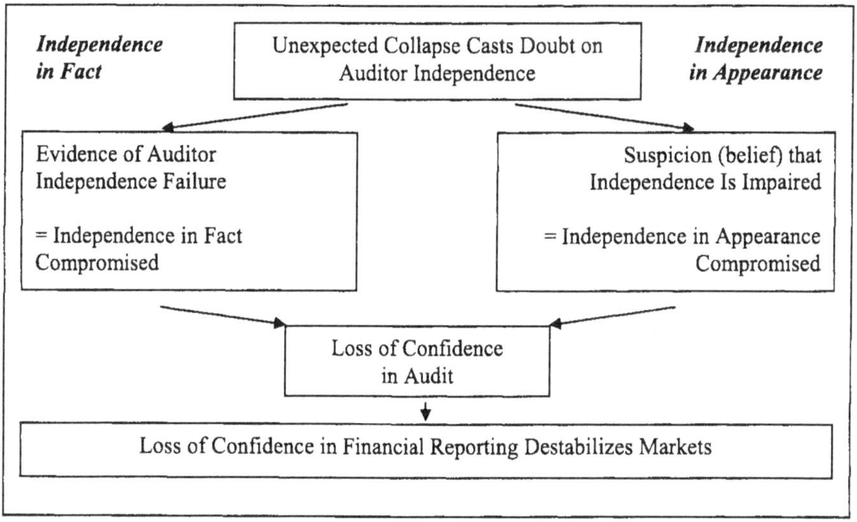

Figure 5: Independence in Fact and Independence in Appearance

B. Economic Changes: The Market of Audit and Non-Audit Services

1. Industry Exposure

A globally expanded client base in the 1950s and 1960s forced audit firms to increase the industry's exposure worldwide. Accounting firms thus evolved from relatively small, manageable partnerships to larger and more profitable businesses. Whereas audit firms used to compete in a national market, by the 1970s global competition lead to the concentration of only a small number of audit firms (through mergers or buyouts) that broadened their geographic coverage to serve the growing number of multi-state and multinational companies. Firms that did not believe in growth through merger sent trusted partners into areas where the firm had no presence in order for them to meet the local civic leaders, find some clients, and then perhaps in a few years open an office (e.g., Price Waterhouse). This decrease in accounting firms resulted in what was referred to as the Big Eight, which dominated accounting for the next 25 years: Arthur Anderson; Lybrand, Ross Bros. and Montgomery; Deloitte; Haskins and Sells; Ernst and Ernst; KPMG Main Hurdan; Peat Marwick; Price Waterhouse and Touche Ross (Brewster 2003: 100-115).[7]

[7] Empirical findings regarding the development of the German audit market are provided by Coenenberg and Marten (1993).

The late 1960s ushered in a period of great change in accounting. Until the mid 1950s, accounts had been as good a personification of diligence and fealty as any professionals. Auditors were respected as sober and trustworthy, although they did not have to work that hard to pull off that image. Third party users of financial statements simply were not considered that important, because there were only a few million investors in stock markets and auditing was not seen to help a company's stock stay afloat (Zeff 2003a: 196).

By the end of the 1960s inflation and stagnation lead to shrinking economies. Many businesses failed, and accounting firms with their hefty insurance coverage became targets for lawsuits. Auditors were threatened by all manner of third-party litigation–by regulators, investors and creditors–as both competence and integrity of the independent auditor were called into question (Brewster 2003: 130).

In addition, through the repeal of rules against competitive practices in 1973, the competition for clients increased significantly. Until the 1970s, global firms were basically splitting up a lucrative pie eight ways, and, consistent with prohibitions on competitive bidding and solicitation, pledging not to steal each other's clients. For a few more years, audit firms held to the ban against advertising and approaching other firm's clients. Eventually, however, the pressure to compete introduced a new dynamic into accounting. The pure technical type of auditing tended not to be enough to maintain competition (Zeff 2003a: 200).

2. Joint Provision of Audit and Non-Audit Services

Following their geographic expansion and increased competition, audit firms were driven towards profitability and growth to maintain competitiveness. The industry had to generate more revenues by securing new audit clients and retaining existing ones. Due to the demand of globally operating clients, other services became alternative profit generators. Thus, a growing percentage of public accounting firms' total revenues began to come from non-audit services such as taxation advice, information system design and implementation, human resource management and general consultancy (e.g., Palmrose 1986, DeFond, Raghunandan and Subramanyan 2002). This increase reflects an absolute growth in non-audit activities and stagnation in the audit service market.

To maintain competitiveness, audit firms started to provide full-service business, cross-selling non-audit services to their audit clients (Zeff 2003b: 269). When contracting is costly, incumbent auditors who possess a comparative advantage over competitors in future periods expect to earn quasi-rents (DeAngelo 1981a). For example, when client-specific start-up costs are significant, the incumbent auditor enjoys a technological advantage on future audits of a given client. On the other hand, transaction costs of changing auditors also create advantages for incumbents. Incumbent auditors can capture future benefits from technological and transaction cost advantages by setting future audit fees above the avoidable costs of producing audits. Competition for initial auditing contracts also became fierce, with many auditors setting audit fees on the initial audit engagement below total current costs (called "low-balling").

3. Auditor as an Opportunistic Agent

Recently, the contemporaneous performance of audit and non-audit services has been regulated worldwide. Monetary incentives for audit firms from providing non-audit services are believed to impair auditor independence. Agency theory explains this phenomenon by the separation of ownership by investors and control by management (Jensen and Meckling 1976). The agency relationship is specified by the contract under which the owners (principals) engage the management (agent) to manage the firm on their behalf. Since both parties to the relationship are utility maximizers, the agent will not always act in the best interest of the principals (Antle 1984: 2). This may result in divergent interests and investor losses due to opportunistic agency behavior.

Use of an external auditor is one control mechanism for reducing the risk of managers' opportunism. However, the external auditor is still hired by the owner as an agent. The auditor-agent has to produce information used in contracting with the manager (Antle 1984: 2). Therefore, the auditor is required to maintain independent from the client management. In considering the impact of non-audit services on auditor independence it needs to be pointed out that where audit and non-audit services are provided to the same client, two different contractual relationships exist (Beattie, Fearnley and Brandt 1999). The non-audit services contractual relationship is with the client while the audit contractual relationship requires that the auditor owes an additional duty to the stakeholders. Moreover, the audit is subject to regulatory oversight. However, the audit firm may perceive the purchase of an audit in the same light as that of any other service and may not distinguish between audit and non-audit services.

The provision of non-audit services to audit clients increases the economic bond between the audit firm and the client. This bond could lead to impaired independence because (1) the audit firm is unwilling to criticize the work done by its non-audit service department; (2) the audit firm does not want to lose lucrative non-audit services provided to the audit client; and (3) the audit firm does not want to lose the audit engagement. In such a situation, the auditor may possibly attempt to agree with management interpretations of accounting issues. Thus, the auditor has her or his own opportunistic incentives which may lead to biased judgments about the nature and scope of the examination (audit work) made and biased reporting as to whether the financial statements fairly represent the financial condition of the audited firm (financial reporting) (Goldman and Barlev 1974).

C. Auditor Independence Risk Models

1. Introduction

A framework conceived by Johnstone, Sutton and Warfield (2001)[8], combines certain incentives affecting independence risk and shows how they interact with situational factors to affect actual or perceived audit quality. This framework articulates the combined effects of direct incentives, indirect incentives and judgment-based decisions involving difficult accounting issues, materiality and audit conduct. Although there are supposed to be effects on independence risk, there may be a variety of factors that mitigate independence risk, including corporate governance mechanisms, regulatory oversight, audit firm policies, audit firm culture and individual auditor characteristics.

A more formal model of independence risk is established by Mock et al. (2005)[9]. Linked to the existing conceptual framework of the Independence Standards Board (2000a), the Securities and Exchange Commission (2001) and the International Federation of Accountants (2004), the model can be used to assess the role of

[8] See Appendix 3 for the complete framework.
[9] Recall the complete model is shown in Appendix 1.

incentives, opportunity and biased integrity possibly impairing auditor independence. The framework also combines judgments about the level of threats identified or the effectiveness of safeguards related to those threats, by using the Dempster-Shafer theory of belief functions, which can accept input judgments related to both quantitative and qualitative evidence.

2. Threats to Auditor Independence

a) Incentives

The first potential factor that can threaten auditor independence is an incentive. Incentives can knowingly affect auditor's decisions to become biased (Mock et al. 2005). The various codes of ethics (e.g. International Federation of Accountants 2001) and regulatory rules (e.g. Securities and Exchange Commission 2001) identify numerous incentives such as financial and employment relationships and non-audit services that may impact independence. Following Johnstone et al.'s (2001) independence risk framework, certain direct or indirect incentives affect independence risk by interacting with situational factors, which can influence actual or perceived audit quality. A potential downside risk to the auditor, in terms of both litigation and impaired reputation, can thus be assumed (Davis and Simon 1992).

Direct incentives involve actual or potential monetary benefits or the possibility that such benefits will be terminated (Johnstone et al. 2001: 5). These may be returns on investments in a firm's securities or mutual funds, contingent fees, potential employment with the client or financial dependence. The latter includes the source, relative magnitude, and continuity of fees[10], low-balling effects[11], and the reputation of the relationship. Financial dependence introduces incentives that threaten the auditor's ability to act without concern that the financial relationship will be terminated.

When the auditor possesses a personal, family or professional relationship with the client, indirect incentives may occur (Johnstone et al. 2001: 5). These incentives also arise when the auditor reviews her or his own work, including the preparation of financial statements, the recommended valuations for financial statement items such as

---

[10] The term "continuity of fees" refers to an auditor's desire not to lose a client. For a general discussion of the notion of auditor financial dependence and its relationship to auditor independence see Wallman (1996).

[11] For academic research concerning the effects of low-balling see DeAngelo (1981a).

in-process research and development, the outsourcing of internal audit services and advice on management decisions.

According to Mock et al. (2005) there are five categories of threats potentially creating an incentive: self-interest, self-review, advocacy, familiarity and intimidation threats. Figure 6 shows the relation between these five categories as they lead to threats and auditor independence risk.

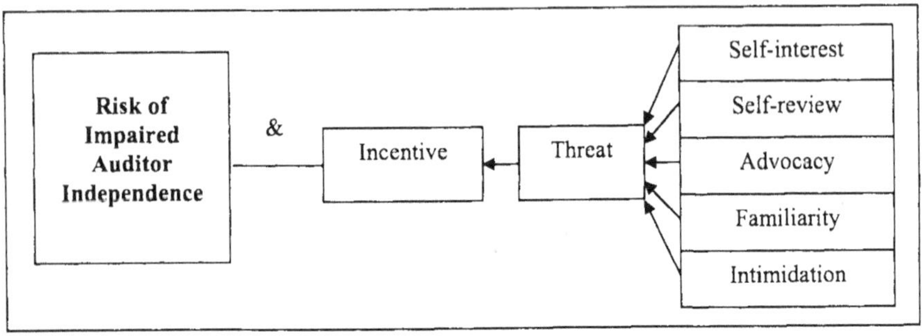

Figure 6: The Risk of Impaired Auditor Independence and Incentives

Similarly, the Institute of Chartered Accountants in England and Wales' framework of auditor independence identifies and elaborates on the same general categories of threats to independence (Institute of Chartered Accountants in England and Wales 2003):

Self-interest threat: occurs when the audit firm or a member of the audit team could benefit from a financial interest in, or other self-interest conflicts with, an audit client. Examples of circumstances that may create this threat include:

- a direct financial interest or material indirect financial interest in an audit client;
- a loan of guarantee to or from an audit client or any of its directors or officers;
- undue dependence on total fees from an audit client;
- concern about the possibility of losing the engagement;
- a close business relationship with an audit client;
- potential employment with an audit client and
- contingent fees relating to audit engagements.

Self-review threat: occurs when the audit firm, or an individual audit team member, is put in a position of reviewing subject matter for which the firm or individual were previously responsible, and which is significant in the context of the audit engagement. Examples of circumstances that may create this threat include:

- a member of the audit team being, or having recently been, a director, officer or other employee of the audit client in a position to exert direct and significant influence of the subject matter of the audit engagement;
- performing services for an audit client that directly affect the subject matter of the current, or a subsequent, audit engagement and
- preparing of original data used to generate financial statements or preparation of other records that are the subject matter of the audit engagement.

Advocacy threat: occurs when the audit firm, or a member of the audit team, promotes, or may be perceived to promote, an audit client's position or opinion to the point where objectivity may be compromised. Examples possibly creating this threat are:

- dealing in, or being a promoter of, shares or other securities in an audit client and
- acting as an advocate on behalf of an audit client in litigation or in resolving disputes with third parties.

Familiarity threat: occurs when, by virtue of a close relationship with an audit client, its directors, officers or employees, an audit firm or a member of the audit team becomes too sympathetic to the client's interest. Examples are:

- a member of the audit team having a close family member who, as a director, officer or other employee of the audit client, is in a position to exert direct and significant influence over the subject matter of the audit engagement;
- long association of a senior member of the audit team with the audit client and
- acceptance of gifts or hospitality, unless the value is clearly insignificant, from the audit client, its directors, officers or employees.

Intimidation threat: occurs when a member of the audit team may be deterred from acting objectively and exercising professional skepticism by threats, actual or perceived, from the directors, officers or employees of an audit client. Examples of circumstances that may create this threat include:

- replacement over a disagreement with the application of an accounting principle;
- pressure to reduce inappropriately the extent of work preformed in order to reduce fees and
- dominant personality in a senior position at the audit client, controlling dealings with the auditor.

b) Opportunities

Following Mock et al. (2005), to risk auditor independence and impact the auditor's report, a second factor necessary in addition to incentives is an opportunity for bias by the auditor. This factor may be present when complex financial transactions need to be depicted or when management must make significant estimates or assumptions. Difficulties in interpretations of generally accepted accounting principles might result in an inappropriate level of reporting materiality. Johnstone et al. (2001) identify three board categories of judgment-based decision situations that affect independence risk: difficult accounting issues, audit-conduct decisions, and materiality decisions. These threats due to client characteristics and audit program judgments are safeguarded by generally accepted auditing standards, audit firm policies, regulation and effective corporate governance. Figure 7 shows the association between threats due to opportunities and auditor independence risk.

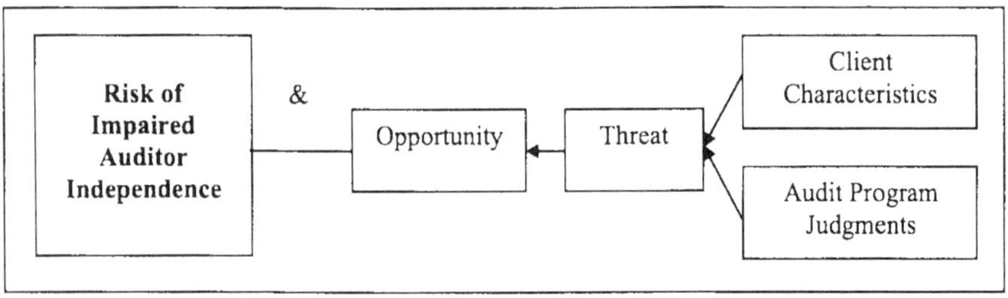

Figure 7: The Risk of Impaired Auditor Independence and Opportunities

c) Integrity

If the auditor engages in inappropriate activities, auditor integrity is impaired (Mock et al. 2005). Auditors are supposed to have high ethical standards (e.g., Ludewig 2003), which lead to their independence in thought and action even when there are strong incentives and available opportunities for improper behavior. The auditor might have positive and negative intrinsic and extrinsic motivators that affect her or his desire and effort to maintain independence (Burke 1997). However, even when intrinsic and extrinsic motivators ensure independence, an auditor's attitude might compromise independence (Mock et al. 2005). An auditor with a weak personality and a weak moral character may have a greater propensity to ignore or inappropriately interpret laws, regulations or professional standards (auditor characteristics). Figure 8 shows the association between auditor integrity and auditor independence risk.

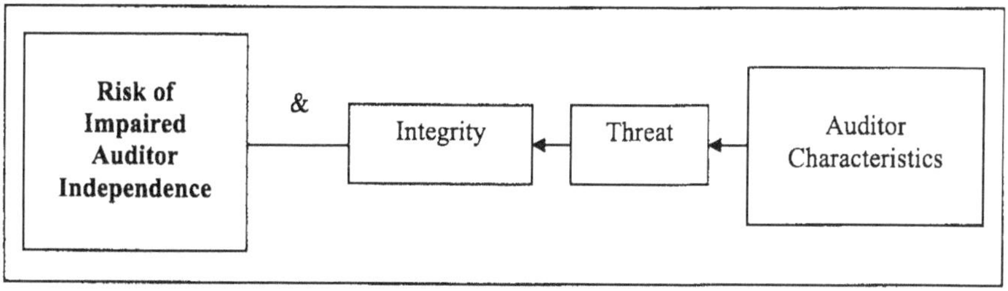

Figure 8: The Risk of Impaired Auditor Independence and Integrity

d) Interrelationships

The three components potentially causing auditors' independence to be impaired can be defined as the independence risk triangle (Mock et al. 2005: 11). Dependence can result from an individual factor or from any combination of the three. For actual impairment of independence, all three components need to be present, but for perceived compromise of independence, there may be one or all three components present. Mock et al. (2005) capture perceived independence risk by including three interrelationships (R) between the threat components as shown in Figure 9.

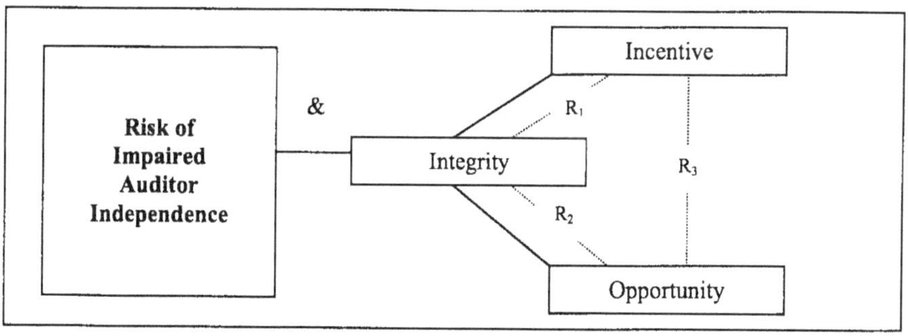

Figure 9: Interrelationships of the Risk Triangle

The three components of independence risk are connected by three relationships (Mock et al. 2005: 12). For example, there may be a perception that the auditor has incentives, due to financial interest in the client, which compromise her and his independence. Through the interrelationship between, for example, incentives and integrity, an auditor may rationalize the impairment of independence. The resulting compromise in integrity may result in the auditor identifying or creating opportunities (Mock et al. 2005: 13).

3. Safeguards to Auditor Independence Threats

When certain threats lead to an individual or interrelated occurrence of incentives, opportunities or biased integrity, effective safeguards should be identified and applied according to the circumstances (Mock et al. 2005: 11). The three categories of safeguards are (1) safeguards created by the profession, legislation or regulation, (2) safeguards within the assurance client, and (3) safeguards within the audit firm's own system and procedures (International Federation of Accountants 2004). Safeguards are installed to reduce threats to auditor independence. The specific safeguards that are identified and applied depend on the significance of the threat, the nature of the audit- and non-audit service engagement, the intended users of the assurance report and the structure of the firm (International Federation of Accountants 2004).

Safeguards created by the profession, legislation or regulation include educational, training and experience requirements for entry into the profession, but they may also consist of continuing education requirements. In addition, there are also professional standards, monitoring and disciplinary processes. An example of monitoring is an external review of an audit firm's quality control system.

The audit client may also install safeguards to avoid auditor dependency. The audit firm may separate the appointment of the auditor and the ratification and approval of the appointment. Furthermore, the client's employees must be competent to make managerial decisions. In addition, the client should implement policies and procedures that emphasize the audit client's commitment to fair financial reporting. These internal procedures shall also ensure objective choices in commissioning non-audit engagements. Finally, there should be a governance structure, such as an audit committee, that provides appropriate oversight and communications regarding the audit firm's services.

If the audit firm wants to keep up with independence requirements, the firm may install quality controls of audit engagements and may try to identify threats to independence such as interests or relationships, reliance on revenues from one client, and the provisions of non-audit services to audit clients. In addition, the firm may prohibit individuals who are not members of the assurance team from influencing the outcome of the assurance engagement. In line with this, the firm may designate members of senior management as responsible for overseeing the adequate functioning of the safeguarding system. Due to multiple service engagements, the firm should arrange the physical and virtual separation of staff involved in conflicting transactions. If there are policies and mechanisms put in place, the audit firm should enact disciplinary procedures to promote compliance whenever necessary.

Chapter III. Prior Research on Auditor Independence

A. Taxonomy

Based on the suggestions of Mock et al. (2005), in this section I will synthesize and evaluate prior research on auditor independence by categorizing research with respect to the type of threat analyzed: incentive, opportunity or compromised integrity. This will also allow me to give an overview of previously investigated safeguards with respect to relevant threats.[12] Section B reviews the research on auditor independence with respect to incentives. Sections C and D examine research on the effects of opportunities and integrity, respectively. In section E I discuss the problems inherent in integrating this body of research. I then conclude by identifying my main research questions.

B. Auditor Independence and Incentives

The European Commission as well as the International Federation of Accountants identify five threats or risks which can compromise auditors' independence (European Commission 2002: 25, International Federation of Accountants 2004: 42): self-interest, self-review, advocacy, familiarity or trust and intimidation threats. Specific circumstances in which threats to independence can arise are financial interests, business relationships and employment with the client, managerial or supervisory role with the audit client, personal relationship, and provision of non-audit services.

1. Self-Interest Threats

The most common self-interest threat arises from the benefit the individual auditor derives from the audit fee paid by the client (Mock et al. 2005). Prior research suggests that low-balling of audit fees is an inherent threat in most audits (DeAngelo 1981a). DeAngelo (1981a) analyzed an audit firm-client model with low-balling as part of a competitive equilibrium and with an incumbent auditor able to exploit the auditor's position and earn positive quasi-rents. The expectation of client-specific quasi-rents

[12] The reviewed literature is presented in Appendix 4 (archival, interview and survey studies on auditor independence risk) and Appendix 5 (experimental studies on auditor independence risk).

from a given relationship led to a lack of indifference with respect to client termination. Therefore, the auditor was not perfectly independent.

Using the percentage of the costs of non-audit services to audit fees, Scheiner and Kiger (1982) examined possible determinants of the type and quantity of non-audit services provided to clients. They found that many non-audit services consist of traditional accounting services like tax assistance. Therefore, the authors concluded that the prohibition of non-audit services would most likely not have a substantial impact on firms. This assumption was made based on fee ratios until 1979. In 1978, the Federal Trade Commission in the United States demanded the American Institute of Certified Public Accountants remove all its rules on advertising, solicitation, fees and even contingent fees. These changes caused a strong growth in accounting firms' provision of non-audit services, which presumably increased the economic bond between the auditor and client. For example, Maher, Tiessen, Colson and Broman (1992) analyzed fee data from 1977 to 1981 and they find a significant decrease in real audit fees between these years. The demand for greater competitiveness and commercialization of audit firms was thus a major precipitating factor in the current problems of the auditing profession.

The link between auditor provision of non-audit services and audit quality has been investigated by several academic studies. However, incentives to compromise auditor independence risk are assessed through various proxy measures. Some assume total fees as the best measure whereas others concentrate on client total, audit, and non-audit fee ranks. Still others claim the ratio of client non-audit to client total fees is the relevant proxy.

Chung and Kallapur (2003) investigated the effect on independence of client importance with respect to incentives, where client importance was assumed to be the ratio of client fees and non-audit fees divided by the audit firm's United States revenues or a surrogate for the audit-practice-office revenues. By using a sample of 1,871 client proxy statements of Big Five audit firms from February 5 to June 30, 2001 they found no statistically significant association between abnormal accruals and any of the client importance measures. The extent of client opportunities and incentives to manage earnings did not affect auditor incentives to compromise independence. There is thus no evidence consistent with auditor independence impairment as a function of different client fee ratios.

Consistent with Reynolds and Francis (2001), DeFond et al. (2002) found no evidence that non-audit service fees impair auditor independence, which is assumed as an auditor's propensity to issue going concern audit opinions. In a separate study, McKinley et al. (1985) located no support for management advisory service provisions affecting bank officers' loan decisions, their perceptions of financial statement reliability or their perceptions of independence. The relation between auditor fees and earnings management and between auditor fees and share values on the date the fees were disclosed was examined by Frankel, Johnson and Nelson (2002). The analysis of data collected from proxy statements showed evidence that non-audit fees affected small earnings surprises and the magnitude of discretionary accruals positively. The opposite was shown for audit fees, as well as between non-audit fees and share values on the date the fees were disclosed. Kinney, Palmrose and Scholz (2004) discovered no consistent evidence of a positive association between either audit firm fees and financial information system design or implementation of internal audit services and restatements, where they assumed that the auditor was lax in enforcing generally accepted accounting principles.

Whether an auditor's objectivity is impaired by non-audit services or by the level of economic dependence on a client was investigated by Reynolds, Deis and Francis (2004). In line with results of Frankel et al. (2002), the authors found no proof that the relative level of non-audit service fees impaired auditor objectivity. In their analysis, they factored in characteristics of small-to-medium sized high-growth firms, especially firms having initial public offerings and in the e-commerce, biomedical, telecommunication, and pharmaceutical industries, as used by Frankel et al. (2002). Somewhat similarly, Ashbaugh, LaFond and Mayhew (2003) investigated the association between auditor fees and firms meeting analyst forecasts. No evidence was discovered that auditors violate their independence as a result of clients purchasing relatively more non-audit services. However, the results of the discretionary accruals tests differed from the findings of Frankel et al. (2002).

2. Self-Review Threats

Competition and merger activities during the last two decades have led increasingly to efforts by audit firms to offer various types of professional services. Whenever a firm's auditor performs additional management services, there is a high risk that her or his previous work might be in the final audited financial statements. This means the auditor might review her or his own work (Mock et al. 2005). This includes work, which was done by the auditor as an external person, as well as a previous director, officer, or influential employee of the client. Whereas most of the research focuses on the dependence bonds which develop as a result of audit fees and non-audit fees, less research is available regarding the risk of a self-review. This may be due to the fact that constructing a measure of the effect of self-reviews is more difficult than assessing quantitative measures like fees.

Swanger and Chewning (2001) examined analysts' perceptions of auditor independence under five different scenarios. They analyzed the evaluation of auditor independence when the audited firm is performing its own internal audit, when the internal audit is outsourced to the current external auditor or to another audit firm, when the staff performing the internal and external audit is separated, and finally when only a part of the internal audit function is outsourced. They found that financial analysts' perceptions of auditor independence were negatively affected when the same audit firm performed the internal and external audits but only if there was no separation of the two audit staffs. Whereas their study examined analysts' perceptions, Lowe, Geiger and Pany (1999) investigated how outsourcing of the internal audit function to an external auditor affected financial statement users' perceptions of auditor independence and financial statement reliability as well as how such perceptions affected the behavior of loan officers. They found evidence that auditor performance of management functions had a significantly negative impact on users' perceptions of auditor independence and financial statement reliability, which resulted in a lower percentage of loan approvals. However, when the staff performing the outsourced internal audit and the financial statement audit was separated, perceptions as well as loan approvals were positively affected.

Including more variables, like competition, management advisory services, audit firm size and tenure, Shockley (1981) examined the decision of former Big Eight audit partners, partners from local and regional audit firms, commercial loan officers, and financial analysts to include audit report users. With respect to performed management advisory services, the authors found that audit firms which provided these services to audit clients were more likely to loose independence than those that did not.

To investigate whether perceived independence could be viewed as a continuum, Bartlett (1993) analyzed four types of consulting activities: assistance in the design and implementation of accounting systems for control of investors, assistance in executive search and hiring of a Chief Financial Officer, assistance in investigation of a significant acquisition and assistance in accounting for complex transactions. The results generated by a questionnaire showed that independence was assumed most when only audit work was performed with no other information about the engagement given. In each of the four cases involving additional management advisory services, compared to auditors, bankers perceived significant reductions in auditor independence.

3. Advocacy Threats

Threats impairing auditor independence may also occur because the auditor is promoting securities for the client or is the client's advocate in litigation or disputes with third parties (Mock et al. 2005). Whenever an auditor behaves in a manner consistent with the client's preferences regarding financial reporting, although the favored treatment may not be the most reliable, auditor independence may be compromised by this advocacy threat.

Gramling's (1999) investigation into client preferences found no evidence that an auditor's use of a client's internal audit department influenced the auditor's initial evaluation of the quality of the internal audit department. In another study, Salterio and Koonce (1997) examined the effect of consistent and mixed accounting precedents on audit judgments and found a larger effect of consistent precedents than of a client's preferred treatment. However, they qualified their results by suggesting that auditors respond to client preferences when generally accepted accounting principles are ambiguous. Trompeter (1994) investigated the impact of client preferences when different levels of ambiguity of generally accepted accounting principles were present. His findings were consistent with Salterio and Koonce's (1997) suggestions of the impact of generally accepted accounting principles. Haynes, Jenkins and Nutt (1998) showed that auditors did not automatically assume an advocacy position. The number of years of audit experience affected the tendency to positively support clients.

4. Familiarity or Trust Threats

Another risk of impaired auditor independence might occur whenever family and personal relationships between the auditor and the audited client exist or there is a long association between the senior audit partner and the assurance client. Independence could also be risked if the auditor receives gifts or hospitability from clients (Mock et al. 2005). Such familiarity or trust threats may affect auditor incentives negatively. Most present studies that examine this threat measure either the effect of employment of former auditors by the client or the effect of the tenure of the auditor-client relationship on (perceived) auditor independence risk.

A survey examining perceived auditor independence of auditors and financial statement users, such as bankers and financial analysts, when an auditor was employed by the client, was first done by Imhoff (1978). He showed a decrease of perceived auditor independence as time elapsed between the audit engagement and the employment. Somewhat similar, there is evidence that independence concerns of middle managers increased as the time period between the last audit and accounting employment decreased (Koh and Mahathevan 1993).

Kaplan and Whitecotton (2001) examined auditors' reporting intentions, particularly when it was revealed that another auditor was considering employment with the client and had failed to comply with ethics rules. They found that auditors' reporting intentions were stronger when personal costs of reporting were perceived to be higher. On the other hand, client perceptions were first studied by Iyer and Raghunandan (2002). They examined the perceptions of company executives and managers about their ability to resolve disagreements with their auditors who happened to be their former employees. The majority of the subjects believed that disagreements were more difficult to resolve if their former audit firm served as an auditor of their current employer.

In addition to other measurements, Shockley (1981) looked at the perceived effect of tenure on the risk of impaired auditor independence. He hypothesized that audit firms which had performed a given client's audit for a period exceeding five consecutive years were perceived as having a greater risk of loosing their audit independence than were firms which had performed the audit for five years or less. The overall results were not significant, which lends support to opponents of mandatory rotation who believe audit reports are better quality when there is a deeper insight and familiarity with the firm. However, with respect to loan officers, these results were significant. Geiger and Raghunandan (2002) found that audit reporting failures were more likely to happen in the earlier years of the auditor-client relationship than when auditors had served these clients for longer tenures. Myers, Myers and Omer (2003) examined the relation between auditor tenure and earnings quality using the Jones-model to calculate abnormal accruals and absolute current accruals as proxies for earnings quality. They concluded that longer auditor tenure results in auditors placing greater constraints on extreme management decisions in the reporting of financial performance.

5. Intimidation Threats

Intimidation threats might occur when the auditor is sued for an actual or threatened litigation, when there is a risk of replacement or when there is high pressure to decrease work performed in order to reduce fees (Mock et al. 2005). Intimidation threats will most likely be relevant when other threats are present. Whenever there is a risk of replacement, it is likely that the auditor will have financial interests in the client. In this situation, auditors' independence might be compromised because of both a self-interest threat and an intimidation threat.

Kaplan and Whitecotton (2001) examined the risk of replacement effects. When the risk of being replaced was lower, costs of reporting were perceived to be low. Consistent with this assumption, the authors found that auditors' reporting intentions were stronger when personal costs of reporting were perceived to be higher. Arnold, Bernardi and Niedermeyer (1999) showed that auditors' decisions were most influenced by stockholders' reliance on the thoroughness of the audit and the fear of loosing the client. The latter decreased with increased country's individualism, resulting in a greater likelihood that there would be more work.

6. Summary of Research on Auditor Incentives

Incentives may compromise auditors' independence in different ways, depending on the threat present. Threats may occur in various circumstances at the same time, yet the identification of the relevant threat is most likely impossible. For instance, if an auditor is sued for a materiality judgment, one will assume that impaired auditor independence might have led to the wrong judgment. However, it is questionable as to which of the theoretical threats may have affected independence negatively. Therefore, research must focus on the most theoretically important threats and depict only a partial aspect of the whole construct of auditor independent risk.

Most research is based on archival data regarding the effect of audit fees and non-audit fees on different dependent variables. Fees are supposed to be highly related to incentives because they demonstrate a quantitative term, which is easy to understand as a financial interest. However, there are different ways to define the measure for incentives that occur from financial interests. Research assuming the total fee as the appropriate variable will most likely find no influence of total fees on audit quality. Furthermore, researchers cannot find a connection between the ranking of fees and effects on going concern opinions, bank loan officer decisions and perceptions of financial statement reliability or share values on the date of fee disclosure. An exception is the finding that non-audit fees positively affect small earnings surprises and the magnitude of discretionary accruals. Whenever a fee ratio was used to measure financial incentives, there was no association with several dependent variables that were investigated. Supported by theoretical evidence these findings may indicate that non-audit services may be beneficial for both the final quality of the audit and the audited financial statements (Ewert 2004: 258).

Research studying different effects on the supply and demand of non-audit services somewhat differs because different independent variables are used. Whereas there is no effect when the amount of auditors present in a market differs, there is a positive effect on the relative use of auditor-provided consultancy services of the percentage of share ownership of directors and stockholders. However, investor needs, client retention, professional values and obligations affecting the decision to do additional work do not affect the demand for consulting services. Overall, the majority of the research on audit fees finds no evidence that fees affect any dependent variable related to auditor independence.

Research focusing on the effects of self-reviewed work on performing the audit shows without any exception a negative association with perceived auditor independence when the staff performing the two services is not separated. With separation, auditors' independence is perceived not to be affected.

There is no evidence that an advocacy threat occurs either when auditors' initial evaluations of the quality of the internal audit department are influenced, or when the preferred litigation disclosures differ from auditors' recommended disclosures. With ambiguous generally accepted accounting principles, auditors are more likely to respond to client preferences. Finally, it can be assumed that the number of years of audit experience affects the treatment of a client. These results show that advocacy threats are not caused by clients' preferences that differ from auditors' favored treatment but from other variables such as accounting standards and experience.

Research regarding the effect on familiarity or trust threats focuses either on the effects of employment of former auditors with the client or on the effect of the tenure of the auditor-client relationship. There is evidence that as time elapses between the audit engagement and the employment, there is a decrease of perceived auditor independence. For example, smaller loans tend to be given to financial directors who were previously employed as an audit partner. Clients' perceptions suggest that company executives and managers are less able to resolve disagreements when the current auditor was a former employee. Research focusing on tenure effects did not support mandatory rotation, except when loan officers' perceptions were studied. Supporting opponents of mandatory rotation, there is evidence that audit reporting failures and auditors placing fewer constraints on extreme management decisions tend to happen in the earlier years of the engagement. Factors affecting audit tenure are assumed to be client-size, client growth rate and type of audit firm.

An examination of the risk of replacement effects as one possible intimidation threat shows that auditors' reporting intentions are stronger when personal costs of reporting are perceived to be higher. Auditors' decisions regarding additional work tend to be most influenced by the fear of loosing the client.

C. Auditor Independence and Opportunity

Opportunities may occur when complex financial transactions are present, when management must make significant estimations or assumptions, when difficult interpretations of accounting principles must be made and applied or when an appropriate level of materiality has to be determined (Mock et al. 2005). These may lead to a threat driven by client characteristics. Mock et al. (2005) describe opportunity as the existence of errors or fraud and of accounting issues requiring judgment. Threats due to audit program judgments can occur by the selection of audit procedures, interpretation of evidence and materiality choices.

1. Client Characteristics

Auditor independence may be compromised due to certain features in the relationship between the current auditor and the client, with the characteristics of the client tending to have more of an impact on this relationship. Such characteristics include the client's industry, size, growth-rate, location, shareholder base and board of directors' structure. If an auditor takes advantage of any of these client characteristics, this can lead to a decrease in the auditor's independence.

In a recent study, Beattie, Fearnley and Brandt (2004) hypothesized six different auditor types (seller types). They found that conforming audit reports were most difficult to achieve when the board's culture was less conservative, the issue was a sensitive one within the company or the firm was disorganized. They thus concluded that ownership and corporate culture have a major impact on attitudes to corporate governance and financial reporting.

Chung and Kallapur (2003) studied the importance of clients in terms of fee amounts. They uncovered no evidence that auditor independence might be compromised by client opportunities and incentives to manage their earnings favorably. Frankel et al. (2002) found no association between fee level and client characteristics, such as small-to-medium sized high-growth firms, especially firms having initial public offerings and which were in specific industries. In Arnold et al.'s (1999) study, factors most influencing an auditor's decision were stockholders' reliance on a client. Finally, Kaplan and Whitecotton (2001) discovered that if there is a risk of replacement, but the competing auditor fails, then the personal costs of reporting of the current auditor are higher, which led to stronger reporting intentions.

2. Audit Program Judgments

An auditor is responsible for making decisions about his or her own audit program including the selection of audit procedures, the interpretation of evidence and any judgments related to materiality choices (Mock et al. 2005). Inadequate decision making in any of these could allow an opportunity threat to occur, thus leading to a decrease in auditor independence.

A study investigating auditors' perceptions of the effectiveness of formal sanctions as incentives for maintaining auditor independence was conducted by Shafer, Morris and Ketchand (1999). The authors analyzed the results of cases involving client pressure, where the moral intensity of the ethical dilemma was manipulated. Their analysis showed that litigation risk and peer-review risk were perceived as significant deterrents to aggressive reporting decisions, but the risk of disciplinary action by professional organizations was not. In another study, Hackenbrack and Nelson (1996) found that when engagement risk was moderate, auditors preferred an aggressive reporting method and forcefully applied relevant financial accounting standards. On the other hand, when engagement risk was high, auditors preferred a conservative reporting method and cautiously applied relevant professional standards. In a similar study, Kadous, Kennedy and Peecher (2003) investigated the effectiveness of regulation designed to reduce auditor acceptance of an aggressive reporting method. They assumed that auditor acceptance would increase with goal commitment, in particular when quality assessment was performed. Following the tendency described by Hackenbrack and Nelson (1996), their results indicated that performing quality assessment amplified the effects of auditors' directional goals on their acceptance of client-preferred methods and on their ratings of the quality of that method. In addition, auditors making quality assessments were more likely to identify the client's method as the most appropriate when they were more committed to their directional goals.

Abbott, Park and Parker (2000) studied whether activity and independence of audit committees reduced the likelihood of fraudulent or aggressive financial statement actions. They compared 78 firms subject to Securities and Exchange Commission's Accounting and Auditing Enforcement Releases with 78 non-sanctioned firms that were similar in size, industry, national exchange and engagement time period. They found that firms with audit committees which met minimum thresholds of both activity and independence were less likely to be sanctioned by the Securities and Exchange

Commission. A study conducted in Malaysia by Teoh and Lim (1996) yielded similar results in that the formation of audit committees had a strong positive impact on enhancing auditor independence.

Jeter and Shaw (1995) investigated the effect of removing bans on direct uninvited solicitation of information dissemination, client-auditor alignment and auditor independence. Their regression analysis showed that auditors in a market allowing solicitation were more likely than those in a market banning solicitation to issue a nonstandard report.

3. Summary of Research on Auditor Opportunity

The nature of the relationship between the current auditor and the client affects the degree to which auditor independence may be compromised, with client characteristics having the most impact. For example, conforming audit reports are most difficult to achieve when the board's culture is less conservative, the issue is a sensitive one within the company or the firm is disorganized. To the extent that clients have opportunities and incentives to manage their earnings favorably, auditor independence will not be compromised. Factors most influencing auditors' decisions are stockholders' reliance on a client. There is evidence that the percentage of share ownership by both a company's directors as well as largest stockholder affects the purchase behavior of consultancy services. In addition, the demand for recurring non-audit services tends to be related to the costs of management ownership and the level of outside investment.

An auditor is able to judge about her or his own audit program depending on several factors. Formal sanctions as incentives for maintaining auditor independence, such as litigation risk and peer-review risk, are perceived as significant deterrents to aggressive reporting decisions while the risk of disciplinary action by professional organizations is not. A moderate engagement risk causes auditors to prefer aggressive reporting methods and application of relevant financial accounting standards. When engagement risk is high, auditors favor conservative reporting methods and application of relevant professional standards. Furthermore, auditor acceptance will increase with goal commitment, especially when quality assessment is performed. In addition, auditors who make quality assessments are more likely to identify the client's method as the most appropriate method when they are more committed to their directional goals.

Activity and independence of audit committees reduce the likelihood of fraudulent or aggressive financial statement actions. Furthermore, the formation of audit committees has a strong positive impact on enhancing auditor independence.

D. Auditor Independence and Integrity

According to Mock et al. (2005), an auditor's integrity is compromised when the auditor faces cultural differences in moral codes. Intimidation threats or other demands by dominant clients may also challenge an auditor's integrity. This may also cause an auditor to be willing to ignore or inappropriately interpret laws and regulations.

1. Cultural Differences

In a study clarifying the linkages between cultural and environmental factors and auditing conducted by Wood (1996) he assumed that the existence of such factors differed among nations and that there must be an empirical association between those factors and auditing practices. His results indicated that the cultural and environmental factors most associated with audit characteristics were literacy, per capita gross national product and legal system origins. Cross-cultural and environmental factors were most associated with auditing experience and examination requirements, codified ethical standards and restrictions on auditor investments and provision of other services to clients. He also found evidence that when a country moved to a common law system, auditor independence issues became more important. The same was true as a population became more literate and affluent.

2. Interpretation of Laws and Regulation

Using a multi period model of the audit market with a single client present, Magee and Tseng (1990) introduced a reporting issue over which the auditor and the client might disagree. Their analytical analysis showed a link between auditor independence and the nature of financial reporting standards. When there was less room for disagreement among auditors regarding the proper application of those standards to client circumstances, the auditor was more likely to behave independently. How companies and their auditors resolve important audit issues was investigated by Beattie et al. (2004). They utilized a grounded theory model of auditor-client negotiation, and their interview evidence showed an audit to be a complex, interactive and judgmental process which required a high level of technical knowledge, integrity and interpersonal skills. A key finding was that aggressive accounting was most affected by financial difficulty, particularly the need to stay within debt covenants. Key sanctions available to an auditor such as qualifying the audit report tended to be ineffective when there was a lack of regulatory clarity and materiality.

That negotiated issues frequently arose because of unclear or non existent generally accepted accounting principles was shown by Gibbins, Salterio and Webb (2001). They further found that accounting negotiation depended on context, including external conditions and constraints such as generally accepted accounting principles, generally accepted auditing standards, statutory power, accountability and deadlines. By manipulating the accounting standard relevant to determining the appropriate reporting method, Hackenbrack and Nelson (1996) discovered that auditors responded to moderate engagement risk by permitting an aggressive reporting method und justifying their choice with aggressive interpretations of accounting standards. The opposite was true for high engagement risk.

Finally, Hussey and Lan (2001) investigated the relevance of separate auditor regulations in the United Kingdom. They found that finance directors who were concerned with the value and benefits of an audit and its impact on their own company in general supported a separate regulation from the accounting profession. However, there was no relationship shown between regulation of external auditors and finance directors' own assessment of the nature of their relationship with their external auditors.

3. Auditor Resistance

Auditor resistance might be compromised when an auditor is unable to resist dominant clients' preferences (Mock et al. 2005). For example, Gramling (1999) found that a high level of fee pressure negatively affected the degree of reliability of an internal audit. That resistance is compromised by the risk of replacement was shown by Kaplan and Whitecotton (2001). Their findings revealed that auditors' reporting intentions were stronger when personal costs of reporting were perceived to be higher. Arnold et al. (1999) found resistance issues such as decision making might be faced when the fear of loosing a client was high.

In a study conducted by Swanger and Chewning (2001), a major result was that financial analysts' perceptions of auditor independence were negatively affected when the same audit firm performed both the internal and external audits without separation of the two audit staffs. Such a situation can be assumed to cause an auditor to have less resistance because future appointments may depend on both the external and internal audit function, thereby putting pressure on the auditor.

In a situation where management attempts to influence its auditors' reporting behavior, it is most important that auditor's resistance is high. Thus, Knapp (1985) studied the perceived ability of auditors to resist client pressure in different contexts. Major results indicated that auditors were perceived as being most susceptible to client pressure in those situations where the client was financially strong and a conflict was not dealt with by precise technical standards.

4. Summary of Research on Auditor Integrity

Cultural and environmental factors most associated with audit characteristics are literacy, per capita gross national product and legal system origins. Cross-cultural and environmental factors are most associated with audit experience requirements, examination requirements, codified ethical standards and restrictions on auditor investments and provision of other services to clients. Furthermore, there is evidence that when a country moves to a common law system, auditor independence issues become more important. The same is true as a population becomes more literate and affluent.

The effects of laws and regulations are taken into account by investigating the association between auditor independence and the nature of financial reporting standards. When accounting standards allow less room for disagreement, the auditor is more likely to remain independent. Interview evidence shows that aggressive accounting was most affected by financial difficulty, particularly the need to stay within debt covenants. Key sanctions available to an auditor, such as qualifying an audit report, tend to be ineffective when there is a lack of regulatory clarity and materiality. Furthermore, accounting negotiation depends on external conditions and constraints, such as generally accepted accounting principles, generally accepted auditing standards, statutory power, accountability and deadlines. Auditors respond to moderate engagement risk by permitting an aggressive reporting method und justify their choice with aggressive interpretations of accounting standards. The opposite occurs with high engagement risk.

Auditor resistance might be compromised when the auditor is unable to resist domineering clients' personnel preferences. A high level of fee pressure negatively affects the extent of the internal audit's reliability. Furthermore, resistance is compromised by the risk of replacement because auditors' reporting intentions tend to be stronger when personal costs of reporting are perceived to be higher. Also, fear of loosing a client will affect an auditor's decisions.

Financial analysts' and other financial statement users' perceptions of auditor independence are negatively affected when the internal and external audits are performed by the same audit firm without separation of the two audit staffs. Where management attempts to influence its auditors' reporting behavior, it is most important that auditor's resistance is high. Results indicate that auditors are thought to be most susceptible to client pressure in those situations where the client is financially strong and the conflict issue is not dealt with by strict technical standards.

E. Discussion and Main Research Questions

Prior research suggests that the nature of financial reporting standards is associated with auditor independence. When standards leave less room for disagreement those standards are more likely applied appropriately and vice versa. Room for improper interpretation and application could lead to auditor's independence become compromised. However, prior research focused only on accounting standards. There is little knowledge on how the nature of auditor independence regulation affects auditor independence. However, the choice of regulation approach has an incremental effect on behavior, since the choice of approach causes the communication accuracy of the regulations to differ (Nelson 2003). A rules-based approach includes both specific prohibitions, such as the prohibition of some, but not all, non-audit services, and specific requirements, such as the pre-approval of non-audit services by the audit committee. Due to this level of detail, decision makers are more likely to gain a clear understanding of what is allowed and what is forbidden. This suggests high communication accuracy. Alternatively, the principles-based approach requires people to interpret the given principles to understand what is prohibited and required. This suggests lower communication accuracy.

Related to the communication accuracy of the regulation approach, the approach affects the potential regulation as to safeguarding auditor independence. Safeguards are mechanisms that are applied to reduce threats to an acceptable level (Mock et al. 2005). These are safeguards created by the profession, legislation or regulation, safeguards within the client and safeguards within the audit firm's own systems and procedures. In this research I attempt to study differences in safeguarding effects due to different regulatory approaches.

Based on prior research and given the two competing regulations, my first research question is:

RQ1: Is the approach to auditor independence regulation associated with the effectiveness of the regulation in reducing risks to auditor independence in fact?

The application of regulation can be characterized as a task which requires a certain amount of knowledge for this cognitive process (Bonner 1994). Therefore, task complexity of the regulation is positively associated with knowledge due to experience in the field or to both training and experience. Because rules-based regulation is written with explicit detail, I argue that less regulatory knowledge is required to apply the regulation as intended. This regulation approach suggests higher communication accuracy and safeguarding quality than a principles-based approach, which requires greater interpretation. Based on these theoretical implications, my second research question is:

RQ2: Is the effectiveness of regulation to reduce auditor independence risk dependent on the knowledge level of the person applying the regulation?

Certain characteristics of the client will influence whether the auditor has an incentive and/or an opportunity to be less independent with respect to her or his professional obligations. The culture of the board of directors affects the audit report in a way that less conservativeness leads to less conforming reports. However, client opportunities and incentives to manage earnings do not necessarily compromise auditor independence. The other institution where opportunities might come from is formal sanctions. Litigation risk and peer-review risk detain auditors to prefer an aggressive reporting method, whereas risk of disciplinary actions by professional organizations has no effect. If goal commitment and quality assessment are present, auditors are more likely to accept the client's accounting method. When there is a high risk of replacement as well as fee pressure, auditors tend to be less resistant, including in their decision making, which is also influenced by management. Furthermore, aggressive reporting is more likely when the engagement risk is moderate. In such a situation, auditors justify their choice with aggressive interpretations of accounting standards.

Based on prior research and given the different audit firm-client engagement characteristics, my second research question is:

RQ3: Is the effectiveness of a regulation to reduce auditor independence risk dependent on the audit firm-client engagement characteristics?

Chapter IV. Auditor Independence Regulation

The need for financial regulation is often justified by the potential for market failure that can result when managers' posses inside information while investors do not, called "information asymmetry," as well as from inappropriate behavior of auditors, called "moral hazard."[13] New laws that attempt to address these issues in the United States (Sarbanes-Oxley Act 2002) and in the European Union (Proposal for a 8th Directive of the European Commission 2004a) indicate that the predominant view among legislators is that we need more regulation, more severe penalties, and larger enforcement budgets to protect financial markets from fraud.

The purpose of this chapter is to describe these two competing regulatory approaches. In section A, I first explain the regulation of the United States of America, provided in the Sarbanes-Oxley Act and the Securities and Exchange Commission's final rules. In section B, I then present the regulation of the European Union; first describing the European Commission's Recommendation and secondly the European Commission's proposal for a revised 8th Directive of the European Parliament and the Council, which was accepted by the European Parlimant and the Council of Economic and Finance Ministers. In section C, I compare the two regulations in terms of differences in single requirements, and, more important for this research, differences in the regulations' approach. Finally, Section D shows Germany's reaction towards the American requirements and European recommended and proposed requirements.

A. Regulation of the United States of America

1. Introduction

The Sarbanes-Oxley Act of 2002 has been the most significant legislative response to corporate scandals such as Enron. The stated purpose of the act, introduced at the second session of the 107th United States Congress, "is to protect investors by improving the accuracy and reliability of corporate disclosures made pursuant to the securities laws, and for other purposes" (Sarbanes-Oxley Act 2002). As a corrective measure in response to significant accounting failures, the Sarbanes-Oxley Act strongly reinforces the position of investors first pronounced by the Securities and

[13] For a detailed discussion on the need of regulation concerning financial reporting and accounting see Watrin (2001).

Exchange Commission. President Bush described the Sarbanes-Oxley Act as "the most far-reaching reforms of American business practices since the time of Franklin Delano Roosevelt" (Bumiller 2002: A1). This Act is applicable to publicly traded companies, and it created the Public Company Accounting Oversight Board under the supervision of the Securities and Exchange Commission (Title I). It also imposes greater restrictions and requirements in terms of auditor independence (Title II).

After the Sarbanes-Oxley Act was issued, the Securities and Exchange Commission had a maximum of 180 days to make final regulations regarding services outside the scope of auditor practices, pre-approval requirements and auditor reports to audit committees (Sarbanes-Oxley Act Section 208 (a)). Title II of the Sarbanes-Oxley Act added new sections (g) to (l) to Section 10A of the Securities Exchange Act of 1934. In the following section, I explain the power and authority of the Public Company Accounting Oversight Board and the requirements concerning auditor independence as outlined in these new sections.

2. Public Company Accounting Oversight Board

The Sarbanes-Oxley Act established the Public Company Accounting Oversight Board (hereafter the Board) and charged it with "oversee[ing] the audit of public companies that are subject to the securities laws, and related matters, in order to protect the interests of investors and further the public interest in the preparation of informative, accurate, and independent audit reports for companies the securities of which are sold to, and held by and for, public investors" (Sarbanes-Oxley Act Section 101 (a)). To carry out this vital charge, the Sarbanes-Oxley Act gives the Public Company Accounting Oversight Board significant powers.

As of July 16, 2003 with the approval of the Securities and Exchange Commission, all United States accounting firms that prepare or issue audit reports for American public companies, or play a substantial role in their audits, must be registered with the Board (Sarbanes-Oxley Act Section 102 (a)). Other core programs are predicated on such registration, and it is critical for the Board's regulatory oversight of public accounting firms. The reason for this is that registration provides the Board with important information about the public accounting firms that apply for registration.

The registration application calls for (1) the names of all issuers for which the firm currently prepares or issues, or expects to prepare or issue, audit reports, (2) the annual fees received from any services by the firm, (3) other requested financial information, (4) a statement of the quality control policies of the firm's accounting and auditing practices, (5) a list of all associated accountants participating in or contributing to the preparation of audit reports, (6) information relating to criminal, civil or administrative actions or disciplinary proceedings pending against the firm or any associated person in connection with the audit report, (7) copies of any periodic or annual disclosure filed by an issuer which discloses accounting disagreements between the issuer and the firm, and (8) other information specified as necessary or appropriate to the public interest (Sarbanes-Oxley Act Section 102 (b) (2) (A)-(H)).

In addition, an annual report has to be submitted to the Board and a company may have to report more frequently or provide the Board with additional information (Sarbanes-Oxley Act Section 102 (d)). To recover the costs of processing and reviewing applications and annual reports, all registered public accounting firms have to pay a registration and annual fee (Sarbanes-Oxley Act Section 102 (f)).

Furthermore, the Board has the power to enforce the compliance of registered public accounting firms and their associated persons with the Sarbanes-Oxley Act, the Board's rules, professional standards and the securities laws relating to the preparation and issuance of audit reports as well as the obligations and liabilities of accountants. The Board can also establish or adopt by rule any auditing, quality control, ethics, independence or other standards relating to the preparation of audit reports for issuers (Sarbanes-Oxley Act Section 103). The auditing standards adopted by the Board require each registered public accounting firm to (1) prepare and maintain audit work papers and other information for a period not less than seven years, (2) provide a concurring or second partner review and approval of such audit report, and concurring approval in its issuance, and (3) describe in each audit report the scope of the auditor's testing of the internal control structure and procedures of the issuer, including the findings, an evaluation and a description (Sarbanes-Oxley Act Section 103 (a) (2) (A)).

In carrying out quality control standards with respect to the issuance of audit reports, the Board can include requirements for every registered public accounting firm relating to monitoring of professional ethics and independence from issuers; consultation within such firms on accounting and auditing questions; supervision of audit work, hiring, professional development and advancement of personnel; the acceptance and continuation of engagements and internal inspections (Sarbanes-Oxley Act Section 103 (a) (2) (B)).

Furthermore, the Board has the authority to adopt other standards like initial and transitional standards (Sarbanes-Oxley Act Section 103 (a) (3)) as well as independence standards, if such rules are deemed necessary or appropriate to the public interest or for the protection of investors (Sarbanes-Oxley Act Section 103 (b)). To evaluate the standards-setting process, the results of these responsibilities and the pending issues agenda for future projects are required to be included in the annual report (Sarbanes-Oxley Act Section 103 (d)).

The Board also has the authority to assess the degree of compliance of each registered public accounting firm and associated persons of that firm with the Sarbanes-Oxley Act, the rules of the Securities and Exchange Commission and professional standards through conducting a continuing program of inspections. These inspections are to be conducted annually with respect to each registered accounting firm that regularly provides audit reports for more than one hundred issuers, and not less than once every three years if audit reports are provided for less than one hundred issuers. Different inspection schedules might be adjusted in accordance with the Sarbanes-Oxley Act, the public interest or the protection of investors or at the request of the Securities and Exchange Commission (Sarbanes-Oxley Act Section 104 (a) and (b)).

Such inspections are meant to ensure the identification of any compliance or violation of the Sarbanes-Oxley Act, the rules of the Securities and Exchange Commission and the firm's own quality control policies or professional standards. If a violation is identified, the Board has to report in written form to the Securities and Exchange Commission and the responsible State regulatory authority and has to begin, if appropriate, a formal investigation or take disciplinary action (Sarbanes-Oxley Act Section 104 (c)). To conduct the investigation, the Board has to inspect and review selected audit and review engagements of the firm and to evaluate the sufficiency of the quality control system of the firm and the manner of the documentation and communication of that system. It also must perform other testing of the audit, supervisory and quality control procedures of the firm (Sarbanes-Oxley Act Section 104 (d)).

3. Rules Regarding Auditor Independence

According to the Sarbanes-Oxley Act, all auditing and non-auditing services provided to a client by the auditor of the client must be pre-approved by the audit committee of the client. Furthermore, the audit committee is established by or amongst the board of directors of a client for the purpose of overseeing the accounting and financial reporting processes of the client and audits of the financial statements of the client (Sarbanes-Oxley Act Section 205 (a) (A)). The audit committee of a client may delegate to one or more designated members of the audit committee who are independent members of the board of directors the authority to grant pre-approvals (Sarbanes-Oxley Act Section 202 (i) (3)).

However, according to Section 202 of the Sarbanes-Oxley Act, the pre-approval requirement is waived with respect to the provision of non-audit services for a client if such services were not recognized by the issuer at the time of the engagement to be non-audit services. Such services must be promptly brought to the attention of the audit committee of the issuer and approved prior to the completion of the audit by one or more members of the audit committee who are on the board of directors and to whom authority to grant such approvals has been delegated. In addition, the aggregate amount of all such non-audit services provided to the issuer are not allowed to constitute more than 5 percent of the total amount of revenues paid by the issuer to its auditor during the fiscal year in which the non-audit services were provided (Sarbanes-Oxley Act Section 202 (i) (1)). Finally, to address investor needs, approval by an audit committee of a client must be disclosed to investors in periodic reports (Sarbanes-Oxley Act Section 202 (i) (2)).

The Sarbanes-Oxley Act also outlines certain obligations for auditors who perform approved audit services. For example, each registered public accounting firm that performs audits for any client is required to report in a timely manner to the audit committee of the client all critical accounting policies and practices to be used, all alternative treatments of financial information which differ from generally accepted accounting principles that have been discussed with management officials of the client, ramifications of the use of such alternative disclosures and treatments and the treatment preferred by the registered public accounting firm. The firm must also report other material written communications between itself and the management of the client, such as any management letter or schedule of unadjusted differences (Sarbanes-Oxley Act Section 204).

Furthermore, according to Section 404 of the Sarbanes-Oxley Act, each annual report shall (1) state the responsibility of management for establishing and maintaining an adequate internal control structure and procedures for financial reporting, and (2) contain an assessment, as of the end of the most recent fiscal year of the issuer, of the effectiveness of the internal control structure and procedures of the issuer for financial reporting. Each registered public accounting firm that prepares or issues an audit report for the issuer shall attest to, and report on, the assessment made by management of the issuer.

In addition, the audit partner rotation requires the leading audit partner or the audit partner responsible for reviewing the audits to rotate a minimum of every five years (Sarbanes-Oxley Act Section 203).

The most prominent subject of the regulations with regard to auditor independence is the implications of services performed outside the scope of standard auditing practice. The Sarbanes-Oxley Act makes it unlawful for a registered public accounting firm (and any associated person of the firm, to the extent determined appropriate by the Securities and Exchange Commission) to provide to a client, contemporaneously with the audit, any non-audit service, including

1. bookkeeping and other services related to accounting records or financial statements,
2. financial information systems design and implementation,
3. appraisal or valuation services and fairness opinions,
4. actuarial services,
5. internal audit services,
6. management functions or human resources,
7. broker-dealer services,
8. legal services, and
9. any other service that the Board determines to be impermissible by regulation.

However, a public accounting firm may engage in any non-audit service for an audit client, including tax services that are not described above, if the activity is approved in advance by the audit committee of the client (Sarbanes-Oxley Act Section 201 (a)).

All of the regulations of the Sarbanes-Oxley Act outlined above have an international impact. They affect foreign accounting firms that conduct audits of both foreign private clients and foreign subsidiaries and affiliates of United States clients. This international impact is discussed controversial throughout the European Member States (for a German perspective, e.g., Ferlings and Lanfermann 2002, Emmerich and Schaum 2003). The fundamental changes regarding the regulation of auditor independence do not completely square with, e.g., German law (Regelin and Fisher 2003). However, they also mandate European audit firms to comply with the requirements relevant for foreign private clients and foreign subsidiaries and affiliates of United States clients. This includes, for example, the need for the registration of European audit firms with the Public Company Accounting Oversight Board (Lanfermann and Maul 2003), accepting the rights of the Public Company Accounting Oversight Board and possible collusions with Member State law (Hilber and Hartung 2003: 1055).

The most critical effects–which caused many European companies to postpone the entrance into the American capital market (Lanfermann and Maul 2003: 349) related to the American thrust concerning auditor independence regulation–are

1. the inharmonic situation concerning auditor independence regulation on a global field, which leads to uncertainty for investors,
2. the additional financial burden and risks caused by the Sarbanes-Oxley Act for none Big Four audit,
3. the fact that the Sarbanes-Oxley Act requires additional clarifying rules, set up by the Securities and Exchange Commission, makes auditor independence regulations less transparent from a European perspective (Institute of Certified Public Accountants in Germany[14] and German Chamber of Public Accountants 2002).

B. Regulation of the European Union

1. Introduction

The role, position and liability of the statutory auditor within the European Union are uncommonly regulated among all Member States. However, the increasing number of important financial failures has given rise to a call for a minimum harmonization of the

[14] The actual German name is Institut der Wirtschaftsprüfer in Deutschland e.V. (IDW); translated by author.

audit. There is increasing belief that the absence of common practices and standards has a negative impact on audit quality and on the freedom to establish and provide services in the audit field (European Commission 1996). Still, before 1996 there were several regulations that existed at the European Union level, including the:

- Fourth Council Directive of July 1978, which requires all companies covered by the Directive to have their annual accounts audited by a qualified professional.
- Seventh Council Directive of June 1983, which extended the audit requirements to all entities which drew up consolidated accounts on the basis of the Directive.
- Eighth Council Directive of April 1984, which concerned the approval of persons responsible for carrying out the statutory audits of accounting documents.

While the Eighth Directive (1984) defined only minimum qualifications of the auditor, it did not contain any specific guidance concerning independence requirements. Although some of the requirements were to be regulated at the national level or were the subject of self-regulation by the accounting profession, there were inevitable differences in the way they were dealt with, including through legislative backing. Therefore, when the Directive was adopted, the European Commission stated that these requirements were not satisfactory and that refinement at a later stage would be necessary. As a response, the Commission issued a Green Paper (European Commission 1996) which was based upon several national and international studies, as the privileged instrument for the consultation of Member States. The Green Paper (European Commission 1996) offered a renewed starting point from which action at a European Union level could be justified. Furthermore, responding to the serious handicap in the negotiations which were taking place at international level, the Commission presented a Communication to the European Council and the European Parliament on "Accounting harmonization: a new strategy vis-à-vis international harmonization" (1995). Furthermore, in 1998 the creation of a European Union Committee on Auditing, which would develop further action in close-cooperation between the accounting profession and Member States, was announced.

Since these documents were issued and the Committee on Auditing created, several serious scandals confirmed the urgency for the envisaged European Union initiatives on auditor independence. Therefore, in 2002 the European Commission issued a Recommendation of a set of fundamental principles regarding the statutory auditors' independence in the European Union (European Commission 2002). This

Recommendation was partly adopted voluntarily by Member States. However, there was no mandatory implementation required as long as the European Commission's recommendations (2002) for new legislation were not passed by the Council and Parliament.[15] The fact that the European Commission proposed a revised Directive to ensure that investors and other interested parties could rely fully on the accuracy of audited accounts and to enhance common protection within the European Union might be an indication that harmonization on a recommended basis was not effective. In the following section I will summarize the main aspects of the 2002 Recommendation.

2. Commission Recommendation

Based on the preparatory work by the Committee on Auditing, the goal of the Commission's Recommendation was "to provide investors and other stakeholders in European Union companies with a uniformly high level of assurance that the statutory auditors perform their audit work independently throughout the European Union" (European Commission 2002: L191/22). To achieve this goal, the European Commission proposed a framework of fundamental principles, which were to be implemented to ensure auditors' independence in fact and in appearance (European Commission 2002: L191/24). The principles were also meant to guarantee the objectivity and professional integrity needed to underlie an auditor's audit opinion on financial statements (Recommendation Section A). As the Recommendation warned, if these overriding principles were not ensured, certain threats and risks, either individually or in combination, could affect an auditor's independence, including self-interest, self-review, advocacy, familiarity or trust, and intimidation threats (Recommendation Section A.3). To reduce these risks of impaired auditor independence, the establishment of different types of safeguards, including prohibitions, restrictions and other procedures, as well as disclosures, were recommended (Recommendation Section A.4).

Such safeguards consisted of audited entities safeguards (Recommendation Section A.4.1), quality assurance (Recommendation Section A.4.2) and the statutory auditor's overall safeguards (Recommendation Section A.4.3). Furthermore, public disclosure was advised for fees (Recommendation Section A.5). In addition, specific circumstances in which auditor independence may be impaired were listed, including

[15] For further details on European Union Law see Craig and DeBurca (2002).

when the auditor has a financial interest in the audit client (Recommendation Section B.1), when certain business relationships between the auditor and the client exist (Recommendation Section B.2), when there is a dual employment of any individual who is in a position to influence the outcome of the audit (Recommendation Section B.3), when an individual who is able to affect the audit outcome owns a managerial or supervisory role in the client (Recommendation Section B.4), when a director or manager of the client establishes employment with the audit firm (Recommendation Section B.5) and when there is any family or personal relationship between the auditor and certain employees of the client (Recommendation Section B.6). Additional risk can arise when the auditor performs certain non-audit services (Recommendation Section B.7), when there are certain fee arrangements made (Recommendation Section B.8), when there is a high risk of litigation (Recommendation Section B.9) or when senior personnel act for a long period of time (Recommendation Section B.10).

The recommendations regarding non-audit services most relevant to this thesis will now be elaborated. In the 2002 document, the European Commission considered the performance of certain non-audit services by an auditing firm as possibly threatening the firm's independence from the client's decision making (European Commission 2002: L191/46). In the Comments to Section B.7, the following services were listed as potentially leading to a specific situation where the level of risk that auditor independence could be impaired might be high: (1) preparation of accounting records and financial statements, (2) design and implementation of financial information technology systems, (3) valuation services, (4) participation in the audit client's internal audit, (5) resolution of litigation for the audit client, and (6) recruitment of senior management.

As mentioned earlier, the Commission's Recommendation was only a voluntary instrument to address auditor independence issues, yet recent scandals confirmed the urgency of unified European Union initiatives on statutory audit and the need for mandatory requirements to ensure a certain level of European regulatory harmonization (Bolkestein 2003). To address these concerns, the European Commission issued a proposal for a revised 8th Directive (2004a), which would be mandatory and would achieve minimum harmonization at the European Union level, because Member States would be allowed to add local requirements.

3. Proposal for a Revised 8th Directive

a) Introduction

According to Bolkestein, "the proposed Directive aims to reinforce the statutory audit function in the Euroepan Union which is one of the crucial elements for underpinning the trust in the functioning of the European capital market" (Bolkestein 2003: 1).

One major goal of the proposal for a revised 8th Directive is the use of international auditing standards for all statutory audits conducted in the European Union. The adoption of these standards, which were developed by the International Auditing and Assurance Standard Board, would be subject to strict conditions. In addition, the proposed Directive aims to reinforce the statutory audit function in the European Union by broadening the scope of the existing 8th Directive that basically deals with the approval of auditors; by introducing a requirement for external quality assurance; by ensuring robust public oversight over the audit profession and by improving co-operation between competent authorities in the European Union (Bolkestein 2003: 1). Moreover, a new decision making structure, including an audit regulatory committee, will allow for swift regulatory responses via the adoption of certain provisions of the proposed Directive.

The proposal for a revised 8th Directive was primary expected to become law by mid-2005, although Member States have a period of 24 months to implement the contents of the Directive as minimum requirements in national law (European Commission 2004b: 1). Finally, the European Parliament (2005) voted in favour of the Commission proposal for the revised 8th Directive on 28 September 2005. The proposed directive changes were also agreed on at the first reading by the Council of Economic and Finance Ministers (2005) on 11 October 2005. The proposal for a revised 8th Directive will replace the existing 8th Directive as of 1984 as soon the formal issuance through the European Council took place.

b) Public Oversight over the Audit Profession

The following elements of the Directive are meant to reinforce public oversight over the audit profession and regulatory cooperation within the European Union and across borders with third countries (European Commission 2004b). First, the proposal requires non-auditing practitioners to control the public oversight system at the Member State level (Proposal Article 31.3). These non-auditing practitioners would have ultimate responsibility for the oversight of (1) the approval and registration of statutory auditors and audit firms, (2) the adoption of standards on ethics, internal quality control of audit firms and auditing and (3) continuous education, quality assurance and investigative and disciplinary systems (Proposal Article 31.4).

According to Article 31.2 of the Proposal, these "home country control" institutes should cooperate, so that audit firms would be principally regulated by authorities in the Member States where they are established. Within this cooperative model, Member States would mutually recognize each other's requirements in the case of audits covering more than one jurisdiction, such as a statutory audit of consolidated accounts or of a company whose securities are traded on a regulated market in a Member State other than where the company has its registered office. To ensure that this cooperative model works properly, procedures for the exchange of information between oversights bodies of Member States need to be established (Proposal Article 32).

The Directive also takes into account the internationalization of European companies, extending the cooperation model to third country auditors with the requirement that they offer reciprocity for European Union auditors. To avoid bilateral working arrangements of individual Member States, the Commission considers assessing the equivalence of third country regulatory systems at a European Level (Proposal Article 33). Furthermore, under exceptional circumstances, the Directive calls for direct access to audit working papers and other documents of authorities of third countries, subject to a number of important safeguards (Proposal Article 31.6).

Currently, the public oversight systems of single Member States do not contain equally effective mechanisms. Thus, the proposal argues a need for a European Union-coordination mechanism to bring together various national systems into a cohesive efficient pan-European network. To achieve this intended convergence of principles and practices, the European Commission's proposal states that regulatory arrangements of Member States shall respect the principle of home country regulation and oversight by the Member State in which the auditor or audit firm is approved and the audited entity has its registered office (Proposal Article 33.1).

Related to the coordination of public oversight, the European Federation of Accountants (2003) developed a framework of legislation and/or standards as well as the application and enforcement of standards, which is shown in Figure 10.

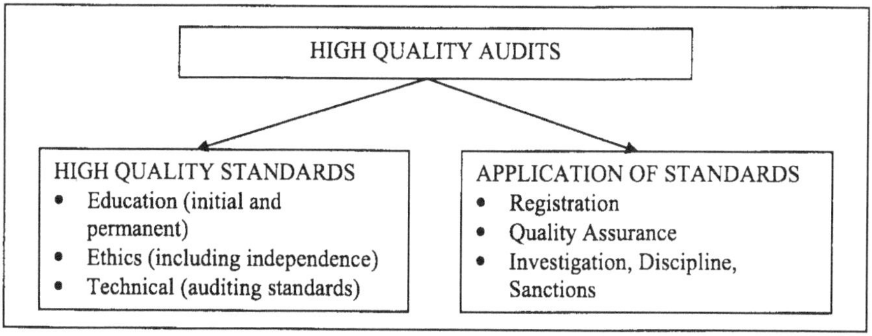

Figure 10: Relationship between High Quality Audits and Standards

To ensure high quality, the Federation recommends that auditing standards should be set by the International Auditing and Assurance Standards Board under global oversight or consultation (European Federation of Accountants 2003: 7). Those setting national standards would then be responsible for making global standards applicable at a national level. Also, ethics and independence standards should be set by the profession under global oversight or consultation. Furthermore, to ensure proper application of standards, the Federation states that auditors must be registered to carry out such a regulated activity, a quality assurance system must be in place to enhance public confidence and investigative and disciplinary proceedings must lead to appropriate sanctions (European Federation of Accountants 2003: 8).

As an interim solution of the European oversight, the European Federation agrees with the European Committee that there should be appropriate stakeholder involvement in a global oversight body. However, the European Federation of Accountants considers a European Co-ordination Audit Oversight Board at the European Union level as a more permanent solution (European Federation of Accountants 2003: 20).

The Federation's framework was adopted by the revised proposed 8th Directive, which means that Member States shall require auditors and audit firms to carry out audits in accordance with international auditing standards adopted by the Commission (European Federation of Accountants 2003, Article 26.1). The adoption of standards will only take place when the standards are developed with proper due process, public oversight and transparency (European Federation of Accountants 2003, Article 26.2 (a)).

c) Auditor Independence Requirements

Among other things, the revised proposed 8th Directive establishes principles concerning auditor independence, yet the requirements of the Directive do not address the auditor directly in this stage of regulation. Moreover, this regulation addresses Member States because they first have to adopt the requirements into national law before they are effective for auditors and other involved parties.

The proposal for a revised 8th Directive requires that public interest entities shall have an audit committee composed of non-executive members of the administrative body or members of the supervisory body of the audited entity with at least one independent member with competence in accounting and/or auditing (Proposal Article 39.1). The audit committee shall among other things: (1) monitor the financial reporting process; (2) monitor the effectiveness of the company's internal control, internal audit where applicable and risk management system; (3) oversee the financial statement audit of the annual and consolidated accounts and (4) review and monitor the independence of the auditor or audit firm and in particular the provision of additional services to the audited entity (Proposal Article 39.2). The auditor or audit firm must report to the audit committee key matters arising from the financial statement audit, in particular any material weakness in internal control in relation to the financial reporting process. The auditor or audit firm must also assist the audit committee in fulfilling its tasks (Proposal Article 39.3). In addition, Member States shall ensure that the statutory auditor or the audit firm disclose to and discuss with the audit committee of the audited entity threats to their independence and the safeguards applied to mitigate those threats, as well as any additional services provided (Proposal Article 40 (a)).

Furthermore, the proposal for a revised 8th Directive states that Member States shall ensure that the auditor or the key audit partner responsible for carrying out the audit on behalf of the audit firm rotates from the audit engagement within a maximum period of five years, or alternatively, the audit firm shall rotate within a maximum period of seven years (Proposal Article 40 (c)).

When a statutory audit is carried out in a Member States, the revised proposed 8th Directive requires that a statutory auditor or the audit firm is independent from the audited entity and is not in any way involved in management decisions of the audited entity. Furthermore, a statutory auditor or an audit firm is prohibited from conducting a statutory audit if there is any financial, business, employment or other relationship, including the provision of additional services, with the audited entity that might compromise the statutory auditor's or audit firm's independence (Proposal Article 23.1). If threats to independence occur, but also if safeguards are applied to mitigate those threats, documentation in the working papers is required. Additionally, fees for audits must be adequate to allow proper audit quality, should not be influenced or determined by the provision of additional services to the audited entity and cannot be based on any form of contingency (Proposal Article 23.2).

C. Comparison of United States and European Union Regulation

1. Requirements

Whereas the Sarbanes-Oxley Act (2002) is intended to address precisely all relevant auditor independence issues and directly audit firms, the revised 8th Directive was proposed to provide a minimum of harmonization for the Member States (European Commission 2004a). This difference is due to the fact that 25 European Union Member States with different national requirements need to have the flexibility to add local requirements where necessary. Therefore, the revised 8th Directive sets minimum standards in form of detailed rules and broad principles which all Member States are obligated to follow, yet it also allows individual governments to expand on those standards. For example, France has more restrictive requirements regarding which non-audit services can be provided to an audit client.[16] However, France would be able to maintain its own national approach even after adopting the new European Directive.

Another difference between the American regulation and the European proposal is that while the Sarbanes-Oxley Act mandates that only 'independent', i.e. non-executive directors, can serve on an audit committee (Sarbanes-Oxley Act Section 202 (i) (2)), the revised 8th Directive allows the audit committee to include executive members with

[16] Report on 'Accounting Standards and the Post-Enron World' (2003) published by the French Conseil d'analyse économique (Council of Economic Analysis) which was created in 1997 as an independent advisory body reporting to the French Prime Minister.

the requirement that there be at least one independent member with competence in accounting and/or auditing (Proposal Article 39.1). However, both the revised 8th Directive and the Sarbanes-Oxley Act require that every listed company have an audit committee and that the powers and responsibilities of the audit committee should be enhanced.

Following the major accounting collapses in the United States, the Sarbanes Oxley Act requires assessment and reporting on the effectiveness of the audit client's internal controls (Sarbanes-Oxley Act Section 404). In comparison, the revised 8th Directive falls far short on this aspect, but nevertheless requires the audit firm to report on key issues arising from the audit, such as weaknesses in internal control mechanisms for financial reporting (Proposal Article 39.3).

Within the area of auditor rotation, the revised 8th Directive goes beyond the requirements of the Sarbanes Oxley Act. While the United States reviewed and rejected the option of the mandatory rotation of entire audit firms as well as senior partners (Sarbanes-Oxley Act Section 202), the European Union has maintained both options (Proposal Article 40 (c)). The European Parliament is currently evaluating whether to support the Commission's proposal or to follow the existing United Kingdom and international approach of rotating only key audit partners (United Kingdom Department of Trade and Industry 2005:10). Only Italy currently has a system of mandatory audit firm rotation, which significantly affects business costs, audit quality in the period immediately after the change of the audit firm and further consolidation of audit work among the largest audit firms (Universita Bocconi 2002). Under the revised 8th Directive, Italy would still be able to maintain current national practice. If the European business and accounting communities are successful in striking out the option of firm rotation, it would indicate that audit firm rotation is not seen as an effective alternative to partner rotation. This might provoke undesirable effects in the case of groups of companies with material subsidiaries subject to conflicting national rotation requirements (European Federation of Accountants 2004).

The Sarbanes Oxley Act and the revised 8th Directive have much in common regarding the performance of additional non-audit services while an audit is performed. Both address the same non-audit services but use different paths to achieve the same goal (e.g., Ferlings and Lanfermann 2002, Schmidt 2003). Whereas the Sarbanes-Oxley Act is based on rules that prohibit the performance of certain non-audit services, the

European requirements are based on basic principles laid down in the Commission's proposal. These principles enhance safeguards against situations leading to damaging conflicts of interest and only become effective when auditor independence might be compromised.

Table 1 shows the key differences between the Sarbanes-Oxley Act requirements and the proposed European requirements.

	Sarbanes-Oxley Act Requirements	**Proposed 8th Directive Requirements**
Audit Committee	Only independent directors can serve on the audit committee	Requires at least one independent member with competence in accounting and/or auditing
Internal Control	Assessment and reporting on the effectiveness of the audit client's internal controls	Requires the audit firm to report on key issues arising from the audit, such as weaknesses in internal control mechanisms for financial reporting
Rotation	Internal rotation of the leading audit partner after five years.	Option of requiring either a change in key audit partner every five years (internal rotation) or change of audit firm every seven years (external rotation).
Non-Audit Services	Prohibited by rules	Interpretation of principles required

Table 1: Sarbanes-Oxley Act versus Proposed 8th Directive Requirements

2. Rules-Based versus Principles-Based Approach to Regulation

The Sarbanes-Oxley Act contains rules which generally prohibit several services, including those outside the scope of standard auditing practice such as bookkeeping and other services related to accounting records or financial statements. Financial information systems design and implementation, appraisal or valuation services and fairness opinions, actuarial services, internal audit services, management functions, human resources, broker-dealer and legal services are also not allowed (Sarbanes-Oxley Act Section 201).

In contrast, the revised proposed 8th Directive follows a principles-based approach of recommendations and does not include a list of non-audit services which statutory auditors or audit firms cannot perform. The revised 8th Directive is based on the belief that a "principles-based approach to statutory auditors' independence is preferable to one based on detailed rules because it creates a robust structure within which statutory auditors have to justify their actions" (European Commission 2002: L 191/23). In such an approach, Member States must ensure that when carrying out a statutory audit, a statutory auditor or the audit firm is independent of the audited entity and is not in any way involved in management decisions of the audited entity. Furthermore, an auditor must refuse any non-audit engagement which might compromise his independence as an auditor (Proposal Article 23).

Table 2 presents the single Sarbanes-Oxley Act rules prohibiting the performance of non-audit services and the European Union principles, which require justification.

Non-audit Services	Rules	Principles
Bookkeeping or other services related to the accounting records or financial statements	Prohibited	Member states shall ensure that when carrying out a statu-tory audit, a statutory auditor or the audit firm is independent from the audited entity and is not in any way involved in management decisions of the audited entity. A statutory auditor or an audit firm shall not carry out a statutory audit if there is any financial, business, employment or other relationship, including the provision of additional services, with the audited entity that might compromise the auditor's or audit firm's independence.
Financial information systems design and implementation		
Appraisal or valuation services, fairness opinions or contribution-in-kind-reports		
Actuarial services		
Internal audit outsourcing services		
Management functions or human resources.		
Broker or dealer, investment adviser or investment banking services.		
Legal services and expert services.		

Table 2: Comparison of Requirements Concerning Non-Audit Services

Another requirement of interest for the research in this dissertation is that concerning an audit committee. Both the Sarbanes-Oxley Act and the revised 8th Directive require publicly listed companies to set up an audit committee to strengthen the independent monitoring of the financial reporting process and of the audit and to help prevent any possible undue influence by the executive management (European Commission 2004a: 8). However, the requirements differ in terms of the level of detail given as well as the level of interpretation required to satisfy the regulation.

The Sarbanes-Oxley Act states that the audit committee of an issuer may delegate to one or more designated members of the audit committee who are independent members of the board of directors, the authority to grant pre-approvals. Furthermore, all auditing and non-audit services provided to an issuer by the auditor of the issuer must be pre-approved by the audit committee of the issuer. This pre-approval requirement is waived with respect to the provision of non-audit services for an issuer if (1) such services were not recognized by the issuer at the time of the engagement to be non-audit services and (2) such services are promptly brought to the attention of the audit committee of the issuer and approved prior to the completion of the audit by one or more members of the audit committee who are also members of the board of directors to whom authority to grant such approvals has been delegated by the audit committee and (3) the aggregate amount of all such non-audit services provided to the issuer constitutes not more than five percent of the total amount of revenues paid by the issuer to its auditor during the fiscal year in which the non-audit services were provided (Sarbanes-Oxley Act Section 202).

In comparison, the revised 8th Directive requires that public interest entities have an audit committee composed of non-executive members of the administrative body or members of the supervisory body of the audited entity with at least one independent member with competence in accounting and/or auditing. The audit committee shall among other things: (1) monitor the financial reporting process; (2) monitor the effectiveness of the company's internal control, internal audit where applicable and risk management system; (3) oversee the financial statement audit of the annual and consolidated accounts and (4) review and monitor the independence of the auditor or audit firm and in particular the provision of additional services to the audited entity. The auditor or audit firm must report to the audit committee key matters arising from the financial statement audit, in particular material weakness in internal control in relation to the financial reporting process. The auditor or audit firm must also assist the audit committee in fulfilling its tasks (Proposal Article 39).

To waive the pre-approval requirement, the Sarbanes-Oxley Act states three preconditions that must be fulfilled. A typical way to set up regulation of a rules-based approach is the implementation of thresholds. This threshold is a clearly stated rule which does not need any interpretation. However, the five percent level might tempt an auditor and his client to structure non-audit service engagements so as to underbid the threshold. In contrast, the revised 8th Directive requires the audit committee to review and monitor the independence of the auditor or audit firm and in particular the provision of additional services to the audited entity. This principle requires audit committee members to justify the independence risk in every single situation and is dependent on audit committees' objectivity and assessment.

D. Germany's Reaction towards the Sarbanes-Oxley Act and the European Recommendation and Proposal

In this section I provide a short summary of Germany's reaction toward the Sarbanes-Oxley Act (2002) and the European Recommendation (2002) and proposal for a revised 8th Directive (2004). This summary will exemplarily show how a Member State addresses requirements that are not mandated to be implemented. However, Member State response was expected by the European Union, since Member States hold the responsibility of maintaining auditor independence on a national level (Lenz 2002: 2275). Thus, many Member States already implemented auditor independence regulation, which will make adjustments necessary after the European proposal for a revised 8th Directive (2004) becomes law. The case of Germany will provide information on how Member States reacted to the American requirements and the recommended and proposed requirements on a European level.[17]

Auditor independence is discussed as being a critical issue in the German profession (e.g., Bormann 2002), academia (e.g., Mandler 2003) and on the regulatory level. The profession's statute already stated in 1961 that the auditor has to perform her or his profession independently (Wirtschaftsprüferordnung 1961: § 43 I Sentence 1). Since then, in Germany several other requirements and recommendations related to auditor independence have been issued.

[17] Empirical Evidence on German requirements is provided by Baetge and Lutter (2003).

Germany has no mandatory requirements for an audit committee, but implementation is strongly recommended by the German Corporate Governance Codex (2002) for listed companies. The main objectives of audit committees in German companies are to maintain independence of audit committee members, improve information quality, increase the efficiency throughout relieving the supervisory board, coordinate monitoring activities, and improve companies' reputation (Bender and Vater 2003).

Since companies have to report incompliance with the Code on any detail, the recommendation is close to law character (e.g., Oser, Orth and Wader 2003). Article 5.3.2 of the German Corporate Governance Codes states that, the supervisory board should set up an audit committee which, in particular, handles issues of accounting and risk management, the necessary independence required for the auditor, the issuing of the audit mandate to the auditor, the determination of auditing focal points and the fee agreement. Furthermore, the chairman of the audit committee should not be a former member of the management board of the company.

The *Bilanzrechtsreformgesetz* was issued in October 2004, and expanded the previous existing regulations concerning auditor independence of the German Commercial Code (*Handelsgesetzbuch–HGB*). This law is discussed as being the direct response to the Sarbanes-Oxley Act (2002) and the European Commission's Recommendation (2002) (e.g., Veltins 2004).

In Germany, an auditor is not allowed to perform the financial statement audit for a client[18] if any business, financial, or personal relationship to the client exists, which may bias the auditor's judgment (§ 319 II HGB). This requirement was issued to cover anything not directly regulated in a situation where auditor's independence might be compromised. Furthermore, an auditor[19] may not be the auditor of the annual accounts if she or he or a person with whom she or he practices her or his profession jointly,

(1) owns shares of or has significant financial interests in the financial statement audit client, or owns shares of any company the client is affiliated with or of a company that owns more than 20% of the client's shares.
(2) is, or in the last three years before her or his appointment was, a legal representative or member of the supervisory board or employee of the client to be

[18] Audit client refers to corporations mandatory to be audited as stated in § 316 HGB as well as to specific partnerships which are being treated as a corporation if § 264a HGB applies.
[19] By using the term auditor I refer to certified public accountants as well as to *Vereidigter Buchprüfer*.

audited or of a company, which is affiliated with the client or owns 20% of the client's shares;

(3) if additional services are provided for a financial statement audit client during the fiscal year the audit takes place or until the audit opinion is issued, such as

   a. bookkeeping or involvement in financial statement preparation,
   b. contribution to the conduction of the internal revision in a significant position,
   c. management or financial services, or
   d. evaluation services, if these services are not of minor importance for the financial statement being audited.[20] This also applies, if these services are provided by a company, where the auditor is a legal representative, is an employee, member of the supervisory board, or shareholder with more than 20% rights of votes.

(4) involves a person in the audit team, who is not allowed to be the auditor related to Numbers (1) to (3).

(5) derived more than 30% of his or her income in the last five years and is expected to earn more than 30% in the current year from being employed with the client or with a company from which the client owns more than 20% of the shares. The possibility of exceptions exists. This rule also applies if the spouse fulfills Numbers (1) to (3) (§ 319 III HGB).

Furthermore, audit firms[21] are not allowed to perform an audit, if they, one of their legal representatives, a shareholder owning more than 20% voting rights, an affiliated company, a shareholder in a position with high responsibilities for the audit or another with this audit firm employed person, who is able to affect the result of the audit, apply to II and III (§ 319 IV HGB). This requirement also applies when a member of the supervisory board is applicable to III Number (2), or when shareholders, owning together more than 20% of the voting right, on their own or together, are excluded by II and III. The reported requirements also apply for auditors of consolidated financial reports (§ 319 V HGB).

Finally, § 319a HGB was issued for companies of public interest and includes specific reasons for exclusion from the audit. An auditor is, beyond the reasons stated in § 319

[20] For a detailed analysis of German interpretations of critical non-audit service see Hagemeister (2002).

[21] By using the term auditor I refer to both audit firms as well as to *Buchprüfungsgesellschaft*.

II and III HGB, also excluded from the audit of a client, using an organized market as defined in § 2 V Securities Trading Act[22] (*Wertpapierhandelsgesetz*) if:

(1) more than 15% of her or his income was derived from the client or from a company, from which the client owns more than 20% of the shares, in the last five years or in the current year,
(2) the auditor has performed tax services additionally to the audit, which include services beyond showing alternatives, and affected the asset, financial, or profit situation in the annual report directly and more than insignificantly,
(3) the auditor has performed services beyond the audit concerning the development, implementation, and establishment of accounting information systems, if this service is not of minor importance or
(4) the auditor has issued the audit opinion (*Bestätigungsvermerk*–§ 322 HGB) for seven or more than seven years. This requirement is waived if there has been a cooling period since the last audit of three or more years.[23]

The Numbers (1) to (3) also applies, when persons, with whom the auditor is working, are applicable to the exclusion reasons. An audit firm also applies to Number (4) if the auditor in charge of the audit is not allowed to perform the audit related to Number (4).[24] The requirements of I also apply for auditors of consolidated financial reports (§ 319a II HGB).

Addressing the need for enforcement, the *Bilanzkontrollgesetz* was issued in December 2004. This law implements two-tier structure enforcement, which shall help to regain public trust in the German capital market (e.g., Pellens, Detert, Nölte and Sellhorn 2004). The objective of the Financial Reporting Enforcement Panel (*Deutsche Prüfstelle für Rechnungslegung*) as the first tier is to serve as the sponsoring organization for an independent body enforcing financial reporting requirements as stated in §§ 342b to 342e HGB.

The Federal Financial Supervisory Authority (*Bundesanstalt für Finanzdienstleistungsaufsicht*) as the second tier essentially pursues three supervisory goals; its

[22] An organised market within the meaning of this Act is a market which is regulated and supervised by state-approved bodies, is held on a regular basis and is directly or indirectly accessible to the public.
[23] A discussion of pros and cons of this requirement is given by Niehus (2003).
[24] § 319 III Number (3) (last part), Sentence 2 and IV also applies for the exclusion reasons stated in Sentence 1.

overall objective is to ensure that the entire financial sector in Germany remains operational. Further sub-objectives are to ensure the solvency of banks and financial services institutions and to ensure the protection of clients and investors.

Lastly, the Auditor Oversight Act (*Abschlussprüferaufsichtsgesetz*) was issued to strengthen independent oversight on German public auditors.[25] Based on the Auditor Oversight Act, effective January 1, 2005, the auditor oversight commission was established. The commission is responsible for overseeing statutory auditors in Germany. Members are appointed for four years and are only non-practitioners.

This section has provided a brief description of two regulatory approaches, the rules-based Sarbanes-Oxley Act and the principles-based 8th Directive of the European Union. It also includes a short summary of the German reaction towards the two regulations. In the following section, I will provide the theoretical construct behind the two competing regulation approaches.

---

[25] For a detailed discussion on how the Auditor Oversight Act will affect German audit firms see Heininger and Bertram (2004)

Chapter V. Task Complexity and Hypotheses Development

A. Introduction

Task complexity can be defined as the amount of cognitive processing a task requires (Bonner 1994: 215) and thus has a major impact on decisions (Libby 1985: 664). Although characteristics of task complexity may seem minor, such as wording of instructions, the effects of these characteristics on decision making can be huge (Libby 1985). In the field of accounting, one area where task complexity is relevant is in decisions of how to apply auditor independence regulations. As such, task complexity deserves additional attention.

In prior research, regulation has been shown to have an affect on the behavior of the decision maker based on how clearly a standard communicates its intended meaning (Nelson 2003: 91). In complexity theory, the communication precision of standards is related to the number of rules in a certain regulation and the usage of thresholds. For example, regulation varies in the extent to which it appears to be rules-based or principles-based. Regulation also differs as to whether precise numerical thresholds are included or probability phrases are given. Principles-based regulation requires that involved parties ensure their decision meets the stated principle rather than just complies with rules. The development of standards requires a tradeoff between including too few rules or too many probability thresholds which communicate too vaguely, and defining too many rules which might decrease discretion and increase complexity.

Aside from different levels of communication accuracy, standards vary in how effective they are at safeguarding auditor independence. If a regulation is communicated ambiguously, what is allowed, prohibited or required is based on interpretation. Thus, in a principles-based setting, a decision maker may be able to interpret the regulation in order to achieve certain objectives which do not conform to the intended compliance. Regulation always has the objective of serving as a safeguard to reduce improper behavior. Therefore, a balance must be struck whereby the content is ambiguous enough to avoid engagement structuring but precise enough to limit inappropriate interpretation.

In the following sections, I further elaborate on these issues. Section B describes the underlying framework of task complexity as it affects communication accuracy and the safeguarding quality of regulations and develops the relevant hypothesis. In section C, the moderating effects of knowledge are explained and the relevant hypothesis is stated. Audit firm-client characteristics, as a measure for perceived litigation risk and monetary incentives, and the final hypothesis is outlined in section D.

B. Task Complexity of Regulation

1. Framework of Task Complexity

Tasks can be defined in terms of the behavioral response of a person in order to achieve some specific level of performance (Wood 1986: 62). This definition includes approaches that focus on critical behaviors; i.e., those necessary for adequate performance (Roby and Lanzetta 1958) as well as on general "behavior requirements" (Miller 1962, Gagne 1964). Since this definition is only an operationalization of the behavior required by the task, properties of the task need also to be considered. Hence, a task can also be defined as a pattern of stimuli impinging on the individual, where task characteristics are "real world" dimensions ("task qua task") which relate to the physical nature of either the stimuli (e.g., stimuli input rate) or the stimulus material (e.g., clarity of instructions) (Hackman 1969). According to Wood (1986), the combination of the "behavior requirements" and "task qua task" has the greatest potential as a theoretical task complexity construct.

This approach leads to the postulate that all tasks contain three essential components: task objective(s) identification, (required) acts and information cues which constitute the input and process component and finally the output component.

Task objectives are the intended result of acts. Acts are the required activity for the creation of a defined product moderated by the knowledge level[26] of the person performing the act. Information cues are pieces of information about the attributes of stimulus objects upon which an individual can base the decisions required in carrying out the task (Wood 1986: 64-65). In my first two experiments, participants were asked to make a decision whether an audit firm is allowed to provide additional non-audit services (task objective identification). They were provided with an extract of the related regulation requirements and a case study describing an audit firm-client

[26] Wood (1986) also refers to skills and resources required for the performance of a certain product. In accordance to my empirical setting, I will only study the knowledge levels.

relationship (information cues) which had to be interpreted (act). This interpretation was related to the knowledge of the participants. The final decision made by the participant is the output component. Figure 11 shows the theoretical task components (Wood 1986: 64-65).

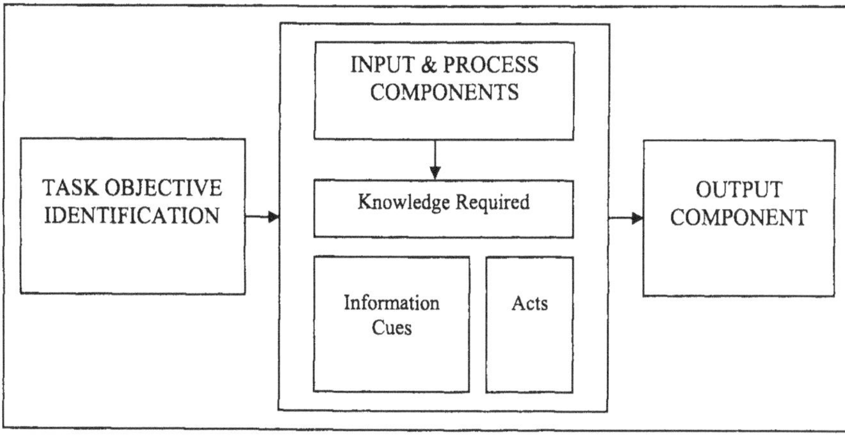

Figure 11: Task Components

According to Wood (1986) total task complexity is determined by task characteristics that affect component, coordinative and dynamic complexity. In the context of auditor independence regulation, component complexity increases with the number of decisions to be made. This number is the same as the number of information cues to be processed in the performance of certain subtasks. Coordinative complexity, on the other hand, increases when information must be combined in complex or unspecified ways while determining whether or not a regulation is satisfied. This is thus related to the number of acts in the task. Finally, dynamic complexity increases when the decisions necessary to satisfy a regulation shift over time, such as the demand for frequent adaptation of changes in the cause-effect chain of a task during performance of the task. Therefore, dynamic complexity is the sum of differences across specified time periods for any or all of the acts, information cues and subtasks required. Total complexity is therefore a function of component, coordinative and dynamic complexity.

Bonner (1994) divides task complexity into the three components of general information processing models: input, processing and output. This model specifies task characteristics incorporated in the information processing model. Thus, this model uses the same input-output structure given by Wood (1986) but views task characteristics as causing different levels of task complexity. These three components are characterized by several task characteristics relating either to the amount or clarity of information.

In this model, the amount of input required is the number of alternatives a decision maker must evaluate and the number of cues or attributes per alternative (Wood 1986, Payne, Bettman and Johnson 1990). The clarity of input is determined by cues not being clearly specified, by cues not being measured (Kerlinger and Lee 2000), by the match between the manner in which information cues are presented and the manner in which they are stored in memory and by the presentation format of information cues.

The amount of processing varies with the alternatives and cues per alternative and the number of steps or procedures that have to be executed to make a decision (Wood 1986, Payne et al. 1990). The clarity of processing is related to the specification of procedures to use (Smith 1988), the level of dependency between the procedures (Campbell and Gingrich 1986), the nature of the individual input-output relations[27], the level of magnitude of the input-output relation (Simnett and Trotman 1989), the sign of functions (Brehmer 1987) and cues which are inconsistent with each other (Brehmer 1987).

The amount of output refers to the number of objectives or solutions per alternative (Campbell 1988). The clarity of output is affected by the specification of an objective or by the decision maker's lack of familiarity with the objective (Campbell and Furrer 1995) and by the lack of objective criteria for testing a proposed solution (Smith 1988). In terms of the information processing level described by Bonner (1994), the task elements of the three complexities stages–input, processing and output–cannot be tested empirically other than through the use of manipulation checks to verify that people's perceptions of task complexity correspond to the definitions. Figure 12 shows the association between task components and factors causing complexity in the component phase model described above.

[27] Lens model research has examined four aspects of these input-output relations: (1) magnitude, (2) sign, (3) consistency among cues as to their relations with output, and (4) functional form (Wood 1986, Campbell 1988).

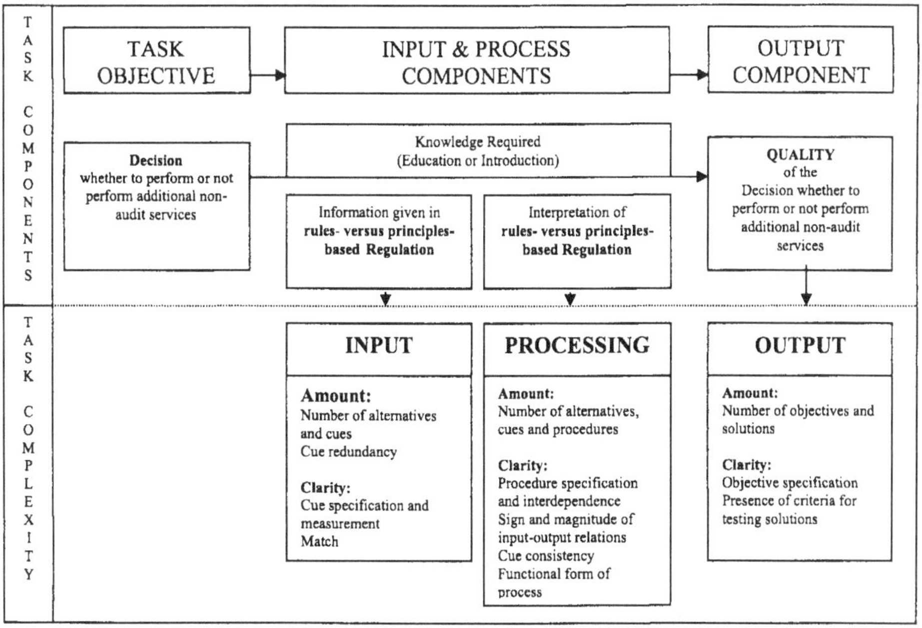

Figure 12: Task Components and Task Complexity in the Context of the Decision Makers Application of Regulation

2. Safeguarding Quality of Regulation

Complexity related to accounting is investigated in many studies. Plumlee (2003) shows that analysts' revision of their forecasts of effective tax rates appear to impound the effects of the less complex tax-law changes but not the more complex changes. Furthermore, she found that the magnitude of the errors in analysts' forecasts of effective tax rates increased with more complex tax-law changes but was unrelated to less complex changes. The influence of tax law requirements and the organization of client facts on professional judgment were studied by Krawczyk (1994). She found that the form of law and the organization of facts interactively influenced the number of cues selected for use in decision making. Form of law also affected which specific cues were selected, which of those were more highly weighted in decision making, and the actual tax decision made. In another study, tax complexity significantly affected tax reporting decisions (Milliron 1995). Boritz (1986) reported significantly different decision making results depending on whether required judgments were made silently or aloud. Similarly, significant variation in decisions depending on the task was reported by Abdolmohammdi and Wright (1987). The effects of task complexity on auditors' performance are studied by Tan, Ng and Mak (2002), who found that performance declines with increasing complexity.

The degree of complexity decreases its communication accuracy. One way to assess the accuracy of a regulation's communication is by comparing subjects' decisions as to whether or not to allow additional services to be preformed in a certain audit firm-client engagement situation, given the intended compliance. I argue that the complexity of a regulation increases the likelihood that subjects' decisions and the intended compliance will differ. If a regulation is very complex, it is more difficult for a subject who reads it to understand what is allowed, prohibited or required. This might result in a heterogeneous interpretation between subjects. Thus, whenever requirements are under-complied they fail to safeguard as intended. Experimental research on communication accuracy as its affects the safeguarding effects of regulation can be divided into two areas. There is little research on how precise standards affect the interpretation of the regulation but a significant amount on the effects of imprecise standards.

Nelson, Elliott and Tarpley (2002) reported evidence that auditors were not likely to require their clients to adjust aggressive reporting that had been specifically structured to meet precise standards because the client could demonstrate compliance with regulation. Magee and Tseng (1990) modeled the link between audit pricing, auditor independence and the characteristics of accounting standards. They hypothesized that when accounting standards were specific, threats by the client to "opinion shop" in the case of a dispute were less effective because it was likely that all auditors would take the same position on an issue. That professional tax preparer responded to a more stringent tax practice standard by interpreting evidence more liberally was found by Cuccia, Hackenbrack and Nelson (1995).

With respect to imprecise standards, Gibbins et al. (2001) demonstrated that clear standards increased auditors' power in auditor-client negotiations while imprecise standards left more room for negotiating. In an experiment using 54 audit partners as participants, Trompeter (1994) found evidence that auditors were less able to resist client pressure for aggressive reporting when there was a wider range of acceptable accounting alternatives. Knapp (1987) reported that audit committees were more likely to support an auditor in a dispute with management when the issue was covered by technical standards. Some evidence of how regulation affects market behavior was shown by Jamal, Maier and Sunder (2003), who found that the most extreme financial reporting frauds happened in the most highly regulated securities market in the world, the United States. A variety of theoretical models indicated that attempts to have very specific accounting and auditing rules can end up hurting the shareholders.

The effects of regulation on the safeguarding of auditor independence depend on the precision of the regulation. This is the degree to which the regulation precisely states what is prohibited, allowed or required in an audit firm-client engagement. Imprecision requires the user to interpret the content, yet her or his interpretation may not be the intended one. In such a situation, principles will not necessarily lead to the intended compliance. In the case of over-compliance, the regulation is satisfied and only the audit firm has to cover the costs of evaded non-audit service fees. If there is under-compliance of a regulation, the regulator and possibly the investor have to bear the costs of auditor independence risk. Under-compliance may place the auditor in a situation where her or his audit work and financial reporting decisions may become biased due to incentives or opportunities threats from unintended decisions making concerning the performance of non-audit services.

Based on theory and such prior research, I argue that the Sarbanes-Oxley Act regulation communicates more accurately than the European Union regulation. This prediction is derived from the idea that adding a certain number of rules that sequence the auditors' necessary decisions could lower total complexity of the regulation by reducing coordinative complexity. The decrease in this type of complexity outweighs the increase in component and dynamic complexity caused by additional rules. However, satisfying the regulation is the prerequisite for ensuring the intended safeguarding quality of the regulation, because subjects' decision making quality affects the safeguarding quality of the regulation. Therefore, I state hypothesis one as follows:

H1: **Subjects' decision making quality based on principles-based regulation will more likely to be compromised (there will be a greater amount or frequency of over- or under-compliance) compared to the decision making quality based on rules-based regulation.**

3. Task Complexity and Decision Making Quality

Decision making quality is negatively related to task complexity (Bonner 1994: 218). As task complexity increases, task performance is thought to decrease, certeris paribus. Furthermore, there are interactive effects of task complexity and a person's knowledge[28] and/or task motivation on decision making quality. Decision making quality in this research is determined by comparing subjects' decision whether to perform or not perform additional non-audit services with the intended outcome.

The relevant range of the theoretical interaction between the effects of task complexity and knowledge on decision making quality is shown in Figure 13 (Bonner 1994: 219).

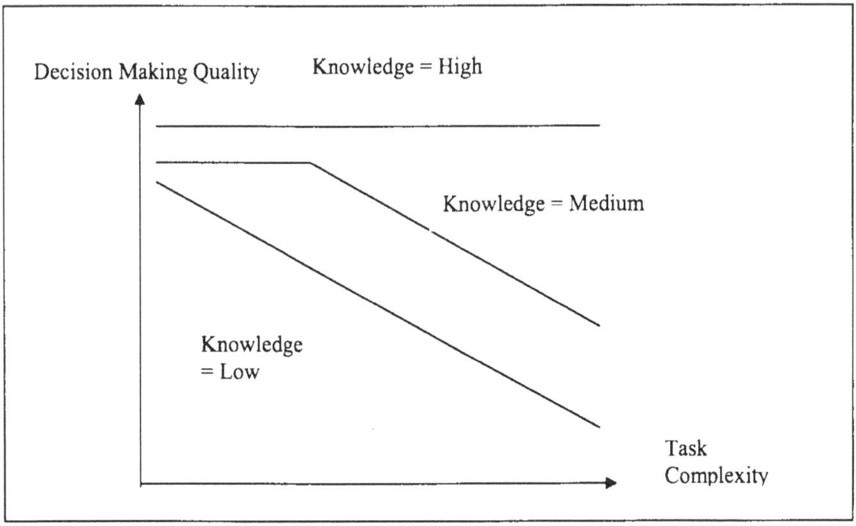

Figure 13: Task Complexity and Knowledge Effects on Decision Making Quality

Knowledge moderates task complexity to affect decision making quality (Bonner 1994). The more complex the task is the greater is the importance of knowledge to good performance.

The affect of task motivation on decision making quality is shown in Figure 14 (Bonner 1994: 219). Task motivation can be intrinsic or extrinsically induced by financial incentives, goals or other techniques (Bonner 1994: 223-224). The relative effect of task motivation decreases as task complexity increases. Related to auditor

[28] Bonner (1994) defines skill as knowledge and abilities. I will only use the term knowledge.

independence regulation, this interaction suggests that when subjects are motivated to apply the regulation as intended (task motivation high), decision making quality measured as the difference between the intended outcome and the subject's decision increases, with task complexity decreasing.

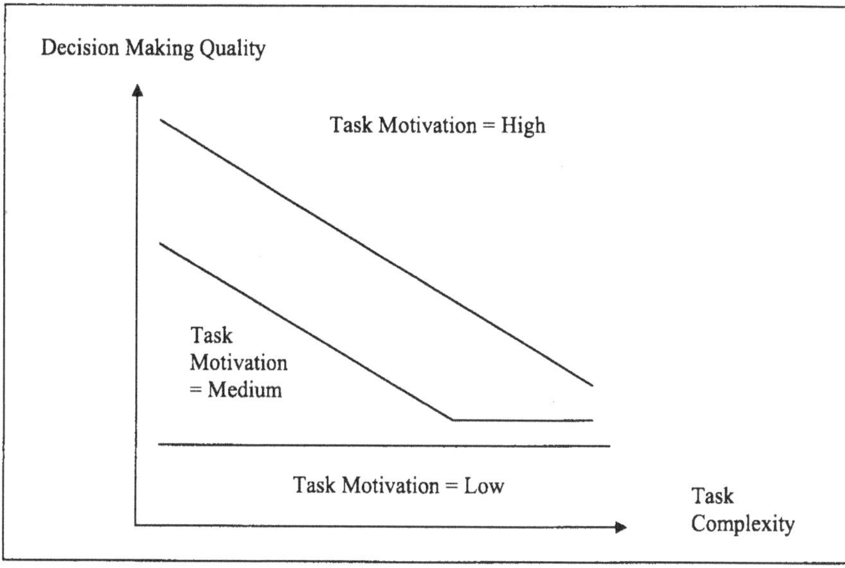

Figure 14: Task Complexity and Task Motivation Effects on Decision Making Quality

In this study, I argue that the final decision about the performance of additional non-audit services will differ, depending on the precision of the information of the given regulation. This is due to the demands on individuals made by complex regulations that may exceed individuals' capacities to decide as intended. In this situation, knowledge and task motivation will moderate this effect. The following sections C and D provide further theoretical information regarding the moderators' knowledge of the decision maker and audit firm-client characteristics as a proxy for task motivation.

C. Knowledge

1. Definition and Characteristics of Knowledge

Knowledge is the information stored in long-term memory, and long-term memory is relatively permanent (Bonner 2005). Knowledge incorporates two relevant characteristics: knowledge content and knowledge structure. The former refers to the quantity and specific pieces of information stored in long-term memory while the latter refers to the extent and the ways in which that information is organized in memory. Although these two characteristics are interrelated, they can have separate effects on decision making quality.

Knowledge content can be divided into semantic and episodic knowledge (Klatzky 1980). Semantic knowledge extracts the underlying meaning of experience, preserves the meaning in the form of concepts and principles and includes an understanding of how the concept is generally to be judged (e.g., good or bad). This knowledge type is either declarative (comprised of facts) or procedural (if-then rules). Episodic knowledge is generated through personal experience, including temporal, spatial and other sensory features of experience, such as affective reactions.

Many classifications of knowledge structure apply to both semantic and episodic knowledge (Markman 1999) and as with semantic knowledge; knowledge structure can be declarative or procedural. The latter is believed to be stored in a simple list format (Anderson 2000). However, declarative knowledge is knowledge about categories, which is structured in the form of a hierarchical network (Markman 1999, Anderson 2000). Declarative knowledge is also believed to be represented via schemas, which are representations of members of a category in terms of what types of objects they are, what parts they tend to have and what their typical properties are (Anderson 2000). Scripts represent regularities about event categories.

Finally, it is important to note how knowledge content and structures are studied in experimental research. Research in accounting has generally used some sort of instruction, practice or feedback proxy to measure knowledge because these factors affect knowledge. Most typically, the proxy is experience, which incorporates instruction, practice and feedback. The majority of studies have divided subjects into groups of experts and novices on the basis of years of experience (e.g., Messier 1983, Frederick and Libby 1986) or have measured expertise by measuring specific types of knowledge and abilities necessary to perform accurately (Bonner and Lewis 1990). Knowledge can also be assessed by using recognition or recall tests. Furthermore, knowledge can be manipulated by varying one or more of the factors that influence knowledge content or structure. For example, an experiment could manipulate the content and amount of instruction subjects receive in order to manipulate knowledge content (e.g., Bonner and Walker 1994).

2. Effect on Decision Making Quality

In a complex task setting, the individual decision makers' characteristics may become important determinants of performance (Bonner 1994). Individuals may perceive task complexity differently and their individual perceptions are likely to affect their proper use of knowledge (e.g., Ho and Rodgers 1993). When tasks are complex, it is more difficult to recognize the embedded concepts and decisions required to solve a problem. In these situations, differences in decision makers' qualifications may become relevant because individuals with task specific knowledge may be able to recognize and apply relevant regulations to solve the problem and perform better (Bonner 1990).

High task complexity decreases the communication accuracy of a regulation. If interpretation of a regulation requires greater effort by those applying the regulation, the task is more complex and is less likely to be carried out accurately. The communication accuracy of a regulation thus decreases as the effort needed for understanding increases. This negative effect is positively moderated by knowledge. For example, task specific knowledge effects can be moderated by providing subjects with the knowledge they lack (Bonner 2005).

In an experimental study, Tan et al. (2002) found that performance declined with increasing complexity but only under combinations of low knowledge and high accountability or high knowledge and low accountability. Similarly, Prawitt (1995) showed that increased environmental complexity resulted in the assignment of more experienced auditors to unstructured firms. Confirming these findings, in another study audit firms assigned more experienced auditors to more complex tasks (Abdolmohammadi 1999). Chang, Ho and Liao (1997) also found that general experience and training significantly affected performance.

Given the research findings above, I argue that transparent information (knowledge) about an audit firm's own policies and procedures helps to increase the precision of the communication of the regulation, thereby decreasing task complexity. If additional knowledge helps the decision maker to understand the regulation, the quality of safeguarding should increase. Negotiating in a certain auditor-client engagement will be less likely because knowledge transmits the information required to determine if a regulation is satisfied. If the regulation is satisfied the audit firm-client engagement structure will be as intended by the regulation. The possibility of arising incentives and opportunity threats is less likely, which mitigates biases in auditor's audit work and financial reporting decisions. However, the additional information must clearly focus on what is allowed or prohibited in an actual engagement. Therefore, hypothesis two is:

H2: Subjects' decision making quality based on auditor independence regulation is less likely to be compromised if additional information is provided to the decision maker (if the decision maker has greater regulatory knowledge).

D. Task Motivation

1. Negative Moderator: Monetary Incentives

Managers consciously or unconsciously make financial reports that are consistent with their interests; however, task motivation can affect an auditors' ability to constrain aggressive and biased reporting by managers. Auditors are supposed to ensure that their clients' financial reporting is fair and reasonable. Nonetheless, auditors may introduce their own errors, as well as biases, if their relationship with the audited client compromises their independence. By providing accurate and specific requirements that do not offer any discretionary power, auditor independence regulations should constitute a safeguard against errors and biases on the part of auditors and managers preparing financial statements.

In a study investigating these issues, Trompeter (1994) found that partners with compensation more closely tied to client retention were less likely to require downward adjustments to income. In another study, Libby and Kinney (2000) conducted two experiments where audit managers estimated reported (audited) earnings conditional on analysts' consensus forecasts, auditing standards and auditor discovery of a quantitatively immaterial earning overstatement. They found that auditors judged overstatement corrections less likely if it would cause a missed forecast, even for objectively measured misstatements. These results confirmed opportunistic corrections to manage earnings to forecasts. The effects of quality assessment and directional goal commitment on auditors' acceptance of client-preferred accounting methods were studied by Kadous et al. (2003). They found that performing a quality assessment amplified the effects of auditors' directional goals on their acceptance of client-preferred accounting methods and on their rating of the quality of that method. Farmer, Rittenberg and Trompeter (1987) provided evidence that the threat of client loss significantly encouraged aggressive reporting for all experience levels. Similarly, competition for the client and client importance tended to encourage aggressive reporting (Lord, Dopuch and Gibbins 1992). In a Dopuch, King and Schwartz (2001) study, mandatory rotation of auditors made auditors less likely to issue audit reports that were consistent with management's intended conclusion.

In this research, I argue that when monetary incentives are high, it is more likely that decisions will be made in favor of the performance of additional non-audit services.

2. Positive Moderator: Litigation Risk

Litigation risk is a significant and increasing concern for audit and assurance services firms. The *ex post* revelation of undetected material misstatements may lead to accusations of negligence against the audit firm resulting in costly litigation (Simunic and Stein 1996).

Pratt and Stive (1994) studied the effects of client characteristics on auditor litigation risk judgments, required audit evidence and recommended audit fees. They discovered that the client's overall financial condition was the primary consideration in an auditor's assessment of litigation risk. Poorer financial conditions were associated with higher levels of litigation risk. Similarly, Simunic and Stein (1996) investigated the relationship between audit pricing and litigation risk. Their results indicated that increased litigation is likely to result in a demand displacement from high quality to low quality auditors. Whether or not the perceived higher quality of a Big Four audit is related to auditor litigation was studied by Khurana and Raman (2004). Their findings suggested that it is litigation exposure rather than brand name reputation protection that drives perceived audit quality. Wilken-Braun (2001) showed that auditors were more likely to waive proposed adjusting journal entries in excess of materiality when there was a potential reward for doing so or when there was little litigation risk from doing so. In line with this, another study found auditors' aggressive reporting decisions were deterred significantly by litigation risk and peer-review risk, but the risk of disciplinary actions by professional organizations had no deterring effect (Shafer et al. 1999).

Related to this body of research, audit firm-client characteristics that affect the likelihood and costs of litigation can lead to conservative decision making. The prediction that litigation costs will lead to audit firm bankruptcy requires some special conditions, such as the audit firm's wealth and the pool of clients in the firm's portfolio may be too small to cover large realized losses (Simunic and Stein 1996). Thus, I will incorporate these findings in the second experiment by manipulating the audit-firm client characteristics as a proxy for task motivation, which may lead to different risk of litigation for the audit firm.[29]

I argue that the perceived litigation risk has possibly an important effect on an audit firm's decision making.[30] However, whether or not the risk of litigation is perceived being more important than monetary incentives of the audit firm needs to be investigated.

3. Audit Firm's Decision Making

When litigation risk is perceived to be higher than the monetary incentives for a given audit firm-client engagement, conservative interpretation of the regulation is more likely. However, if monetary incentives are more important, it is more likely that auditor independence regulation will be interpreted in favor of performing additional non-audit services. This means that monetary incentives must be smaller than the costs

[29] I will not consider different liability systems, which may also affect an audit firm's decision making concerning the performance of additional non-audit services in real world settings. Since subjects of the experiments one and two are students it can assumed that the effect of the liability systems is insignificant. For a detailed comparison of auditor's legal liability in the USA and selected European Countries see Baker and Quick (1996) and Heppe (2003a, b). For an economical analysis see Ewert (1999).

[30] By the client or other involved parties; however this will not be specified for this research.

of potential litigation to ensure the safeguarding quality of regulation. In addition, regulation must be imprecise enough to allow a decision maker a range of interpretation.

Simunic (1980) developed a model identifying elements of the audit firm's decision making when accepting an audit client. He stated that in a competitive market, audit fees will be equal to the audit firm's expected costs. I extend the model by including additional non-audit fees and thus analyzing an audit firm's decision making when accepting to perform non-audit services for a financial statement audit client.

In a highly regulated market, the audit firm will perform the following procedures before deciding whether to perform additional critical non-audit services: (1) assess the costs (monetary and reputation costs) and the likelihood of a potential litigation if the decision does not conform to regulatory requirements, (2) assess the costs of performing the additional services in terms of resources and opportunity costs and (3) assess the expected total fees and the relevance of these fees for the audit firm. The following Equation 1 shows the audit firm's decision making.

$$E_{TF} \text{ X } E_R \quad \gtreqless \quad E_{CL} \text{ X } E_D + C \qquad (1)$$

E_{TF}	=	Expected Total Fees
E_{CL}	=	Expected Cost of Litigation (Monetary and Reputation Costs)
$E_D = E_R$	=	Expected Likelihood of Litigation = Relevance of Fees (Related to Client and Audit Firm Characteristics)
C	=	Costs of Performing the Additional Non-audit Services (Related to Client and Audit Firm Characteristics)

Equation 1: Audit Firm's Decision Making

An audit firm's decision making model is therefore affected by certain reward and risks factors (Wright and Wright 1997). One of these factors is the client's relative fees (reward factor). Client-specific quasi rents naturally arise from a multi-period relationship in which auditors invest in the current period with the expectation of future returns (DeAngelo 1981a, b). Audit firms operate in a competitive market where retaining a current client is important to their firm's future revenue base. Thus, audit firms may be more willing to avoid potential client loss by improperly interpreting auditor independence regulation when the client accounts for a relatively large share of the audit firm's fees (perceived monetary incentives).

A reverse effect arises due to risk factors from an asymmetric power-dependence relation between an audit firm and a client (Emerson 1962, Goldman and Barlev 1974). These factors can derive from client characteristics and audit firm characteristics (perceived litigation risk). Several studies have shown that auditors' actual and perceived exposure to legal liability increases with client's size (Schultz and Gustavson 1978, St. Pierre and Anderson 1984). Auditors' tend to disclose more conservatively when engagement risk is high (Hackenbrack and Nelson 1996).

The audit firm can only perform the foregoing decision procedures when regulation is ambiguous and imprecise enough to allow an opportunity for unintended interpretation. Related to prior research and the theory of audit firm's decision, I state my final hypothesis as follows:

H3: Subjects' decision making quality based on auditor independence regulation is expected to be higher (lower) when the costs of litigation are perceived to be greater (less) than the monetary returns from the additional non-audit service fees.

E. Summary

This Chapter presented the theory and hypotheses which were tested in two 2 x 2 between subjects design. The three independent variables are

1. the task complexity of the regulation;
2. the knowledge level created by additional information; and
3. the audit firm-client characteristics (affecting litigation risk and monetary incentives) as a proxy for task motivation.

Each of these were manipulated between subjects. In the first experiment I manipulated task complexity and knowledge level. The second experiment contained task complexity and audit firm-client characteristics (affecting litigation risk and monetary incentives) manipulations. European and Sarbanes-Oxley Act regulation, which proxy for principles- or rules-based regulation respectively were the manipulation for different task complexity levels. Knowledge and audit-firm client characteristics were manipulated at two levels (low and high).

The experiments were conducted using 39 undergraduate and 54 graduate students, respectively. The experimental task was to decide whether an audit firm is allowed to provide additional non-audit services for a financial statement audit client given different regulation approaches. The decisions concerning additional non-audit services provide measures of the communication accuracy and safeguarding quality of the regulation as dependent variables. Manipulations check questions were used to test the success of the manipulations. A summary of hypotheses, dependent and independent variables is presented in the Table 3.

	Hypotheses	**Dependent Variable**	**Independent Variables**
H1	Subjects' decision making quality based on principles-based regulation will more likely to be compromised (there will be a greater amount or frequency of over- or under-compliance) compared to the decision making quality based on rules-based regulation.	Subjects' Decisions	Regulation Approach
H2	Subjects' decision making quality based on auditor independence regulation is less likely to be compromised if additional information is provided to the decision maker (if the decision maker has greater regulatory knowledge).	Subjects' Decisions	Knowledge
H3	Subjects' decision making quality based on auditor independence regulation is expected to be higher (lower) when the costs of litigation are perceived to be greater (less) than the monetary returns from the additional non-audit service fees.	Subjects' Decisions	Audit Firm-Client Characteristics (Litigation Risk & Monetary Incentives)

Table 3: Summary of Hypotheses and Experimental Variables

Chapter VI. Empirical Studies on Auditor Independence Regulation

The purpose of this chapter is to study regulation approach as it affects the safeguarding quality of auditor independence regulation. Related to the model of auditor independence risk, this research will provide further information on whether the regulation approach itself may lead to its own risk of impairing auditor independence in fact[31] instead of maintaining auditor independence as intended.

In section A, research results of an experimental pilot test of regulation approach and knowledge are presented. In section B I then study the effects of regulation approach and audit firm-client characteristics as they affect perceived costs of litigation risk and monetary returns in a second experiment. Education related knowledge effects are presented and discussed in section C. Finally, in section D I study relevant threats by performing regression analysis of subjects' assessments on auditor independence risk and the level of threat from audit, tax and IT fees.

A. Experiment on Regulation Approach and Knowledge

In this first experiment, which serves a pilot test, I study differences in subjects' decision making based on rules-based or principles-based auditor independence regulation. Since, while designing experiments, some critical issues need to be considered, such as demand effects and validity of responses, I consider this experiment as being a pilot test. This is the first attempt to answer research question one, which asked whether the approach of auditor independence regulation is associated with the effectiveness of the regulation in reducing risks to auditor independence. More specific, subjects' decisions will be analyzed to investigate hypothesis one, which predicts that subjects' decision making quality based on principles-based regulation will more likely be compromised (there will be a greater amount or frequency of over- or under-compliance) compared to the decision making quality based on rules-based regulation.

---

[31] This chapter focuses on the possibility that in an experimental setting, subjects may compromise their decisions. Thus, unless indicated, the terms 'independence risk', 'lack of independence' and 'impaired independence' all refer to impaired independence 'in fact'.

Furthermore, I investigate whether the effectiveness of regulation to reduce auditor independence risk is dependent on the knowledge level of the person applying the regulation, which is research question two. Related to this research question, hypothesis two predicts that subjects' decision making quality based on auditor independence regulation is less likely to be compromised if additional information is provided to the decision maker.

1. Participants

Participants in my first experiment were 39 undergraduate students from Germany and the United States with some auditing experience who were attending a one week workshop. Almost all participants have experience in financial statements analysis or have completed an audit class, so that understanding of the case study can be assumed. However, the students self-assessed little knowledge about auditor independence regulation (mean=2.3, scale 1 to 7 indicating low to high knowledge, respectively).

2. Research Design and Procedures

The two independent variables, regulation approach and level of knowledge, were manipulated in a 2 x 2 between subjects design, where subjects were assigned to one version randomly.[32] Furthermore, as a manipulation check, I asked subjects to indicate the complexity of the given regulation requirements. This provides further information about how accurate regulation is perceived to be communicated. Throughout the whole questionnaire I use numerical rating scales with seven response categories. These scales types are easiest to construct and use, whereas they also yield numbers that can be used directly in statistical analysis (Kerlinger and Lee 2000).

All subjects were given some background information in auditor independence regarding the increase in violations of auditor independence by several auditing firms and the economic damage to the capital markets possibly caused by impaired independence. They were presented the following information as an introduction:

---

[32] The results of a performed one way ANOVA on subjects' knowledge level indicate that random assignment of subjects to versions was effective ($F=0.14$, $p=0.93$).

Recent worldwide financial scandals have emphasized that the financial statement audit is an important element in ensuring the credibility and reliability of companies' financial statements. However, significant economic damage to the capital markets and the economy has resulted from alleged impaired auditor independence. Auditor independence is impaired when audit decisions or judgments are biased in favor of the client. Independence is considered the profession's main means of demonstrating to the public and regulators that auditors and audit firms are performing their task at a level that meets established ethical principles, particularly those of integrity and objectivity.

An example of the importance of auditor independence is demonstrated by the bankruptcy of the energy giant Enron Corporation and the demise of its auditor – Arthur Andersen, LLP. As the Enron case shows, a lack of auditor independence can lead to catastrophic consequences for investors, audit firms and financial markets. The effects on audit firms of problems related to independence have not been limited to Arthur Andersen. In January 2002 another Big 4 firm, KPMG, was censured because it purported to serve as an independent auditing firm for an audit client at the same time that it had made substantial financial investments in that client. Regulators found that KPMG violated the auditor independence rules by engaging in such conduct. In another case, in a ruling by an administrative-law judge, Ernst & Young was called "reckless," "highly unreasonable" and "negligent" because it formed a business venture with one of its audit clients, PeopleSoft. Ernst & Young was PeopleSoft's independent auditor and business partner from 1994 through 1999. Its audit fees during this period were $1.7 million, and revenue from its PeopleSoft partnership was $425 million. The Securities and Exchange Commission is investigating PricewaterhouseCoopers for a possible violation of auditor independence rules. In a press release announcing its quarterly results, the Royal Bank of Canada said it has received a subpoena from the U.S. securities regulator regarding PwC, which resigned as one of the bank's auditors in September 2004.

Following this information, recent changes regarding auditor independence regulation were specified by giving the exact wording of either Sarbanes-Oxley or European requirements concerning the regulation of non-audit services. To avoid biased assessment, subjects were not informed about whether the requirement was Sarbanes-Oxley Act or European Union regulation which proxy for rules-based or principles-based regulation, respectively. Subjects of the rules-based condition were given the following Sarbanes-Oxley Act regulation extract:

Requirements Concerning the Regulation of Non-audit Services

A public accounting firm (and any associated person of that firm) can not perform for a financial statement audit client, contemporaneously with the audit, any of the following non-audit services:

1. *bookkeeping or other services related to the accounting records or financial statements of the audit client;*
2. *financial information systems design and implementation;*
3. *appraisal or valuation services, fairness opinions, or contribution-in-kind reports;*
4. *actuarial services;*
5. *internal audit outsourcing services;*
6. *management functions or human resources;*
7. *broker or dealer, investment adviser, or investment banking services; or*
8. *legal services and expert services unrelated to the audit.*

However, the public accounting firm may engage in any non-audit service, including a tax service that is not described above for an audit client, if the activity is approved in advance by the audit committee of the client.

Subjects within the principles-based condition were provided with the following European Union regulation extract:

Requirements Concerning the Regulation of Non-audit Services

When carrying out a financial statement audit, both the auditor and the audit firm must remain independent from the client and not be in any way involved in management decisions of the client. The auditor and audit firm can not carry out a financial statement audit if there is any financial, business, employment or other relationship, including the provision of additional services, with the client that might compromise the auditor's or audit firm's independence.

The experiment was done using a case study dealing with an audit firm-client relationship. In addition to performing the audit for the client for four years, the audit firm is also performing IT and tax services. All participants were provided with the following information:

Auditor

Roberts & Partner (R&P) is a large, American registered independent public accounting firm. The firm was founded in 1963 and is headquartered in New York. Including its affiliations in Europe and Asia, R&P employs over 6,000 people. The firm is primarily involved in financial statement audit services applying US-GAAP. In addition, as a result of its expansion into Europe and Asia, the firm specializes in financial statement audit services applying international accounting standards. Furthermore, R&P also offers non-audit services in order to maintain its competitiveness in the audit market.

As part of an ongoing quality control and improvement process, R&P is proactive in keeping up with the ever-changing professional and regulative requirements. These activities include training of audit partners to satisfy additional education requirements, and developing its own audit practice improvement system. To help insure that R&P meets the profession's independence guidelines, last year R&P developed its own independence compliance system (RPICS®).

Client Information

R&P's Boston office has performed the financial statement audit for Kelly & Co for the last seven years. After the first three years there was a change of the key audit partner (partner in charge of the audit engagement), because the former audit partner retired. Currently, the key audit partner is John Miller, who has led the audit for the last four years. The annual audit fee is currently around $3,000,000. This fee represents 6% of the average annual revenue of the Boston office of R&P and 30 % of John Miller's annual billings.

In addition, to performing the annual financial statement audit, R&P's Information Technology Department is developing new software for Kelly & Co's management information system. The new software is designed to improve strategic flexibility, to facilitate short run decision making, and to support internal operations. Senior management believes that significant efficiencies can be achieved through savings in product costs through automation reduced data processing, more effective management of inventory and reduced raw materials waste. The new system is designed to provide more timely, relevant, and concise information to the decision making process, and improved system integration of accounting and financial reporting.

Although R&P's Information Technology Department is responsible for the development and implementation of the system, Kelly & Co's management is responsible for establishing, maintaining, operating and evaluating the information system. Kelly & Co's information technology manager Clara Becker manages the development and implementation process. An R&P employee, Arthur Kellerman an IT specialist, oversees the project and its staff. Reporting lines for audits and IT projects within R&P are completely separated. It is expected that the fee for providing the system design and implementation service will be around $700,000. This fee represents 1.4 % of the average annual revenue of R&P's Boston office. R&P also provides tax consultancy to Kelly & Co regarding planning and ensuring regulatory compliance. Kelly & Co's audit committee approved the tax service. The annual fee for this service is $750,000, which is 1.5% of the average annual revenue of the R&P's Boston office.

To test for possible subject reactions toward additional information, subjects in the high level knowledge cell received specific information about the audit firm's own independence compliance system. Recall that knowledge can be manipulated through an introduction into the task specific area (Bonner 2005). In comparison, subjects of the low level knowledge version were informed that such a compliance system was in place without any further description. The additional 'high-level' information treatment contained the following:

RPICS® is an online system that assists the firm in identifying and resolving potential independence issues affecting the firm. For example, the system features an investment tracking system that enables each auditor to search a database to determine if any of their investments are with current clients and thus are restricted according to SEC rules. The independence compliance system also notifies professionals when a previously unrestricted investment becomes restricted as a result of a company becoming a new audit client. In addition, R&P has a positive assurance conflict-checking database in place that provides data on all audit and non-audit services being provided to each current client. The system provides a warning message for any engagements that may violate current legal or professional requirements regarding the provision of non-audit services to audit clients. Finally RPICS® monitors each auditor's compliance with R&P risk management policies and procedures and current legal and professional audit requirements relating to auditor independence. RPICS® also provides a monthly report of audits that require lead partner auditor rotation within the next 12 months. This enables R&P to plan for auditor rotations by assigning another partner to the audit engagement so the auditor can become familiar with the client before the actual lead partner rotation occurs. Tests of RPICS® have shown it to work properly for all the partners and managers tested.

The participating subjects per experimental treatments are shown in Table 4.[33]

		Regulation Approach	
		Rules	Principles
Level of Knowledge	High	11	9
	Low	10	9

Table 4: Experimental Treatments and Treatment Sample Sizes (Experiment 1)

Subjects decision making quality was measured by asking subjects to decide whether the performance of the additional IT and/or tax service should be prohibited. To assess subjects' attitude I use the forced-choice scaling method where subjects have to choose among alternatives (Kerlinger and Lee 2000). Subjects had to read the given regulation extract carefully to decide about the performance of additional services. Therefore, they were allowed to go back to the case study and the regulation extract. This task required subjects to interpret the content of the given regulation before deciding. Depending on the complexity of the regulation approach, this task had different levels of difficulty. I will compare subjects' decisions with the intended outcome, to investigate whether the regulation leads to intended compliance, under-compliance or over-compliance.

The intended outcome is determined by analyzing the Securities and Exchange Commission's final rule (2001) and the European Commission's Recommendation (2002) and proposal for a revised 8th Directive (2004a). One category of prohibited non-audit services included in the Sarbanes-Oxley Act is financial information systems design and implementation, which I refer to as IT service.

The Securities and Exchange Commission's final rule (2001) related to this service prohibits the audit firm from "designing or implementing a [...] software system that aggregates source data or generates information that is 'significant' to the financial statements taken as a whole. In this context, information would be 'significant' if it is reasonably likely to be material to the financial statements of the audit client" (2001:

[33] The research instrument is shown in Appendix 6.

IIB). Particularly, an auditor "would not be independent of an audit client for whom the [audit firm] designed an integrated Enterprise Resource Planning or similar system since the system would serve as the basis for the audit client's financial reporting system" (2001: IIB). Similar, the European Commission's Recommendation (2002) states "that there are engagements where the [audit firm] takes on [...] responsibilities for the [financial information technology]-systems design and implementation project, [which] would clearly result in an unacceptable level of independence risk" (2002: 7.2.2).

In the case study R&P designed and implemented new software to improve strategic flexibility, to facilitate short run decision making, and to support internal operations, which would lead to significant efficiencies through savings in product costs through automation, reduced data processing, more effective management of inventory and reduced raw materials waste. Since, the new system is designed to provide timely, relevant, and concise information to the decision making process, and improved system integration of accounting and financial reporting, thus serves as a basis for the client's financial reporting system, the auditor would not be independent. Thus, the intended outcome for the IT service as related to the Securities and Exchange Commission rule (2001) and the European Commission's Recommendation (2002) would be to prohibit the performance of this service.

Regarding the performed tax service the Securities and Exchange Commission's final rule (2001) states "any non-audit service, including tax services, that is not described as a prohibited service, can be provided by the auditor without impairing the auditor's independence 'only if' the service has been pre-approved by the issuer's audit committee" (2001: IIB).

The European Commission (2002, 2004a) allows the performance of tax services. Neither the European proposal for the revised 8th Directive (2004a) nor the Recommendation (2002) discussed tax services as causing potential threats.

The case study states that the tax service performed by R&P includes planning and ensuring regulatory compliance, which was approved by Kelly & Co's audit committee. Thus, the intended outcome for the tax service would be to allow its performance.

To obtain each subject's decision the following question was asked, whereas a "Yes" was coded seven, a "No" was coded one and a "Not sure" was given four:[34]

> Given the preceding regulation requirements, do you believe that
>
> a. R&P should be prohibited from providing the IT service to Kelly & Co?
> YES NO NOT SURE
>
> b. R&P should be prohibited from providing the Tax service to Kelly & Co?
> YES NO NOT SURE

I then asked one question as a manipulation check which results will be provided later in this chapter. Finally, I collected subjects' demographic information. I asked whether subjects had completed an audit class and also asked them to indicate their self-assessed knowledge of auditor independence regulation on a seven point Linkert-scale.

3. Results

a) Decision Making Quality and Safeguarding Effects

Subjects had to decide whether the IT and/or the tax service should be prohibited or not. The correct decision would have been to prohibit the IT service. However, the tax service was approved by the audit committee and therefore the regulations allow the tax service to be performed. Thus, the correct decision would have been to allow this service. Descriptive statistics of means and standards deviations (Std. Dev.) are shown in Table 5.

Scale 1 to 7		Regulation Approach				Marginals	
Means (Std. Dev.)		Rules		Principles			
		IT	Tax	IT	Tax	IT	Tax
Level of Knowledge	High	4.81 (2.71)	2.36 (2.46)	4.67 (2.91)	4.67 (2.91)	4.75 (2.73)	3.4 (2.85)
	Low	4.6 (2.75)	4 (3.16)	4 (3)	4 (3)	4.31 (2.8)	4 (3)
Marginals		4.17 (2.67)	3.14 (2.87)	4.33 (2.89)	4.33 (2.89)		

Table 5: Descriptive Statistics of Subjects' IT and Tax Decisions (Experiment 1)

[34] I used a seven point scale to code subjects' responses because this will make the data of experiment one comparable with the data of experiment two.

Descriptive statistics show that subjects are unsure about the decision concerning the IT service in the rules-based setting (mean=4.17) as well as in the principles-based setting (mean=4.33). However, there is a pattern which shows a weak trend towards prohibition of the IT service. From low knowledge-principles-based setting (mean=4) to low knowledge-rules-based setting (mean=4.6) prohibition becomes a little more likely. From high knowledge-principles-based setting (mean=4.67) to high knowledge-rules-based setting (mean=4.81) this trend holds on.

Hypothesis one asks whether subjects' decision making quality based on principles-based regulation will more likely to be compromised (there will be a greater amount of frequency of over- and under-compliance) compared to the decision making quality based on rules-based regulation. Results of a performed two way ANOVA in Table 6 indicate that subjects decisions on the performance of the IT service did not differ significantly when the rules-based or principles-based requirements were given ($F=0.17$, $p=0.68$). Thus, hypothesis one is rejected, since subjects' decision making quality and thereby the safeguarding quality of a regulation is not higher when it is rules-based.

Source of Variance	df	F-statistic	p-value
Regulation Approach	1	0.17	0.68
Level of Knowledge	1	0.22	0.64
Regulation Approach x Level of Knowledge	1	0.06	0.8

Table 6: Two Way ANOVA Results of the Effects of the Treatments on Subjects' IT Decisions (Experiment 1)

Under the Sarbanes-Oxley Act, the performance of tax services during a financial statements audit is allowed when this service is approved by the audit committee in advance. The service was pre-approved in all versions of the case studies. Descriptive statistics are shown in Table 5. In line with the intended outcome, subjects within the rules-based treatment tended to recommend that the tax service be permitted (mean=3.14). However, results indicate that subjects were unsure about the tax service under the principles-based regulations (mean=4.33).

Again, hypothesis one states that subjects' decision making quality based on principles-based regulation will more likely to be compromised (there will be a greater amount of frequency of over- or under-compliance) compared to the decision making quality based rules-based regulation. The differences are not statistically significant as shown in Table 7 (F=1.65, p=0.2). However, there is a weak support for hypothesis one (p=0.2), which might indicate that the decision making and thereby safeguarding quality of the rules-based regulation is higher than that of the principles-based regulation.

Source of Variance	df	F-statistic	p-value
Regulation Approach	1	1.65	0.2
Level of Knowledge	1	0.38	0.53
Regulation Approach x Level of Knowledge	1	1.55	0.22

Table 7: Two Way ANOVA Results of the Effects of the Treatments on Subjects' Tax Decisions (Experiment 1)

Descriptive statistics in Table 5 indicate that the prohibition of the IT service is slightly more probable in the high knowledge treatment (mean=4.75) than in the low knowledge treatment (mean=4.31). Considering the intended outcome for the IT service, which is prohibition of the service; this might indicate that higher knowledge helps to remedy complexity. Similar, the tax service, given the regulation allows this service, was more likely allowed in the high knowledge treatment (mean=3.4) than in the low knowledge treatment, where subjects' were unsure (mean=4).

Hypothesis two states that subjects' decision making quality based on auditor independence regulation is less likely compromised if additional information is provided to the decision maker. However, the additional information did not provide subjects with the knowledge needed to increase the communication accuracy of regulation and thereby the safeguarding quality of the regulation, which was measured by comparing subjects' decisions with the intended outcome. For both the IT (F=0.22, p=0.64) and the tax decision (F=0.38, p=0.53) the results are statistically insignificant as shown in Table 6 and 7, respectively; therefore, hypothesis two is not supported, since the decision making quality based on the regulation is not higher when additional information about an audit firm's own policies and procedures is provided to the decision maker.

Finally, individual results capturing the interaction of regulation approach and knowledge level in Table 5 indicate the additional information (high knowledge treatment) to have an effect on the decision making quality based on the regulations. The most interesting result is the allowance of the tax service under Sarbanes-Oxley Act regulation (mean=2.36) and the trend towards prohibition of the tax service when the European regulation is applied (mean=4.67). A performed t-test of the two means indicates a significant difference ($t=1.85$, $p=0.04$). These findings indicate that the high knowledge level may affect the way regulation is applied, but only for the tax service decision.

b) Manipulation Check

The manipulation check asked subjects to assess the complexity of the given regulation extract. Therefore the following question was asked:

> Another issue of concern to the accounting and auditing profession is how the nature of regulations affects the audit. For example, some regulations are rules that are quite straightforward, some are very complex rules and some are general principles. Thinking back to the background information on auditor independence as to the stated description of the regulation non-audit services (page three), please complete the following sentence by circling the appropriate number:
>
> | | Low | | | Moderate | | | High |
> |---|---|---|---|---|---|---|---|
> | The <u>complexity</u> of the regulation regarding the performance of additional non-audit services is ... | 1 | 2 | 3 | 4 | 5 | 6 | 7 |

Descriptive statistics are shown in Table 8. Results indicate that there is a difference in the complexity assessment depending on the underlying regulation approach. The complexity of the rules-based regulation was assessed as being smaller (mean=3.81) than that of the principles-based regulation (mean=4.72).

Scale 1 to 7 Means (Std. Dev.)		Regulation Approach Rules	 Principles	Marginals
Level of Knowledge	High	3.18 (1.72)	3.89 (1.45)	3.5 (1.61)
	Low	4.5 (1.43)	5.55 (1.33)	5 (1.45)
Marginals		3.81 (1.69)	4.72 (1.6)	

Table 8: Descriptive Statistics of Subjects' Complexity Assessment

Results of the performed two way ANOVA on subjects' complexity assessment in Table 9 indicate a significant effect of regulation approach (F=3.57, p=0.0673). Thus, the selected rules-based requirement tends to be less complex than the selected principles-based requirement. That is, the number of rules seems to be more informative than principles.

As results in Table 8 indicate the complexity was assessed as being lower when the level of knowledge was higher through additional information provided (mean=3.5) than when the level of knowledge was low (mean=5). The knowledge level is significant at a 95% level (F=9.41, p=0.0041) as shown in Table 9.

These findings indicate that there is an important effect of additional information. The fact that the compliance system provides a warning message for any engagements that may violate current legal or professional requirements regarding the provision of non-audit services to audit clients, might have caused the significant difference between the low and high knowledge situation. Unconsciously subjects evidently included their knowledge through additional information while assessing the complexity of the two different requirements.

Source of Variance	df	F-statistic	p-value
Regulation Approach	1	3.57	0.0673
Level of Knowledge	1	9.41	0.0041
Regulation Approach x Level of Knowledge	1	0.13	0.7208

Table 9: Two Way ANOVA Results of Subjects' Assessments on Complexity of Regulations

4. Discussion

The results of the first experiment, which was conducted as a pilot test of the instrument and of the experimental approach, indicate little effects of the regulation approach in terms of communication accuracy as it influences the safeguarding effects of regulation concerning auditor independence risk. In this setting, the complexity of the contending non-audit services regulations as a measure of communication accuracy depends not on the nature of regulation. However, principles regulation tends to communicate less accurately to some degree, whereas rules tend to state more precisely the services addressed by a single rule. Therefore, the decision process of subjects in the European Union regulation treatment may be to some degree compromised. However, results are not significant.

Although not significant, the results of the Sarbanes-Oxley Act treatment tend to be more likely conforming to the intended compliance. The European Union treatment might lead subjects to compromised, over-complied decision making. The results also indicate that the information given helped to mitigate complexity (manipulation check). However, although subjects assessed the complexity being lower in the high knowledge setting, it did not influence subjects' decision making significantly.

The weak results of experiment one might be explained by the fact that subjects were undergraduate students and related to a demand effect caused by the fact that the decision concerning the performance of additional services had already been made by the audit firm. The fact that the decision concerning the performance of the IT and the tax service was not entirely left to subjects, might have compromised they decision towards allowing the services. Subjects' low knowledge about auditor independence regulation might have increased this demand effect additionally. However, both of these possible weaknesses were remedied in the design of experiment two. In the second experiment more experienced subjects were obtained and the subjects were asked to decide whether the audit firm should undertake any of the additional non audit services. The audit firm-client setting of experiment two leaves the performance decision entirely to the subjects, meaning more analysis for the subjects and less likelihood of any demand effect.

In addition, I added regulations concerning the implementation of an audit committee to increase the overall task complexity and also to increase the task complexity differences between the two regulation approaches. Beside the question where subjects had to decide about the performance of the IT and tax service, I ask them two additional questions to control for the validity of the responses regarding the performance decision. Asking more than one question is an important means to increase the overall validity. I then perform an exploratory factor analysis of subjects' decision based on the responses of all three questions, whereas responses are weighted depending on their exploratory power.

B. Experiment on Regulation Approach and Audit Firm-Client Characteristics

In experiment two I also study differences in subjects' decision making related to rules-based or principles-based auditor independence regulation. Again, this experiment provides some evidence on whether the approach of auditor independence regulation is associated with the effectiveness of a regulation in reducing risks to auditor independence as stated in research question one. Thus, subjects' decisions will be analyzed to investigate whether their decision making quality based on principles-based regulation will more likely be compromised compared to the decision making quality based on rules-based regulation (hypothesis one).

In addition, I ask whether the effectiveness of a regulation to reduce auditor independence risk is dependent on the audit firm-client engagement characteristics in research question three. Hypothesis three predicts that subjects' decision making quality of auditor independence regulation is expected to be higher (lower) when the costs of litigation are perceived to be greater (less) than the monetary returns from the additional non-audit service fees.

1. Participants

Participants in the second experiment were 54 graduate accounting students from the United States. Students self-assessed moderate knowledge about auditor independence regulation (mean=3.98, scale 1 to 7 indicating low to high knowledge, respectively). All participants indicated some experience in financial statements analysis and completed an audit class. Thus, when compared to the pilot study subjects, these subjects are probably both more experienced and more knowledgeable.

2. Research Design and Procedures

Regulation approach and audit firm-client characteristics (affecting perceived litigation risk and monetary incentives) as independent variables were manipulated in a 2 x 2 between subjects design. I assigned subjects randomly to one version.[35] Subjects were asked first to read the case study and the given regulation extract, either Sarbanes-Oxley Act or European Union requirements, concerning the performance of non-audit services for a financial statement audit client and then to make a decision whether the IT and/or the tax service performance should be recommended based on the regulation extract given. Furthermore, subjects were asked to indicate the dependency the audit firm has on the client and to indicate the maximum percentage that non-audit fees could be of total fees from the client such that no pre-approval would be required, whereas these assessments served as manipulation checks. I used numerical rating scales with seven response categories (Kerlinger and Lee 2000).

Subjects were given a short introduction into how impaired auditor independence possibly caused recent financial scandals. They were presented the following background information:

Recent worldwide financial scandals have reinforced the argument that the financial statement audit is an important element in ensuring the credibility and reliability of financial statements. However, significant economic damage to the capital markets and the economy has resulted from alleged impaired auditor independence. Auditor independence is impaired when audit decisions or judgments are biased in favor of the client. Independence is considered the profession's main means of demonstrating to the public and regulators that auditors and audit firms are performing their task at a level that meets established ethical principles, particularly those of integrity and objectivity.

Following this information, subjects were provided with the exact wording of the requirements concerning the regulation of non-audit services and the implementation of an audit committee. The extract contained either Sarbanes-Oxley or European requirements concerning the regulation of non-audit services and of audit committee implementation, whereas subjects were not told which requirement they were given. The rules-based Sarbanes-Oxley Act extract stated the following:

[35] The results of a performed one way ANOVA on subjects' knowledge level indicate that random assignment of subjects to versions was effective (F=0.04, p=0.99).

Part A: Regulation of Non-audit Services

A public accounting firm (and any associated person of that firm) can not perform for a financial statement audit client, contemporaneously with the audit, any of the following non-audit services:

1. *bookkeeping or other services related to the accounting records or financial statements of the audit client;*
2. *financial information systems design and implementation;*
3. *appraisal or valuation services, fairness opinions, or contribution-in-kind reports;*
4. *actuarial services;*
5. *internal audit outsourcing services;*
6. *management functions or human resources;*
7. *broker or dealer, investment adviser, or investment banking services; or*
8. *legal services and expert services unrelated to the audit.*

However, the public accounting firm may engage in any non-audit service, including a tax service that is not described above for an audit client, if the activity is approved in advance by the audit committee of the client.

Part B: Audit Committee Regulation

The audit committee of an issuer may delegate to 1 or more designated members of the audit committee who are independent directors of the board of directors, the authority to grant pre-approvals.

Furthermore, all auditing services and non-audit services provided to an issuer by the auditor of the issuer shall be pre-approved by the audit committee of the issuer. This pre-approval requirement is waived with respect to the provision of non-audit services for an issuer, if

1. *such services were not recognized by the issuer at the time of the engagement to be non-audit services; and*
2. *such services are promptly brought to the attention of the audit committee of the issuer and approved prior to the completion of the audit by the audit committee of by 1 or more of the audit committee who are members of the board of directors to whom authority to grant such approvals has been delegated by the audit committee; and*
3. *the aggregate amount of all such non-audit services provided to the issuer constitutes not more than 5 percent of the total amount of revenues paid by the*

issuer to its auditor during the fiscal year in which the non-audit services were provided.

The European Union principles-based regulation was provided as follows:

Part A: Regulation of Non-audit Services

When carrying out a financial statement audit, both the auditor and the audit firm must remain independent from the client and not be in any way involved in management decisions of the client. The auditor and audit firm can not carry out a financial statement audit if there is any financial, business, employment or other relationship, including the provision of additional services, with the client that might compromise the auditor's or audit firm's independence.

Furthermore, the auditor or audit firm shall annually disclose to and discuss with the audit committee of the audited entity threats to their independence and the safeguards applied to mitigate those threats, as well as the additional services provided. The auditor or the audit firm shall also annually confirm in writing their independence to the audit committee of the audited entity.

Part B: Audit Committee Regulation

Public interest entities shall have an audit committee, composed of non-executive members of the administrative body or members of the supervisory body of the audited entity with at least one independent member with competence in accounting and/or auditing. The audit committee shall among other things:

a. Monitor the financial reporting process;

b. Monitor the effectiveness of the company's internal control, internal audit where applicable, and risk management system;

c. Oversee the financial statement audit of the annual and consolidated accounts;

d. Review and monitor the independence of the auditor or audit firm and in particular the provision of additional services to the audited entity.

The auditor or audit firm must report to the audit committee key matters arising from the financial statement audit, in particular on material weakness in internal control in relation to the financial reporting process, and shall assist the audit committee in fulfilling its tasks.

The experiment was done using a case study, dealing with an audit firm-client relationship. In addition to performing the audit for the client, the auditing firm is considering performing IT and/or tax services. Since the service descriptions were the same as in experiment one, the expected outcome of subjects' decisions regarding the performance of the IT and tax service if they interpret the regulations as intended, is that they decide not to provide the IT service and to provide the tax service

To possibly elicit different decisions given differences in litigation risk and monetary incentives, I used two different audit firm-client relationships. The high litigation risk manipulation was done by describing a small audit firm in terms of employees, services offered and international presence, and a large client in terms of employees, international presence, market position and management tenure. In addition, the relative non-audit and audit fee amounts represented a significant portion of the total revenues the office as well the particular engagement partner is earning. This manipulation captures both a weak position for the auditor in a potential litigation situation if the regulation is applied incorrectly, as well as an engagement where monetary incentives are strong.

In comparison, subjects of the low litigation risk and monetary incentives version were informed that the client is small and the audit firm is large, using the same characteristics such as employees, international presence, market position and management tenure. Thus, litigation risk and monetary incentives were manipulated at two levels, high and low.

In the high litigation risk and monetary incentives condition participants received the following information:

Audit Client

Kelly & Co is a large corporation headquartered in Boston and listed on the New York Stock Exchange. The company was founded in 1980 and employs approximately 5,600 people in 23 offices in the United States. The Company is the leading supplier of luxury bath equipment, such as shower heads, faucets and lamps. Customers in both Europe and North America include retailers as well as direct customers. Kelly & Co has recently expanded into five additional European countries.

Management and Board of Directors

Günther Blauch has been the CEO of Kelly & Co for ten years. Blauch, a CPA, earned a master's degree in accounting and has 20 years of professional experience. The Board of Directors of Kelly & Co is comprised of Blauch and two other executive members and seven non-executive members. The Audit Committee is comprised of three non-executive directors, where one Committee member holds substantial accounting and auditing qualifications. The Audit Committee is regulated by a formal written charter, which conforms to all regulation requirements and is approved by the Board of Directors. The Audit Committee reports to the Board of Directors after each meeting. The external and internal auditors have direct access to the Audit Committee.

External Auditor

The external audit firm of the parent company, Kelly & Co, is Streich & Holz (S&H). S&H is a small, American accounting and assurance services firm. The firm was founded in 1923 and is headquartered in New York. S&H employs around 1,100 people. The firm is primarily involved in financial statement audit services applying US-GAAP. Furthermore, S&H is considering performing non-audit services in order to compete in the audit market.

S&H's Boston office is performing the financial statement audit for Kelly & Co the first time. The managing partner of this audit is Wilhelm Schulz. The annual audit fee is currently $3,000,000. This fee represents 12% of the average annual revenue of the Boston office of S&H and 65% of Wilhelm Schulz's annual billings.

Additional services opportunities

In addition to performing the annual financial statement audit, S&H has the opportunity of performing two additional services for Kelly & Co. First, S&H's Information Technology Department has the opportunity of developing new software for Kelly & Co's management information system. The new system would be designed to provide more timely, relevant, and concise information to the decision making process, and to improve system integration of accounting and financial reporting. Although S&H's Information Technology Department would be responsible for the development and implementation of the system, Kelly & Co's management would be responsible for establishing, maintaining, operating and evaluating the information system. One of S&H's information technology partners, Armin Kellerman, would manage the development and implementation process. Anneliese Becker, a Kelly & Co *employee and IT specialist, would oversee the project and its staff. Reporting lines for audits and IT projects within S&H are completely separated. It is expected that the fee for providing the system design and implementation service would be around $300,000. This fee would represent 30% of Armin Kellerman's annual billings.*

The second opportunity is for Nikolaus Knubel, a tax partner, to provide tax advisory services for Kelly & Co regarding tax planning and regulatory compliance. Kelly & Co considers this service to be part of the audit, so they see no need for pre-approval by their Audit Committee. However, it is expected that Kelly & Co's audit committee would approve this service. The expected annual fee for this service would be $150,000, which would represent 20% of Nikolaus Knubel's annual billings.

Within the low litigation risk and monetary incentives condition, participants were given similar information. Thus, subjects were provided with the following information:

Audit Client

Kelly & Co is a medium-sized corporation headquartered in Boston and listed on the New York Stock Exchange. The company was founded in 1980 and employs approximately 1,200 people in 9 offices in the United States. The Company is one of many suppliers of luxury bath equipment, such as shower heads, faucets and lamps. Customers in North America include retailers as well as direct customers.

Management and Board of Directors

Günther Blauch was recently hired as Kelly & Co's CEO. Blauch, a CPA, earned a master's degree in accounting and has 20 years of professional experience. The Board of Directors of Kelly & Co is comprised of Blauch and two other executive members and seven non-executive members. The Audit Committee is comprised of three non-executive directors, where one Committee member holds substantial accounting and auditing qualifications. The Audit Committee is regulated by a formal written charter, which conforms to all regulation requirements and is approved by the Board of Directors. The Audit Committee reports to the Board of Directors after each meeting. The external and internal auditors have direct access to the Audit Committee.

External Auditor

The external audit firm of the parent company, Kelly & Co, is Streich & Holz (S&H). S&H is a large, American accounting and assurance services firm. The firm was founded in 1923 and is headquartered in New York. Including its affiliates in Europe and Asia, S&H employs over 6,000 people. The firm is primarily involved in financial statement audit services applying US-GAAP. In addition, as a result of its expansion into Europe and Asia, the firm conducts financial statement audits applying international accounting standards. Furthermore, S&H also performs non-audit services in order to maintain its competitiveness in the audit market.

S&H's Boston office has performed the financial statement audit for Kelly & Co since the company's inception. The managing partner of this audit is Wilhelm Schulz. The annual audit fee is currently $3,000,000. This fee represents 0.5% of the average annual revenue of the Boston office of S&H and 10% of Wilhelm Schulz's annual billings.

Additional services opportunities

In addition to performing the annual financial statement audit, S&H has the opportunity of performing two additional services for Kelly & Co. First, S&H's Information Technology Department has the opportunity of developing new software for Kelly & Co's management information system. The new system would be designed to provide more timely, relevant, and concise information to the decision making process, and to improve system integration of accounting and financial reporting. Although S&H's Information Technology Department would be responsible for the development and implementation of the system, Kelly & Co's management would be responsible for establishing, maintaining, operating and evaluating the information system. One of S&H's information technology partners, Armin Kellerman, would manage the development and implementation process. Anneliese Becker, a Kelly & Co employee and IT specialist, would oversee the project and its staff. Reporting lines for audits and IT projects within S&H are completely separated. It is expected that the fee for providing the system design and implementation service would be around $300,000. This fee would represent 5% of Armin Kellerman's annual billings.

The second opportunity is for Nikolaus Knubel, a tax partner, to provide tax advisory services for Kelly & Co regarding tax planning and regulatory compliance. Kelly & Co considers this service to be part of the audit, so they see no need for pre-approval *by their Audit Committee. However, it is expected that Kelly & Co's audit committee would approve this service. The expected annual fee for this service would be $150,000, which would represent 3% of Nikolaus Knubel's annual billings.*

Participating subjects per experimental treatment are presented in Table 10.[36]

		Regulation Approach Rules	 Principles
Litigation Risk and Monetary Incentives	High	13	14
	Low	13	14

Table 10: Experimental Treatments and Treatment Sample Sizes (Experiment 2)

Subjects were asked to decide whether the performance of the additional IT and/or tax service is recommended. Furthermore, subjects were asked to indicate the degree to which the likelihood that the audit firm's independence could be impaired assuming either or both of these services are performed. Similarly, subjects were asked to indicate the significance of threats to independence from the service fees if the service was performed. The latter two questions are a control for subjects' decision making validity and will be used for additional exploratory factor analysis.

Based on the described audit-client setting and the assistant's findings concerning applicable regulations, please answer the following questions. (Please check or circle)

What would you recommend that S&H performs
(1) both the IT and TAX services ( )
(2) only the IT service, ( )
(3) only the Tax service or ( )
(4) neither of these services? ( )

[36] The research instrument is presented in Appendix 7.

Please indicate the degree to which you believe the following factors influenced your recommendation as to whether S&H should perform or should not perform the additional non-audit services:

	Low influence			Moderate influence			High influence
The likelihood that S&H's independence could be impaired assuming S&H performs the IT service:	1	2	3	4	5	6	7
The likelihood that S&H's independence could be impaired assuming S&H performs the Tax service:	1	2	3	4	5	6	7

Please assess the significance of the following threats to audit independence assuming S&H perform all three services:

	Low Significance			Moderate Significance			High significance
The threat to audit independence from the IT service fees ($300,000).	1	2	3	4	5	6	7
The threat to audit independence from the tax advisory service fees ($150,000).	1	2	3	4	5	6	7

Two manipulation check questions were then presented (the results are reported later in this chapter). Since the two additional control questions are scaled from one to seven, the answers of the first question were coded separately with a seven indicating that the IT or tax service was prohibited and with a one indicating that the subject recommended providing the service. Through this coding, the responses of all three questions can be used in exploratory factor analysis. Finally, I collected subjects' demographic information concerning whether they had completed an audit class and their self-assessed knowledge of auditor independence regulation on a seven point Linkert-scale.

3. Results

a) Decision Making Quality and Safeguarding Effects

The case study reflected the same engagement situation as in experiment one. Again, the correct decision would have been to prohibit the IT service and to provide the tax service.

Descriptive statistics are shown in Table 11.[37] The higher the mean, the more likely it is that the subjects recommended the prohibition of the service. The rules-based auditor independence regulation led subjects' to, on average, recommending not providing the IT service in both the litigation risk and monetary incentives settings (mean=5.65). Under principles-based regulation the IT service tended to be prohibited only in the high litigation risk and monetary incentives setting (mean=5.12). Unexpectedly, the low litigation risk and monetary incentives setting increased the likelihood of under-compliance with the regulation, meaning that the subjects, on average, tended not to recommend the performance of the IT service (mean=3.62).

Scale 1 to 7		Regulation Approach				Marginals	
Means (Std. Dev.)		Rules		Principles			
		IT	Tax	IT	Tax	IT	Tax
Litigation Risk and Monetary Incentives	High	5.56 (4.17)	3.72 (5.59)	5.12 (2.59)	4.45 (4.63)	5.33 (3.44)	4.10 (5.14)
	Low	5.74(3.05)	3.72 (4.75)	3.62 (4.81)	4.36 (5.59)	4.64 (5.14)	4.05 (5.20)
Marginals		5.65 (3.59)	3.72 (5.09)	4.38 (4.43)	4.40 (5.04)		

Table 11: Descriptive Statistics of Subjects' IT and Tax Decisions (Experiment 2)

Hypothesis one asks whether the decision making quality based on principles-based regulation will more likely to be compromised compared to the quality based on rules-based regulation. In Table 12 results of a performed two way ANOVA of subjects' decisions regarding the IT-performance are shown. As for the IT service, the overall

[37] Descriptive Statistics show the means and standards deviations based on all three questions.

difference between the two regulatory systems is significant (F=7.57, p=0.008). Thus, this significant difference in the regulation approaches implies that subjects' decisions differ n the settings. As descriptive statistics show the safeguarding quality of the principles-based regulation is being compromised, since the regulation was under-complied in the low litigation risk setting.

Furthermore whether subjects' decision making quality based on auditor independence regulation is expected to be higher (lower) when the costs of litigation are perceived to be greater (less) than the monetary returns from the additional non-audit service fees was asked in hypothesis three. As shown in Table 12 there are significant differences in the effects of the two litigation risk and monetary incentives settings on subjects' decisions (F=4.77, p=0.03). Therefore, hypothesis three is supported, meaning that the decision making quality based on the regulation differs depending on the level of perceived litigation risk and monetary incentives.

Source of Variance	df	F-statistic	p-value
Regulation Approach	1	7.57	0.008
Litigation Risk and Monetary Incentives (LR/MI)	1	4.77	0.03
Regulation Approach x LR/MI	1	4.43	0.04

Table 12: Two Way ANOVA Results of the Effects of the Treatments on Subjects' IT Decisions (Experiment 2)

Furthermore, the results in Table 12 indicate a significant interaction effect of regulation approach and litigation risk and monetary incentives on subjects' decision making (F=4.43, p=0.04). Descriptive statistics in Table 11 of the interaction variables indicate two main different interactions: first, the low litigation risk and monetary incentives treatment lead subjects to tent to prohibit the IT service in the rules-based setting (mean=5.74) but not in the principles-based setting (mean=3.62). Secondly, subjects in the principles-based setting tended to recommend the IT service in the low litigation risk and monetary incentives setting (mean=3.62) but tended to prohibit the IT service in the high litigation risk and monetary incentives setting (mean=5.12).

Table 13 presents a t-test analysis to investigate which of the four possible settings is responsible for the interaction effect found for the IT service.

Scale 1 to 7 Means (Std. Dev.)		Regulation Approach		
		Rules		Principles
		IT		IT
Litigation Risk and Monetary Incentives	High	t=0.126 p=0.45	t=0.326, p=0.62	t=1.261 p=0.11
	Low		t=1.65, p=0.058	

Table 13: T-test for Comparison of Means (Table 11) for Subjects' IT Decisions (Experiment 2)

The results in Table 13 indicate that subjects in the principles-based setting made their decisions based on their assessment of litigation risk. If litigation risk was low, subjects were more likely to recommend the IT services, thus monetary returns evidently outweighed the costs of potential litigation. If litigation risk was perceived as being higher, subjects' decisions were more likely to be consistent with the regulations, thus this implies that potential monetary returns were perceived as being too risky. However, the difference in means is insignificant as shown in Table 13 (t=1.261, p=0.11). Subjects in the rules-based setting made their decision as intended also when litigation risk was low whereas subjects of the principles-based setting did not decide as intended. This leads to a significant difference in means for the low litigation risk and low monetary incentives setting and both regulation approaches (t=1.65, p=0.058). In conclusion, differences in applying the two regulation approaches in the low litigation risk and monetary incentives seem to be responsible for the interaction effect found for the IT service.

Results in Table 11 indicate that the tax service was allowed under rules-based auditor independence regulation (mean=3.72) in both settings. In comparison, there is a very weak trend towards prohibition the service with an increase in litigation risk in the principles-based setting (mean increases from 4.36 to 4.45).

Hypothesis one asks whether subjects' decision making quality based on principles-based regulation will more likely to be compromised compared to the quality based on rules-based regulation. To address this hypothesis, results of a performed two way ANOVA are shown in Table 14. Results indicate that there is a weak difference in subjects' decision making dependent on the regulation approach. Thus, there is some support for hypothesis one for the tax service. However, the difference between the regulation approaches is insignificant (F=1.76, p=0.19). Thus, safeguarding effects, measured by comparing subjects' decisions with the intended outcome of rules-based regulation, is to some extend higher than that of the principles-based requirements. However, hypothesis one is not supported.

Hypothesis three states that the decision making quality based on auditor independence regulation is expected to be higher (lower) when the costs of litigation are perceived to be greater (less) than the monetary returns from the additional non-audit service fees. Results in Table 14 indicate that differences are insignificant (F=0.29, p=0.59). Thus, hypothesis three is not supported indicating that the decision making quality based on a regulation is not significantly affected by perceived litigation risk or monetary incentives for the tax service.

Source of Variance	df	F-statistic	p-value
Regulation Approach	1	1.76	0.19
Litigation Risk and Monetary Incentives (LR/MI)	1	0.29	0.59
Regulation Approach x LR/MI	1	0	0.98

Table 14: Two Way ANOVA Results of the Effects of the Treatments on Subjects' Tax Decisions (Experiment 2)

b) Additional Exploratory Factor Analysis

Performing an exploratory factor analysis on responses to the six questions (three for each service) will determine the number of constructs measured by this six questions as well as the nature of those constructs. The measured constructs should be two, one for the IT service and one for the tax service.

Responses to the six item questionnaire (three questions for each service) for the two additional non-audit services were subject to an exploratory factor analysis using squared multiple correlations as prior communality estimates. If the responses of the three questions regarding each service load on one factor, subjects' decisions are valid on average. If the factor analysis would show that the three questions for each service do not load on one factor, this might be an indication that subjects did not understand the task they were asked to perform.

The principal factor method was used to extract the factors, and this was followed by a varimax (orthogonal) rotation to get uncorrelated factors. Only the first two factors displayed eigenvalues greater than one (1.54 and 1.18), and the scree test suggested one meaningful factor for each service,[38] so only these two factors were retained for rotation.

In interpreting the rotated factor pattern, an item was said to load on a given factor if the factor loading was 0.5 or greater for that factor. Using this criterion the first construct was found, which was labeled 'IT-performance'. It compromises three items detailing the overall decision whether the IT service should be performed, the first measured on a forced-choice scale and the other two on a seven-point scale. All responses were unified to categorical numbers from one to seven for exploratory factor analysis. Specifically, the factor captures the decision whether the IT service should be performed or not (question one), the likelihood that the firm's independence could be impaired assuming performance of the IT service (question two) and the assessment of the significance of the threat to independence from the IT service fee (question three).[39] Thus, all three questions capture the same underlying theoretical construct.

The scoring coefficients were used to perform a two way ANOVA. If ANOVA based on factor scores indicate the same results as the performed ANOVA for the service decision only, subjects' decision validity is supported. Results are presented in Table 15.

Source of Variance	df	F-statistic	p-value
Regulation Approach	1	14.1	0.005
Litigation Risk and Monetary Incentives (LR/MI)	1	4.09	0.048
Regulation Approach x LR/MI	1	6.03	0.017

Table 15: Two Way ANOVA Results of the Effects of the Treatments on the IT-Performance Factor Scores (Experiment 2)

ANOVA results based on factor scores are essentially the same ANOVA results based on subjects' decisions. Thus, this adds additional validity to the experimental findings. The second construct, labeled as 'Tax-performance', reflects the decision whether the tax service is allowed to be performed or not. It comprises three items detailing the

---

[38] See Appendix 8.

[39] The resulting construct, IT-performance, has Cronbach's coefficient alpha of 0.69. IT-performance captures 46% of the variation. Questionnaire items and corresponding factor loadings are presented in Appendix 9.

overall tax-performance decision. Specifically, the factor captures the decision whether the tax service should be performed or not (question one), the likelihood that the firm's independence could be impaired assuming performance of the tax service (question two) and the assessment of the significance of the threat to independence from the tax service fee (question three).[40]

Again, the scoring coefficients were used to perform a two way ANOVA as shown in Table 16.

Source of Variance	df	F-statistic	p-value
Regulation Approach	1	2.15	0.14
Litigation Risk and Monetary Incentives (LR/MI)	1	0.01	0.91
Regulation Approach x LR/MI	1	0.01	0.91

Table 16: Two Way ANOVA Results of the Effects of the Treatments on the Tax-Performance Factor Scores (Experiment 2)

Again, ANOVA results of the single measure of subjects' decision and the measurement based on factor scores indicate essentially the same findings.

[40] This construct has Cronbach's coefficient alphas of 0.73 and captures 60% of the variation. Questionnaire items and corresponding factor loadings are presented in Appendix 9.

c) Manipulation Checks

To investigate whether the manipulation of the audit firm-client characteristics as they affect the perceived litigation risk and monetary incentives was successful, one manipulation check was asked. Subjects had to indicate the level of dependency between the audit firm and the client. The question was stated the following:

Please indicate the level of dependency that S&H has on Kelly & Co assuming S&H performed all three services:						
Low			Moderate			High
1	2	3	4	5	6	7

Results indicate that subjects assess a difference in the level of dependency the audit firm has on the client. Descriptive statistics in Table 17 show that dependency was assessed as being higher in the 'high-litigation risk and monetary incentives' audit firm-client setting where the client was large in terms of employees, international presence, market position and management tenure and the audit firm was small in terms of employees, services offered and international presence (mean=5.92) as opposed to the reverse, 'low-litigation risk and monetary incentives' setting (mean=4.18).

Scale 1 to 7 Means (Std. Dev.)		Regulation Approach Rules	 Principles	Marginals
Litigation Risk and Monetary Incentives	High	5.84 (0.8)	6 (0.81)	5.92 (0.78)
	Low	4.46 (1.39)	3.92 (1.63)	4.18 (1.52)
Marginals		4.96 (1.64)	5.15 (1.31)	

Table 17: Descriptive Statistics of Subjects' Dependency Assessment

Overall results in Table 18 indicate a significantly different assessment of dependency ($F=28.02$, $p=0.00$). This result shows that subjects assessed the dependency level as it was manipulated in the experiment. Thus, the manipulation of audit firm-client characteristics was successful.

Source of Variance	df	F-statistic	p-value
Litigation Risk and Monetary Incentives	1	28.02	0.00

Table 18: One Way ANOVA Results of the Effects of Litigation Risk and Monetary Incentives on Subjects' Dependency Assessment

Furthermore, I asked subjects to assess the maximum percentage of non-audit fees to total fees from the client such that no pre-approval would be required. With this manipulation check, I investigate whether subjects read the regulation extracts as they were asked. Only the rules-based regulation states a maximum percentage of non-audit fees to total fees such that the pre-approval is waived. If subjects of the rules-based setting performed the task with the demanded effort, they should assess the percentage to be somewhat close to what was stated in the regulation extract. Thus, a second question was asked as follows:

> Some regulations suggest requiring pre-approval of non-audit services by the Audit Committee. At the same time, regulators have discussed the possibility of waiving the pre-approval requirement under certain circumstances. Please indicate the maximum percentage that non-audit fees could be of total fees from the client such that no pre-approval would be required.
>
> 0 5 10 15 20 25 30 35 40 45 50 55 60 65 70 75 80 85 90 95 100%
>
> 0% means you would never waive the pre-approval requirement.
>
> Total amount of fees from audit and non-audit services performed. (= 100%)

Interestingly, subjects in the Sarbanes-Oxley Act setting tend to waive the requirement around a 10% threshold (mean=9.8) which is somewhat close to the 5% stated in the Sarbanes-Oxley Act regulation. Subjects in the European Union setting were more likely to accept a higher percentage (mean=15.17). Table 19 shows descriptive statistics.

Scale 0 to 100% Means (Std. Dev.)		Regulation Approach Rules	Principles	Marginals
Litigation Risk and Monetary Incentives	High	9.69 (10.61)	15.35 (13.93)	12.59 (12.58)
	Low	10 (9.59)	15 (13.3)	12.59 (11.71)
Marginals		15.17 (13.36)	9.8 (9.94)	

Table 19: Descriptive Statistics of Subjects' Waiving Pre-approval Assessment

Overall results in Table 20 indicate a significantly different assessment of the pre-approval requirements (F=2.77, p=0.1). Thus, the manipulation of the regulation approaches was successful.

Source of Variance	df	F-statistic	p-value
Regulation Approach	1	2.77	0.1

Table 20: One Way ANOVA Results of the Effects of Regulation Approach on Subjects' Waiving Pre-approval Assessment

4. Discussion

The results of experiment two show a different effect of the accuracy of the regulation's communication which affects the safeguarding effects of a regulation. This difference seems to depend on the precision of the regulation. Overall rules-based regulation tends to be communicated more accurately than principles-based requirements. Related to this, the communication accuracy seems to affect the regulations' safeguarding quality.

Furthermore, the level of perceived litigation risk affects differences in subjects' decision making concerning the performance of the IT service. There is some evidence that the monetary incentives in the form of additional fees overweight expected costs of low litigation risk to the extent that principles-based regulation is under-complied with by these subjects. In a high litigation risk setting, subjects' decisions are more conservative relative to the cost of litigation, which means that principles-based regulation is complied as intended, possibly because costs related to the perceived risk of litigation is higher than monetary incentives. The interpretation of rules-based regulation is unaffected by litigation risk or monetary incentives, and therefore decisions meet the intended compliance.

Figure 15 presents the results of experiment two with respect to the regulation compliance-litigation risk relation for the IT service decisions.

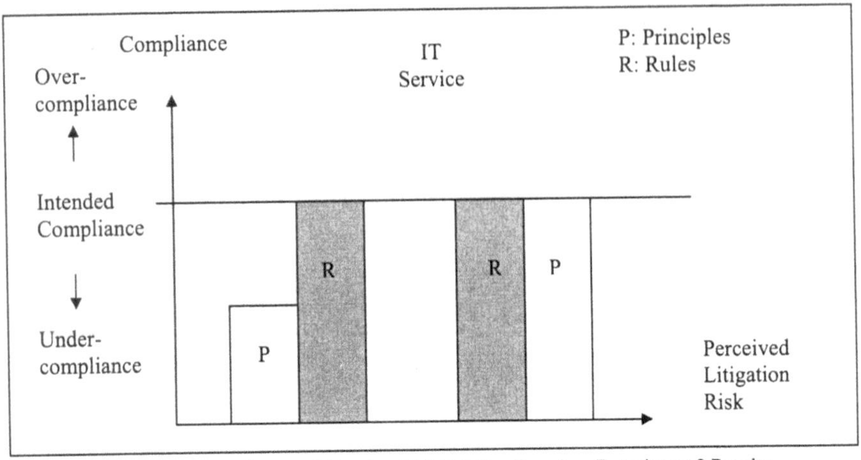

Figure 15: Regulation Compliance – Litigation Risk Relation Based on Experiment 2 Results

Regardless of the perceived litigation risk, rules-based regulation is interpreted as intended for the IT service. This implies that rules are accurately communicated and interpreted, meet the intended compliance vis-à-vis the intended safeguarding effect and lead to the intended decisions.

On the other hand, the decision based on principles-based regulation is related to the litigation risk level, rather than to monetary incentives for the IT service. This implies that principles are less accurately communicated, do not always meet the intended compliance vis-à-vis safeguarding effect and may lead to unintended decisions about the performance of the additional IT service. First, in the second experiment, when if litigation risk was low, the requirements were interpreted as favoring the performance of additional non-audit services, perhaps because the monetary incentives from the additional fees outweigh the expected cost of risk of litigation. Second, if litigation risk is higher, the requirements tended to be interpreted conservatively, possibly because the risk of litigation and the cost of additional service performance are perceived to be higher than the additional fees.

Furthermore, findings on interactions between the regulation approach and the litigation risk/monetary incentives suggest a certain level of perceived litigation risk where principles-based regulation is satisfied. Figure 16 presents the expected compliance of principles associated with the litigation risk for the IT service.

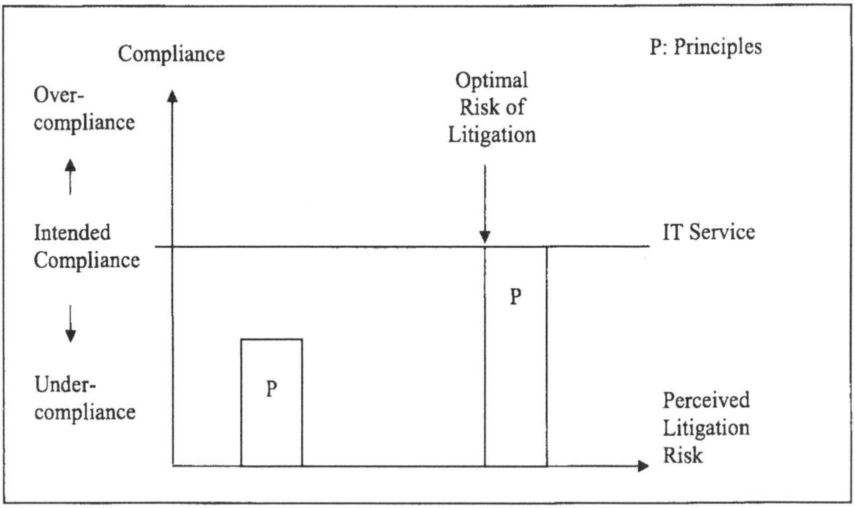

Figure 16: Principles Compliance – Litigation Risk Relation Based on Experiment 2 Results

Whereas over-compliance of regulation is only important in terms of opportunity costs and switching costs, under-compliance may lead to more serious problems. With respect to the experimental results, an engagement where regulation was under-complied with might increase the risk of auditor independence instead of decreasing it, because a service is performed where requirements intend to prohibit the performance. This shows how imprecise and complex regulation can introduce its own unintended consequences by not communicating accurately. Thus, the intended safeguarding effect might be compromised.

C. Regulation Approach and Educational Knowledge Effects

To study education level related knowledge effects, I aggregated data of the first and second experiments. Recall, that undergraduate students participated in the first experiment, whereas the second experiment was conducted with accounting graduate students. Therefore, there might be an education related knowledge effect on how the regulation is interpreted and applied. With the first experimental setting, I studied the effects of either rules-based or principles-based regulation and the effect of additional information as provided by information about audit firm's own policies and procedures.

Thus, I try to provide further evidence on whether the approach to auditor independence regulation is associated with the effectiveness of the regulation in reducing risks to auditor independence in fact (research question one) and whether the effectiveness of regulation to reduce auditor independence risk is dependent on the knowledge level of the person applying the regulation (research question two).

More specific, hypothesis one asks whether subjects' decision making quality based on principles-based regulation will more likely to be compromised compared to the decision making quality based on rules-based regulation. Additionally, hypothesis two predicts that the safeguarding quality of auditor independence regulation is less likely compromised if the decision maker has higher regulatory knowledge.

1. Research Design

Since there was no significant knowledge effect in experiment one, I will use the complete dataset (39 undergraduate students) for the following comparative analysis. From the main experiment I will use the data generated from the two low litigation risk and monetary incentives versions (27 graduate students), in which the case study is in accordance with the first experimental setting in terms of audit firm-client characteristics. Furthermore, I only used the forced decisions concerning the performance of additional non-audit services of both experiments (question one of experiment one and two). Table 21 demonstrates the experimental treatment regulation approach as well as the assumed knowledge levels.

	Regulation Approach	
	Rules	Principles
Graduate Students (moderate knowledge)	13	14
Undergrad Students (low knowledge)	20	19

Table 21: Experimental Treatment Regulation Approach, Knowledge Levels and Sample Sizes (Comparative Analysis)

The assumption that the knowledge level of undergraduate and graduate students differs is supported by a significant difference in means of the knowledge assessment.

Undergraduate students self-assessed the knowledge as relatively low (mean=2.3), whereas graduate students indicated their knowledge as being moderate (mean=4). A performed t-test analysis indicates a significant difference in means (t=12.92, p=0.0006).

2. Results

Descriptive statistics are given in Table 22. Note that the higher the mean, the more likely is a prohibition of the certain service. Students prohibited the IT service more often in the rules-based setting (mean=4.63), as compared to the principles-based setting (mean=3.54). When the knowledge level was moderate the IT service was more likely prohibited (mean=5) than when the knowledge level was low (mean=3.46).

Scale 1 to 7 Means (Std. Dev.)		Regulation Approach				Marginals	
		Rules		Principles			
		IT	Tax	IT	Tax	IT	Tax
Level of Knowledge	Moderate	6.51 (1.66)	3.31 (3.04)	3.57 (3.08)	4.42 (3.08)	5 (2.88)	3.88 (3.05)
	Low	3.4 (3.68)	4.75 (2.89)	3.52 (2.87)	3.84 (2.91)	3.46 (2.74)	4.3 (2.9)
Marginals		4.63 (2.78)	4.18 (2.99)	3.54 (2.91)	4.09 (2.95)		

Table 22: Descriptive Statistics for Subjects' IT and Tax Decisions (Comparative Analysis)

Results of a two way ANOVA are shown in Table 23. Hypothesis one states that subjects' decision making quality based on principles-based regulation will more likely to be compromised (there will be a greater amount or frequency of over- or under-compliance) compared to the quality based on rules-based regulation. As the means already indicated, there is a statistical significant difference of subjects' decision related to the regulation approaches for the IT service (F=4.51, p=0.037). Thus, hypothesis one is supported, indicating that principles-based regulation is more likely compromised.

Source of Variance	df	F-statistic	p-value
Regulation	1	4.51	0.037
Knowledge	1	5.66	0.02
Regulation x Knowledge	1	5.35	0.02

Table 23: Two Way ANOVA Results of the Effects of Regulation Approach and Knowledge Levels on Subjects' IT Decisions (Comparative Analysis)

Hypothesis two asked whether the subjects' decision making quality of auditor independence regulation is less likely compromised if the decision maker has higher regulatory knowledge. Results in Table 22 indicate that subjects with a moderate knowledge level prohibited the IT service (mean= 5), whereas a low knowledge level led to allowance of the IT service (mean=3.46). Related to this findings, results in Table 23 indicate a significant education related knowledge effect (F=5.66, p=0.02). As for the IT service, hypothesis two is supported, which means that the safeguarding quality auditor independence regulation is less likely compromised if the decision maker has higher regulatory knowledge.

Furthermore, results in Table 22 indicate that subjects with moderate knowledge prohibited the IT service in the rules-based setting (mean=6.51) followed by the same subjects with moderate knowledge in the principles-based setting, who allowed the performance (mean=3.57). All subjects of the low knowledge level allowed the performance of the IT service independent of whether principles were given (mean=3.52) or rules were provided (mean=3.4). These interactions are significant as shown in Table 23 (F=5.35, p=0.02).

Table 24 presents a t-test analysis to investigate which of the four possible settings is responsible for the interaction effect found for the IT service.

<table>
<tr><td colspan="2" rowspan="3">Scale 1 to 7
Means (Std. Dev.)</td><td colspan="3">Regulation Approach</td></tr>
<tr><td colspan="2">Rules</td><td>Principles</td></tr>
<tr><td colspan="2">IT</td><td>IT</td></tr>
<tr><td rowspan="2">Level of
Knowledge</td><td>Moderate</td><td rowspan="2">t=4.15
p=0.0002</td><td>t=3.149, p=0.0053</td><td rowspan="2">t=0.047
p=0.96</td></tr>
<tr><td>Low</td><td>t=0.135, p=0.89</td></tr>
</table>

Table 24: T-test for Comparison of Means (Table 22) for Subjects' IT Decisions (Comparative Analysis)

Results in Table 24 indicate a significant difference between the interpretation of rules when different knowledge levels are present (t=4.15, p=0.0002). This indicates that rules only ensure decision making as intended as long as the regulatory knowledge is high enough. Furthermore, there is a significant difference between the means when graduate students with moderate knowledge made their decisions regarding the IT service based on either rules or principles (t=3.149, p=0.0053). This finding indicates that regulatory knowledge only helps to apply the regulation as intended as long as it is rules-based. The insignificant difference between the means of both regulations for the undergraduate students with low level knowledge (t=0.135, p=0.89) implies that no matter which regulation is given, the knowledge level is not high enough to make the decision as intended. Lastly, the fact that principles-based regulation lead to insignificant decision making in both knowledge settings (t=0.047, p=0.96) indicates that decision are not as intended with either moderate or low knowledge being present.

The results in Table 22 also indicate that graduate students allowed the tax service (mean=3.88), but undergraduate students did not (mean=4.3). The regulations approaches led to similar result. This means the tax service was prohibited in both regulation settings (mean=4.18 and 4.09).

That subjects' decision making quality based on principles-based regulation will more likely be compromised (there will be a greater amount or frequency of over- or under-compliance) compared to the quality based on rules-based regulation was predicted in hypothesis one. Results of a performed two way ANOVA for subjects' decisions on the performance of the tax service are presented in Table 25. There is no different effect on subjects' decision making related to the regulation approach (F=0.02, p=0.9). Thus, hypothesis one is not supported.

Source of Variance	df	F-statistic	p-value
Regulation	1	0.02	0.9
Knowledge	1	0.33	0.57
Regulation x Knowledge	1	0.13	0.99

Table 25: Two Way ANOVA Results of the Effects of Regulation Approach and Knowledge Levels on Subjects' Tax Decisions (Comparative Analysis)

Hypothesis two states that subjects' decision making quality based on rules-based regulation is less likely compromised than the quality based on principles-based regulation if the decision maker has higher regulatory knowledge. For the tax service, there is also no knowledge effect (F=0.33, p=0.57) as presented in Table 25. Thus, hypothesis two needs to be rejected.

3. Discussion

In the pilot study, the manipulation of certain knowledge related to regulations did not result in any significant effects. However, in the main experiment, as Figure 17 demonstrates, a moderate knowledge level ensures higher decision making quality (intended compliance) only to a certain level of complexity. Where moderate knowledge ceases to overcome the level of complexity, regulation switches from rules to principles. Thus, this association depicts the interaction effects of knowledge level and regulation approach, which were significant for the IT service.

The results indicate that a higher knowledge level helps to remedy complexity to some extend, but only for the IT service decision. Graduate students apply the Sarbanes-Oxley Act requirements as intended for the IT service, but fail to apply the European requirements as intended. Undergraduate students allowed the IT service in both regulation settings, which leads to under-compliance of the regulations.

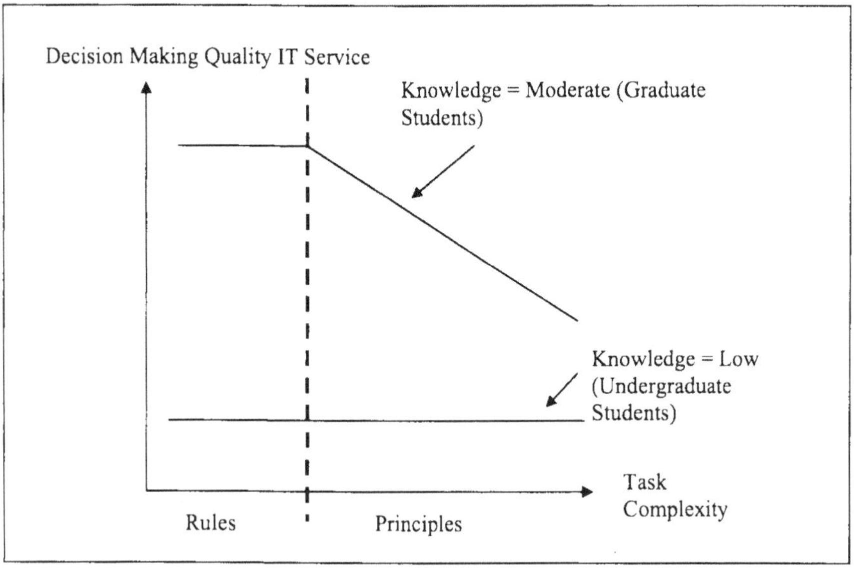

Figure 17: Decision Making Quality – Knowledge Relation for the IT Service

D. Regression Analysis to Identify Significant Fee Threats

Beyond the findings of the previously discussed experiments, where the IT service decision was compromised under some circumstances, I try to investigate whether the decisions based on the regulations concerning the two non-audit services can be empirically supported by further analysis. Thus, I asked in research question four, what are the significant threats, represented by fees, to auditor independence risk in a multi audit firm-client engagement? Based on the results of experiment one, I try to answer research question five which asks whether auditor independence regulation safeguards against significant threats. Thus, I will compare subjects' decision as they indicate the safeguarding effect of the regulation with the findings of regression analysis regarding the fee threats.

1. Research Design and Procedures

Additional statistical analysis was undertaken based on two post-experimental questions from experiment one, because the assessment of the fee threats is only free of manipulation in this setting. The question asked the 39 subjects to indicate the significance of listed threats to the risk of impaired auditor independence, which were given with respect to the case study: audit service fees, tax service fees and IT service fees. This analysis facilitates examining the relationship between these threats, as independent variables, and auditor independence risk as dependent variable. The questions were stated the following:

What is your assessment of the risk that R&P's independence may be impaired, when auditing Kelly & Co's financial statement?

	No Risk			Moderate Risk			High Risk
Assessment of risk of impaired independence:	0	1	2	3	4	5	6

There are a number of factors, often called threats that may increase the risk of impaired auditor independence. Please rate your perception of the significance of the listed threats on the scale below:

	Insignificant			Moderately significant			Strongly significant
The threat to audit independence from the fees for the financial statement audit service ($3,000,000).	0	1	2	3	4	5	6
The threat to audit independence from the fees for the Tax service ($700,000).	0	1	2	3	4	5	6
The threat to audit independence from the fees for the IT service ($700,000).	0	1	2	3	4	5	6

The Johnstone et al.'s (2001) and Mock et al.'s (2005) auditor independence risk models provide a fundamental basis for analyzing the main threats potentially impairing auditor independence. Both models deal with the relevance of fee incentives as one factor overruling the safeguarding efforts made by regulators, accounting and assurance firms and the client.

The most suggested reason for self-interest threats being present is the benefit for the individual auditor from the audit fee paid from the client (Mock et al. 2005). Prior research suggests these pricing phenomena, such as of low-balling (DeAngelo 1981a), as an inherent threat in most audits. DeAngelo (1981a) analyzed an auditor-client model with low-balling as part of a competitive equilibrium and with an incumbent auditor able to exploit auditor's position and earn positive quasi-rents. The expectation of client-specific quasi-rents from a given relationship leads to a lack of indifference with respect to client termination. Therefore, the auditor is not perfectly independent. The relations between the fees, threats, incentives, and the risk of impaired auditor independence are shown in Figure 18.

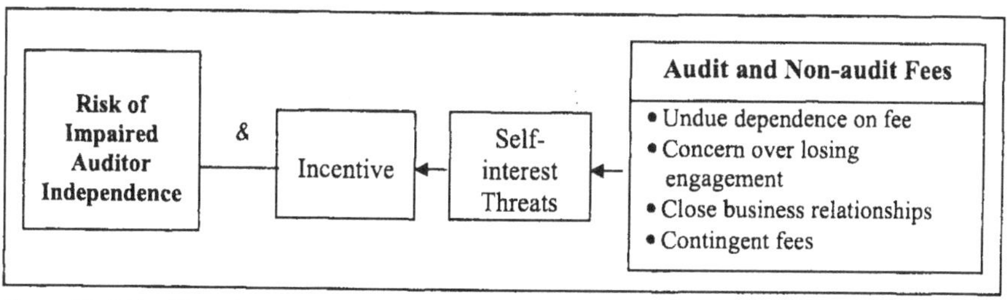

Figure 18: Risk of Impaired Independence and Audit and Non-audit Fees

The additional analysis will provide further evidence for the following research questions:

RQ4: What are significant threats, represented by fees, to auditor independence risk in a multi service audit firm-client engagement?

RQ5: Does auditor independence regulation safeguard against significant threats?

The following Equation 2 represents the association between auditor independence risk and fee threats to auditor independence.

$$\textbf{AI Risk} = \beta_0 + \beta_1\,\textbf{AF} + \beta_2\,\textbf{TaxF} + \beta_3\,\textbf{ITF} + \textbf{u}$$

Dependent Variable
AI Risk: Auditor Independence Risk
Independent Variables
AF: Threat to Auditor Independence Risk through the Audit Fees
TaxF: Threat to Auditor Independence Risk through the Tax Fees
ITF: Threat to Auditor Independence Risk through the IT Fees
β: Beta Coefficient (Intercept or Slopes)
u: Error Term (captures the effects of all omitted variables)

Equation 2: Regression Model of the Effect of Subjects' Assessment of Fee Threats on Auditor Independence

2. Results

Descriptive statistics of the dependent and independent variables are shown in Table 26. The mean and standards deviations (Std. Dev.) of the assessed auditor independence risk is 3.48 (1.33); the means of the independent variables are audit fees 3.28 (1.92), tax fees 2.56 (1.23) and IT fees 3.3 (1.36). This is due to other threats potentially present risks which may impair auditor independence.

Variable Type	Name	Mean	Std. Dev.
Dependent	Auditor Independenc Risk	3.48	1.33
Independent	Audit Fees	3.28	1.92
	Tax Fees	2.56	1.23
	IT Fees	3.3	1.36

Table 26: Descriptive Statistics of Subjects' Assessment of Fee Threats to Auditor Independence

The Pearson correlation co-efficient values for the dependent and independent variables are shown in Table 27. The correlations between the dependent variable and the independent variable are moderate. However, there are weak correlations between the independent variable, which negates the presence of multicollinearity.

Variable Type		AF	TaxF	ITF
Dependent	Auditor Independenc Risk (AIR)	-0,13	0.42**	0,13
Independent	Audit Fees (AF)		-0,21	0,24
	Tax Fees (TaxF)			0.33**
	IT Fees (ITF)			

** indicate significance at the 5 percent level.

Table 27: Pearson Correlation and Significance Levels of Assessed Fee Threats to Audi Independence

Regression results of Equation 2 are significant at a 10% level with F=2.56 (p=0.07) as shown in Table 28. The predictive and explanatory value of the four variables is R-square 0.18. Thus, the model explains 18% of the variance in the assessment of auditor independence risk. Table 28 also shows the coefficient data of all variables. The results indicate that the IT fees are significant (t=2.4, p=0.02). This result is conforming to my first experimental setting, where the IT service was prohibited in both regulation treatments. Furthermore, the intercept β_0 is significant (t=3.08, p=0.004). However, the tax fees and the audit fees are not significant (t=0.03, p=0.97 and t=-0.23, p=0.81, respectively).

	Sum of Squares	df	Mean Square	F-statistic	p-value
Regression	12.18	3	4.06	2.56	0.07
Residual	55.56	35	1.59		
Total	67.74	38			

		β	t-statistic	p-value
0	Intercept	2,22	3,08	0,004
1	Audit Fees	-0,03	-0,23	0,81
2	Tax Fees	0,004	0,03	0,97
3	IT Fees	0,4	2,4	0,02

Table 28: Regression Results and Coefficients Data of Assessed Fee Threats

3. Discussion

Related to Mock et al.'s (2005) auditor independence risk model, incentives might compromise auditor independence. I use different fee types to investigate this relationship. My results indicate that only the IT fees affect the assessment of the risk that the auditor is not independent significantly. Furthermore, the audit fees and the tax fees are not affecting the assessment of auditor independence risk.

The experimental results of experiment one weakly indicate which services are perceived to be prohibited based on the nature of regulation. In comparison, the additional analysis shows which fees are perceived most likely to impair auditor independence. Related to Mock et al. (2005), threats to auditor independence might be prevented by safeguards, such as regulation. Thus, I will contextualize the results of the experimental settings with additional regression results.

To understand how I want to contextualize the two lines of empirical findings, Table 29 summarizes the main findings.

	Assessed Threat from Fees (Results of Regression Analysis)	**Intended Compliance Based on the Given Regulations**
IT	YES (t=2.4, p=0.02)	Prohibition
TAX	**NO** (t=0.03, p=0.97)	Allowance

Table 29: Assessed Fee Threats versus Intended Compliance

Based on the results of additional regression analysis, the IT service was a significant threat, whereas the tax service was not affecting auditor independence risk significantly (see the column labeled Assessed Threat from Fees). I then repeated the intended compliance (see the column labeled Intended Compliance). This is how regulation was required in both experiments. The comparison shows that subjects' felt the IT fees to be a threat, but not the tax fees. This is conforming to the intended compliance, which is that the IT service is prohibited, but the tax service is not.

Table 30 repeats the safeguarding intention in form of the intended compliance (see the column labeled Intended Compliance) and repeats whether subjects assessed the fess to be a threat (see the column labeled Perceived Threats from Fees) in comparison to the achieved compliance based on subjects' decisions in the first experiment (see the column labeled Subjects' Decision). Although the tax fees was assessed to not affecting the risk of impaired auditor independence (see the cell labeled NO→Allowance), subjects were unsure about the decision whether to allow or to prohibit the tax service.

	Perceived Threat from Fees → Intended Compliance	**Subjects' Decision**	
		Rules-based Approach	Principles-based Approach
IT	YES → Prohibition	YES	YES
TAX	**NO → Allowance**	NO	**UNSURE**

Table 30: Assessed Fee Threats versus Subjects' Decisions

Chapter VII. Consequences from the Empirical Findings for the European Capital Market

In this chapter I deduce consequences for European Union Regulation setting. Section A compares national requirements of Germany, France and the United Kingdom to investigate whether national regulation approaches and requirements differ significantly from what is being proposed by the European Union. This is, whether Member States use a rules- or principles-based national regulation approach and whether regulation differs in terms of the requirements' content. I found differences in national regulation approaches and requirements, which may lead to audits of different quality throughout the European Union and therefore to differences in the risk of impaired auditor independence. I then describe possible effects of impaired auditor independence on the European capital market. Since one mechanisms to align information asymmetries concerning audits and thereby decreasing deficiencies in capital markets is greater transparency, the influence of transparency on impaired auditor independence risk as studied in a third experiment is presented in section B.

A. Evaluation of the Conceptual Principles-Based Approach

1. Introduction

The European Commission argues that "[a] principles-based approach to statutory auditors' independence is preferable to one based on detailed rules because it creates a robust structure within which statutory auditors have to justify their actions". Furthermore the Commission assumes that a principles-based approach "provides the audit profession and its regulators with the flexibility to react promptly and effectively to new developments in business and in the audit environment" by "avoid[ing] the highly legalistic and rigid approach to what is and is not permitted, which can arise in a rules-based regime. A principles-based approach can cater to the almost infinite variations in individual circumstances that arise in practice and in the different legal environments throughout the European Union". Thus the Commission concludes that "a principles-based approach will better serve the needs of European capital markets (European Commission 2002: L 191/23)".

Empirical findings of experiment two do not support this and other statements supporting a conceptual approach. The results of my research show that principles need more clarifying adjustments than rules do. Furthermore, the principles require an audit firm to conscientiously consider providing additional non-audit services, whether or not the performance of additional services would involve threats which would impede the observance of the principles. Where such threats exist, the audit firm must put in place safeguards that reduce the threats to clearly insignificant levels. If the audit firm is unable to implement fully adequate safeguards, the additional services are not allowed to be performed (European Federation of Accountants 2001: 5).

Results of experiment two indicate that principles lead to under-compliance of regulation when audit firm's litigation risk was low. The findings do not automatically cause auditor's independence to be impaired, but rather increase the risk of impairment. If an auditor were to appear before a disciplinary tribunal, charged with a breach of the given principles-based requirements of experiment two, it would not be a sufficient defense to demonstrate the particular examples of threats and safeguards, since those are only illustrative. The auditor would need to be able to demonstrate that, in the particular circumstances under consideration, the principles had in fact been observed.

Related to the findings in experiment two and to the statement by the European Commission concerning a principles-based regulation approach, in the following I study national requirements of Germany, France and the United Kingdom to investigate whether national regulation approaches and requirements differ to some degree from what is being proposed by the European Union.

2. National Auditor Independence Regulation of Germany, France and the United Kingdom

So far, national systems of auditor independence regulation have different approaches to imposing requirements on auditors in order to avoid situations where their independence would be threatened. Public interest protection systems involve law (a clear statement of what is not permissible), education, detection (receipts of complaints or structured systems of inspection), and discipline (penalties) (European Federation of Accountants 2001: 4). However, in this section, I focus on national requirements corresponding to the requirements proposed by the European Union.

The European Commission is planning to issue auditor independence requirements, serving as a minimum harmonization for all Member States and protecting public interest against the self-interested actions of auditors. These requirements are based on broad statements of principles. Member States are free to go beyond the European requirements in order to add local requirements. As already shown for Germany, many Member States responded to the Sarbanes-Oxley Act (2002) and to the European recommendations (2002) and proposal (2004). However, Member States may use different approaches (rules or principles) to implement requirements. Furthermore, the content of requirements may differ.

Germany, France and the United Kingdom are three Member States with differences in their financial systems, corporate governance culture and more importantly, in their auditor independence regulation approaches and requirements (Baker, Mikol and Quick 2001, Piot 2005). In the following I will provide an overview about the requirements concerning audit committee composition, audit partner and audit firm rotation and non-audit services for Germany, France and the United Kingdom. I then use the outline of these requirements to study the regulation approaches and the content of the requirements. A summary is presented in Table 31, where I also repeat the proposed European requirements for completeness.

	European Union Proposal	**Germany**	**France**	**United Kingdom**
Audit Committee Composition	Composed of non-executive members, at least one independent member with competence in accounting/auditing (Proposal Article 39 (1)).	Recommended, committee chairman should not be former member of supervisory board (Corporate Governance Codex 5.3.2).	Recommended, composed of independent directors to at least two-third, no corporate officer (*Association Française des Entreprises Privées* 14.1).	Recommended, at least three members, all independent non-executive officers, at least one member with financial experience (Smith Report 2003).
Audit Partner Rotation	Required after five years (Proposal Article 40 c).	Required after seven years for auditors of clients using an organized market as defined in II (5) *Wertpapierhandelsgesetz* (§ 319a I (4) HGB).	Individual auditors and signing members of auditing firms are prohibited from auditing the accounts of legal entities which make public issues for more than six consecutive financial years (§ L822-14 Commercial Code).	After five years for audit engagement partner and after seven years for other key audit partners (Coordinating Group on Audit and Accounting Issues: 17).
Audit Firm Rotation	Alternative to audit partner rotation after seven years (Proposal Article 40 c).	---	----	----
Non-audit Services	Member states shall ensure that when carrying out a statutory audit, a statutory auditor or the audit firm is independent from the audited entity and is not in any way involved in management decisions of the audited entity, when the auditor refuses any non-audit engagement which might compromise his independence as an auditor (Proposal Article 23).	Business, financial, personal relationship to client, which may impair independence (§ 319 II HGB); additional services prohibited, such as bookkeeping, internal revision, management or financial services, evaluation services, if not of minor importance (§ 319 III (3) HGB). Performance of audit or other appraisal services prohibited if self-review (§ 23 *Satzung der Wirtschaftsprüferkammer*).	Auditors are prohibited from providing any advice or other service to the person who entrusts them with the auditing of their accounts (§ L822-11 Commercial Code).	Internal audit services only under exceptional circumstances Review of circumstances for the following services: Valuation services, Taxation services, design and supply of IT and financial information technology systems (Coordinating Group on Audit and Accounting Issues: 28-31).

Table 31: European Union Proposal and National Requirements in Germany, France and the United Kingdom

The European proposal for the revised 8th Directive (2004) requires companies of public interest to have an audit committee composed of non-executive members, with at least one independent member with competence in accounting and/or auditing. So far, all selected countries have no mandatory requirement for an audit committee, but they do have a voluntary recommendation to have an audit committee as one important corporate governance mechanism (e.g., Klein, Schaum and Tielmann 2003).

The German Corporate Governance Code (2002) recommends an audit committee with a chairman that is not a former member of the supervisory board. This recommendation has law character since listed companies are required to report noncompliance with the Code. However, audit related tasks are still treated as supplementary (Köhler 2005). France recommends an audit committee composed of at least two-thirds independent directors and no corporate officer (*Association Française des Entreprises Privées* 2002); the United Kingdom proposes at least three members, all independent non-executive officers with at least one member with financial experience (Smith Report 2003). Member States will have to fully comply with the European Union requirements concerning the audit committee. This means not only fundamental changes within the composition of the audit committee (e.g., as for the United Kingdom not all audit committees have an independent member), but moreover, a cost-intensive legislative initiative for putting a mandatory requirement in place (e.g., the United Kingdom estimated the cost for changes to be up to a total of $22 million) (United Kingdom Department of Trade and Industry 2005:10).

Audit partner rotation is already mandated in all three selected European Countries; Germany requires auditor rotation after seven years, France after six years and the United Kingdom (in line with the European Proposal) after five years.[41] Whereas the United Kingdom generally requires the auditors of listed companies to rotate, Germany will have to expand the coverage of the national requirements to address all required listed companies. None of the selected European countries have set up the alternative audit firm requirement as the European proposal requires. If the European Proposal is issued with this requirement included, all selected Member States would have to adopt it, although the alternative audit firm rotation is criticized as possible decreasing audit quality and increasing audit costs and the risk of audit failure (e.g., German Chamber of Public Accountants 2004).

[41] For a detailed new institutional economics analysis based on principal-agent theory, see Herzig and Watrin (1995).

Finally, the requirements concerning non-audit services are based on principles in the European Union proposal as shown before. The German requirements are also fairly broad, but specific rules are given to address particular services, if these services are not of minor importance. These are bookkeeping and financial statement preparation, internal revision services, management or financial services and evaluation services. Still, there is some scope of discretion as to whether the performed service is of minor importance. Furthermore, the performance of audit or other appraisal services are prohibited if their performance poses a review of work previously performed by the auditor. This principle leaves room for the audit firm to decide whether the existing business, financial, personal relationship to the client may impair independence. Hence, the German conceptual approach is similar to that of the European Union regulation.

The French regulation is very restrictive, by prohibiting book keeping, valuation, involvement of litigation, and involvement in the management, legal, tax, financial consultancy or services incurring significant risks with general auditing. The French approach is basically a rule-based approach.

Finally, United Kingdom regulation allows internal audit services to be performed only under exceptional circumstances. Internal audit services as defined in these regulations are mainly taxation services, the design and supply of information technology and financial information technology systems. Thus, I see the United Kingdom requirements between a German and European principle, versus the French and American detailed rules.

The preceding comparison indicates significant differences between the national regulation approaches and requirements. Since the approach of auditor independence regulation may affect auditor's decisions concerning audit work and ultimately their client's financial reporting (see the Figure 1), different national approaches and requirements may lead to different levels of impaired auditor independence risk.

The European Union can be regarded as a single market, since many companies operate in more than one European country. Furthermore, a lot of effort is being expended by European Union institutions to accelerate the process of developing one strong single market (e.g., issuance of a uniformed currency and discussion on a uniformed corporate tax system[42]). However, different levels of auditor independence risk throughout the 25 Member States from a complex European principles-based regulation approach and different national regulation approaches and requirements might lead to deficiencies in this market as is next discussed.

3. Effects of Auditor's Impaired Independence on the European Capital Market

Auditor's impaired independence can affect the quality of the performed audit. The audit should serve as an expert and impartial analyses for the financial positions of companies, which stakeholders have an interest in (European Federation of Accountants 2001: 3). A company can seek to raise capital from outside investors for the purpose of expanding its operations, whereas the outcome of the investment depends on several factors, including audit quality (Schwartz 1997).

After the auditor issues the audit report, the investor decides whether or not to invest and at what level (Antle and Nalebuff 1991). Based on the reliability and creditability of the financial information, investors make rational choices, which affect the efficiency of capital markets. Thus, unreliable financial information will act as a brake on economic progress through harming interests of individuals. Hence, governments regard audit quality as a public interest and try to maintain audit quality with auditor independence regulations.

The efficiency of auditor independence regulation depends upon how regulation impacts the level of investment through affecting audit quality (Marten 1999). Recent studies found legal requirements to have an impact on the development of capital markets (Ali and Hwang 2000, La Porta, Lopez-de-Silanes, Shleifer and Vishny 2000). These studies suggest that the legal protection of investors' rights is the crucial element in understanding the pattern of corporate finance and the role of financial information worldwide (La Porta et al. 2000, Bushman and Smith 2001). A recent study by Newman, Patterson and Smith (2005) found that markets with relatively greater auditor penalties for audit failures have larger investment levels.

[42] Watrin, Sievert and Strohm (2004) give an overview on European-wide corporate taxation.

With respect to findings in experiment two, it is questionable whether a conceptual approach based on principles is preferable to one based on detailed rules. On a European Union-Member State audit market level, it may provide European and national regulators with the flexibility needed to react promptly and effectively to new developments in the business and audit environments. This conceptual approach avoids the highly legalistic and rigid approach to what is and is not permitted, which can arise in a rules-based regime. Thus, the overall approach seems to fit into a 25 Member State market, where only a broad concept is manageable. Furthermore, this approach leaves Member States with highly demanded national authority, because they still have the possibility to add local requirements. However, this approach alone will not serve as a step towards harmonization, since many clarifying adjustments from the revised European 8th Directive are required on the Member State Level to ensure that the auditor independence requirements are complied with as intended and thus to serve as effective safeguards to the risk of impaired auditor independence.

On a Member State-auditor level, a principles-based approach may create a robust structure, within which statutory auditors are able to justify their actions. Legalistic effort will be required on a national level, since Member States have to ensure that auditors are able to interpret the requirements as intended. Thus, these principles (e.g., France extended the principles-based requirement concerning non-audit services by stating rules-based restrictions) can be adjusted for the individual needs of each Member State. However, not only important is the possibility to adjust requirements addressing national characteristics; my findings in experiment two also show the need for Member States to adjust the content of principles to become more detailed and more rules-based to be effective. Thus, as for the comparison of Germany, France and the United Kingdom all three Member States issued more detailed requirements than the European Union proposal. However, there are still differences between the level of detail given (e.g., France and Germany).

The fact that Member States are free to add local requirements may lead to 25 different auditor independence regulations. How much national regulations differ was shown in the comparison of German, France and the United Kingdom regulation approaches and requirements. Given these challenges to regulation, the European Union has considered various mechanisms to support the principles-based regulation approach such as requiring additional transparency.

According to the European Federation of Accountants, the key of a successful principles-based regulation approach is effective mechanisms, which apply at three levels (European Federation of Accountants 2001: 7): particular cases addressed in single requirements, the risk of detection, and the work environment.

In this thesis I provide further evidence regarding the effectiveness of specific requirements as related to particular cases, such as questions regards the performance of additional non-audit services as studied in the two experimental studies previously reported. The risk of detection is reflected in the duty to report breaches of ethical requirements, to draw attention to unprofessional behavior, and in professional arrangements for monitoring by the professional bodies, which itself is subject to external supervision.

Finally, the broadest level of mechanisms is the work environment and includes educational requirements, which include the initial training for auditor qualification and in subsequent compulsory continuing professional education (European Federation of Accountants 2001: 6). Furthermore, the systems of corporate governance are playing a growing role in ensuring that auditor independence threats do not exist (e.g., Bushman and Smith 2001). Most importantly, with respect to audit quality, are legal and regulatory requirements for the involvement of persons independent of companies' management in decisions on audit, such as audit committee composition and reporting requirements to the audit committee. Related to auditors' risk of damaged business reputation are disciplinary penalties put in place by Member States. Lastly, transparency is an important factor to provide investors with relevant information, such as audit and non-audit fees. In this part of the dissertation, I study the effects of greater transparency.

B. Experiment on Transparency Effects on Perceived Auditor Independence Risk

1. Proposed Transparency Report

The previous discussion showed possible deficiencies of the proposed European Union requirements, which in experiment two led to over-compliance of regulations concerned with the provision of non audit services to financial statement audit clients. In experiment three, based on the audit firm's published information regarding important safeguards, stakeholders assess the level of impaired auditor independence risk.[43] One important source of information for outside stakeholders is the information provided by the client itself and the client's audit firm. This limited information leads to an asymmetric information structure and to an information gap. Such an information gap between auditors and other client's stakeholders may lead auditor independence in appearance to differ between stakeholders, whereas the assumed functional associations are presented in Figure 19 (Mock et al. 2005).

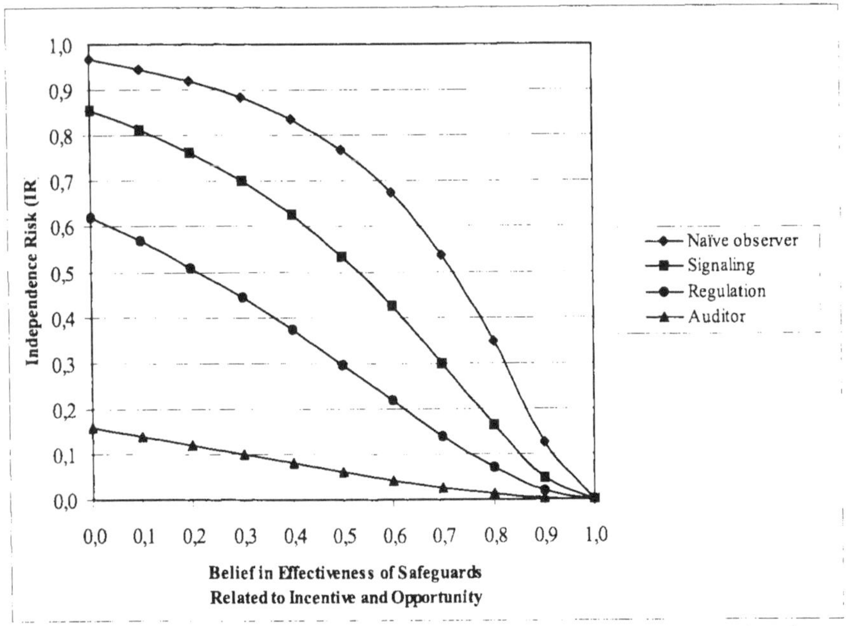

Figure 19: Independence Risk as a Function of Perceived Effectiveness of Safeguards against Threats Related to Incentives and Opportunities for Different Levels of Transparency and Existence of Regulations and Laws

Independence risk: Plausibility of impaired independence

Naïve observer:	Plausibility of impaired independence as perceived by an observer having minimal information about the relationship between the independent auditor and the audit client or about the effectiveness of safeguards affecting that relationship

[43] Unless indicated, the terms 'independence risk', 'lack of independence' and 'impaired independence' all refer to impaired independence 'in appearance' for section B.

Signaling: Plausibility of impaired independence perceived by an observer after increased signaling by independent auditor regarding nature of threats and the effectiveness of safeguards

Regulation: Plausibility of impaired independence perceived by an observer after increased signaling by the profession and regulators regarding nature of threats and effectiveness of safeguards and after implementation of increased regulations and laws, such as Sarbanes-Oxley Act of 2002

Auditor: Plausibility of impaired independence self-assessed by independent auditor

Assuming the auditor is able to assess the level of independence in fact, this may also lead independence in appearance and in fact to differ. In addition, providing investors with more reliable information about the auditor-agent of public companies has an effect on the overall economic performance. Based on reliable information investors more likely detect investment opportunities in the European capital market.

A still growing body of evidence indicates that the development of financial markets facilitates its performance, but also depends on the level of corporate transparency. Ewert (1989) found that for the market of financial reporting publicly available information is beneficial for all stakeholders. Love (2000) found that financial development affects growth by decreasing information related imperfections in the capital markets. Furthermore, financial information helped clients and owners overcome moral hazards and adverse selection problems as related to auditors (e.g., Rajan and Zingales 1998). As argued by Black (2000) and Ball (2001), strong financial accounting regimes focusing on the credibility and accountability of information are a prerequisite to the very existence of vibrant securities markets.

To address the need for greater transparency as one major mechanism, the European Commission (2004a) also proposed the requirement for audit firms to publish a transparency report annually. The requirement states that Member States shall ensure that audit firms carry out audits of public interest entities and publish on their website an annual transparency report that includes at least the following:

1. A description of the legal structure and ownership;
2. Where the audit firm belongs to a network, a description of the network and the legal and structural arrangements in the network;
3. A statement on the governance structure of the audit firm;
4. A description of the internal quality control system of the audit firm and a statement by the administrative or management body on the effectiveness of its functioning;
5. An indication of when the last quality assurance review took place;
6. A listing of public interest entities for which an audit has been carried out during the last year by the audit firm;
7. A statement about the audit firm's independence practices, which also confirms that an internal review of independence compliance has been conducted;
8. A statement on the policy followed by the audit firm concerning continuous education of auditors;
9. Financial information showing the importance of the audit firm, such as the total turnover divided into fees from the audit of annual and consolidated accounts, and fees charged for other assurance services, tax advisory services and other non-audit services and
10. Information about the basis for the partner remunderation (Article 38).

The proposed transparency report is viewed differently throughout the European Union by various Member States. For example, the German Chamber of Public Accountants (2004) is generally supportive towards more transparency, but questions the level of detail proposed. Furthermore, the German position points out that this report is only proposed for audit firms and not for individual auditors. They also argue that the date of the last quality assurance review is not very expressive. According to the German position it would be more important to know if the quality assurance review was completed successfully.

The United Kingdom government is more supportive of the proposed transparency regulation. The United Kingdom delegation believes that the proposed report is an appropriate compromise between all of the stakeholders' interests. There are also costs implications; the benefits of greater transparency should outweigh those costs (United Kingdom Department of Trade and Industry 2005: 10).

If reporting on all listed safeguards of the transparency report is mandatory, audit firms would be faced with a cost-intensive implementation phase after the proposed requirement becomes law. Furthermore, national regulators would have to bear the costs of the legislative implementation of this requirement into national law.

However, audit firms might be willing to provide the information concerning important safeguards on a voluntary basis (e.g., in 2005, KPMG and in 2004 and 2005, Grant Thornton published a transparency report on a voluntary basis), which would prevent some of the audit firms' costs as well as the regulators' implementation costs. The disadvantage of a voluntary publication would be that transparency reports might not be as comparable as desired between audit firms. For example, in 2005, KPMG focused mainly on corporate governance, whereas Grant Thornton's report covered information related to independence, integrity and quality controls. Hence, audit firms' available information would most likely vary throughout the European Union. Furthermore, a voluntary provision may lead to different transparency reports in different audit firm years. For example, Grant Thornton's report in 2004 focused on independence, professionalism, integrity and responsibility. The 2005 report provided information related to independence, integrity and quality controls.

High costs would be caused by implementing a mandatory transparency report, but at the same time comparable reports would be assured. Or, based on an audit market constraint, audit firms could issue a transparency report on a voluntary basis, which would then most likely lead to non-comparable reports between audit firms and between different audit firm years. This decision should be based on the transparency report user's assessment concerning the effectiveness of a mandatory versus a voluntary transparency report. This discussion leads to the question: Should the disclosure of the most effective safeguards be mandatory, and should reporting on additional, less important, information be voluntary?

The European Federation of Accountants (2003: 17) believes that a transparency report would only provide reliable information with appropriate oversight in place. This view is related to the question about non-audited information, such as a transparency report, wherein reliability can be assumed (e.g., Herzig and Watrin 1995). A transparency report, which is not reviewed by an external institution, might be in danger to contain a lot of unreliable information on the safeguards. Furthermore, a transparency report which is not reviewed might focus on information which emphasizes the audit firm's activities to maintain auditor independence, but at the same time might ignore any weaknesses that could possibly compromise auditor independence. For example, KMPG's transparency report (2005) focuses on corporate governance, whereas Grant Thornton (2005) reports on independence and integrity.

Related to this discussion, the main objective is to find the balance between doing justice to the audit firms' demand for self-regulation (Marten 1999) and the need of enforcement for reliable transparent reporting. The latter uses high quality signals to decrease information asymmetries between audit firms and stakeholders (Helm, Mark and Fischer 2003). External reviews are discussed as being important to ensure high quality audits and public confidence in transparent quality controls (Marten, Köhler and Meyer 2003). Therefore, appropriate oversight, such as a detailed review process might be necessary to ensure the effectiveness of the reported safeguards (Houghton and Trotman 2003). Hence, I asked the question: Does a reviewed report better serve as an overall framework to improve an audit firm's independence?

Related to prior research that suggests greater transparency helps to mitigate imperfections in markets and to address the controversial discussion throughout Member States, I state the following research questions:

RQ6: Would a mandatory rather than a voluntary transparency report better serve as an overall framework to improve an audit firm's independence?

RQ7: Would a reviewed report better serve as an overall framework to improve an audit firm's independence?

RQ8: Which of the proposed disclosures are viewed as being relatively more important?

RQ9: Which of the reported safeguards contribute significantly to stakeholder assessments of the maintenance of auditor independence?

2. Participants

Subjects of the experiment were participants in a conference on current regulatory developments organized by the University of Southern California. The research was conducted as an experiment, but was distributed to all 800 conference participants. 62 questionnaires were completed at the conference and 29 were mailed afterwards. Subjects had professional experience in auditing, accounting and/or finance with an average of 21 years. Subjects indicated their knowledge about auditor independence regulation at a relatively high average of 5.45 (scale 0 to 6, indicating low to high knowledge, respectively).

3. Research Design and Procedures

The two independent variables, the regulation approach of the transparency report (mandatory/voluntary) and a possible oversight arrangement to ensure high quality transparency reports (review/no review), were manipulated in a 2 x 2 between subjects design, where subjects were assigned to one version randomly.[44] Subjects were asked to assess the effectiveness of the transparency report as an overall framework to improve the audit firm's independence. Table 32 shows the experimental treatments, including the number of subjects within each treatment (cell).

		Oversight Arrangement	
		Review	No Review
Regulation Approach	Mandatory Transparency Report	23	22
	Voluntary Transparency Report	22	24

Table 32: Experimental Treatments and Treatment Sample Sizes (Transparency Report)

Each subject received a copy of the research instrument as part of the conference materials.[45] An announcement requesting subjects to voluntarily participate in the study was made by the conference director. Since there was no specific time scheduled during the conference to complete the research materials, subjects were also provided

[44] The results of a performed one way ANOVA on subjects' knowledge level indicate that random assignment of subjects to versions was effective ($F=1.27$, $p=0.29$).

[45] The research instrument is provided in Appendix 9.

with a self-addressed envelope in case they preferred to mail their response instead of completing the instrument during the conference.

Within the research instrument, there first was an introduction to the current debate in Europe, as to whether or not a transparency report about audit firm's own policies and procedures should be required. They were informed that European Union Member States have a broad range of opinions on whether the report should be mandatory or voluntary. The discussion includes concerns over the details required and cost versus benefit implications. Thus, the instrument contained the following information:

The use of such a transparency report is currently quite controversial. In the European Union one of the many discussions revolve around whether the report should be mandatory or voluntary. The discussion includes concerns over the details required and cost versus benefit implications. With this study we want to provide evidence concerning:

1. *whether a mandatory versus a voluntary transparency report would better serve as an overall framework to improve an audit firm's independence and*
2. *which of the proposed disclosures are viewed as being relatively more important?*

We believe this study will be of interest to both the European Standard-setters and to the PCAOB. The study will only take around 5 to 10 minutes to complete.

This information was followed by a case study of a hypothetical audit firm R&P, LLP which is located in the United Kingdom. The case study contained the following description of R&P:

Roberts & Partner, LLP (R&P) is a large, British independent accounting firm. The firm was founded in 1923 and is headquartered in London. Including its affiliates in the USA, Europe and Asia, R&P employs over 6,000 people. The firm is primarily involved in financial statement audit services applying International Accounting Standards. Furthermore, R&P also performs non-audit services in order to maintain its competitiveness in the audit market.

Two groups of subjects were told to assume that in the United Kingdom the regulations include the mandatory publication of an annual transparency report on its own homepage to document the policies and procedures that R&P carries out to maintain auditor independence (mandatory). The other two groups were told to assume that in the United Kingdom the professional guidance include the voluntary publication of an annual transparency report on its own homepage to document the policies and procedures that R&P carries out to maintain auditor independence (voluntary). Subjects in the mandatory condition got the following information:

As part of an ongoing quality control and improvement process, R&P is proactive in keeping up with the ever-changing regulation. Assume that in the UK the regulation include the mandatory publication of an annual transparency report on its own homepage to document the policies and procedures that R&P carries out to maintain auditor independence.

The voluntary condition contained the same information; only the report was voluntary published:

As part of an ongoing quality control and improvement process, R&P is proactive in keeping up with the ever-changing regulation. Assume that in the UK the professional guidance include the voluntary publication of an annual transparency report on its own homepage to document the policies and procedures that R&P carries out to maintain auditor independence

As for the review treatment, subjects were told that R&P has engaged two independent experts to review their policies and procedures and that the final report of these experts is posted on R&P's homepage. Furthermore, subjects were informed that after having reviewed the policies and procedures as described in the transparency report, the two experts stated the following: "Based on our review, no significant issues have come to our attention that would cause us to believe that R&P's policies and procedures to maintain auditor independence is not operating properly" (review). The version without a review did not include any review information (no review). Subjects of the review condition got the following information, which was not provided for subjects of the condition with no review:

Furthermore, R&P has engaged two independent experts to review their policies and procedures. The final report of these experts is posted on R&P's homepage. After having reviewed the policies and procedures as described in the transparency report, the two experts state the following: "Based on our review, no significant issues have come to our attention that would cause us to believe that R&P's policies and procedures to maintain auditor independence is not operating properly."

After having read the introduction and the case study, subjects were asked to assess whether or not the policies and procedures described in the transparency report[46] provided an overall framework to improve the firm's independence. Specifically, they were asked the following question:

Based on the information about R&P, the mandatory/voluntary transparency report and the conclusion as stated by the reviewer, please answer the following questions: The policies and procedures listed in the transparency report are usually thought as being safeguards to auditor independence risk. What is your viewpoint on how these policies and procedures provide an overall framework to improve the firm's independence?						
Not effective			Moderately effective			Very effective
0	1	2	3	4	5	6

As a post experimental question, subjects were asked to indicate which of the safeguards might be more effective than the others in order to maintain auditor independence. Subjects were allowed to go back to the transparency report to reread the information. The question was:

[46] The description of the legal structure, ownership, and information about where the audit firm belongs to a network, a description of the network and the legal and structural arrangements in the network, as proposed information details in the transparency report were dropped from the research instrument because of lack of relevance to my research questions.

How important are each of the individual safeguards as related to each other? In other words, which of the safeguards might be more effective than the others? (See the prior page for complete descriptions of each safeguard):

	Not Important			Moderate Important			Very important
1: Governance Structure	0	1	2	3	4	5	6
2: Internal Quality Control	0	1	2	3	4	5	6
3: Quality Assurance	0	1	2	3	4	5	6
4: Audited Entities	0	1	2	3	4	5	6
5: Independence Practice and Compliance	0	1	2	3	4	5	6
6: Continuing Professional Education	0	1	2	3	4	5	6
7: Fee Information	0	1	2	3	4	5	6

Finally, I collected subjects' demographic information. I asked for their professional auditing, accounting or/and finance experience in years and for their self-assessed knowledge of auditor independence regulation on a seven point Linkert-scale. To ensure a precise self-assessment the scale ranging from 'little knowledge' and 'moderate knowledge' to 'high knowledge' was labeled with examples such as 'Casual Investor' as an example for a little knowledge and 'Certified Public Accountant and Audit Committee Member' for high knowledge.

4. Results

Research question six asked whether a mandatory versus a voluntary transparency report is viewed by stakeholders as better serving as an overall framework to improve an audit firm's independence. Whether a reviewed report versus a not reviewed report improves an audit firm's independence was asked in research question seven. The descriptive statistics of the question, where subjects were asked to indicate their viewpoint on how the information given in the transparency report provided an overall framework to improve the firm's independence, are shown in Table 33. Subjects felt both a mandatory (mean=3.8) and a voluntary (mean=3.89) transparency report to be moderately effective in improving auditor independence. However, a reviewed report (mean=4.02) was viewed as being slightly more effective than a report not reviewed (mean=3.67).

Scale 0 to 6		Oversight Arrangement		
Means (Std. Dev.)		Review	No Review	Marginals
Regulation Approach	Mandatory Transparency Report	3.91 (1.08)	3.68 (1.29)	3.8 (1.18)
	Voluntary Transparency Report	4.14 (1.25)	3.66 (1.27)	3.89 (1.27)
Marginals		4.02 (1.16)	3.67 (1.26)	

Table 33: Descriptive Statistic of Subjects' Assessment of the Effectiveness of a Transparency Report

The results of a two way analysis of variance are shown in Table 34. As indicated, there is no significant difference in the subjects' assessments as to whether or not the transparency report is more effective to maintain auditor independence whether the transparency report was mandatory or voluntary (F=0.13, p=0.72). Results also indicate that the oversight treatment of a required review of the transparency report was assessed to be more effective although the difference is not statistically significant using conventional significance thresholds (F=1.87, p=0.17).

Source of Variance	df	F-statistic	p-value
Regulation Approach	1	0.13	0.72
Oversight Arrangement	1	1.87	0.17
Regulation Approach x Oversight Arrangement	1	0.22	0.64

Table 34: Two Way ANOVA Results of the Effects of the Treatments on Subjects' Assessment of the Effectiveness of a Transparency Report

Research question eight asked which of the proposed disclosures are viewed as being relatively more important. One post experimental question asked subjects to indicate the importance in the transparency report of each listed safeguards as related to each other. The importance of each safeguard was measured on a scale from 0 to 6, indicating that the single safeguard is not important to very important. Descriptive statistics are shown in Table 35.

Variable Type		Mean	Std. Dev.
Dependent	Auditor Independence	3.85	1.22
Independent	Independence Practice and Compliance	4.84	1.28
	Internal Quality Control	4.78	1.32
	Quality Assurance	4.59	1.26
	Continuing Professional Education	3.86	1.49
	Corporate Governance Structure	3.79	1.65
	Audited Entities	3.2	1.75
	Fee Information	2.78	1.88

Table 35: Descriptive Statistics of Subjects' Assessment of the Importance of the Proposed Safeguards

A statement about the audit firm's independence practice, which also confirms that an internal review of independence compliance has been conducted, is viewed as being the most important safeguard (mean=4.84). Slightly less important is a description of the internal quality control system of the audit firm and a statement by the administrative or management body on the effectiveness of its functioning (mean=4.78). An indication of when the last audit firm's quality assurance review took place (mean=4.59) is felt to be important. A statement on the policy followed by the audit firm concerning continuous education of auditors (mean=3.86) is assessed to be important, as well as a statement on the governance structure of the audit firm (mean=3.79). Of at least moderate importance is a listing of public interest entities for which an audit has been carried out during the last year by the audit firm (mean=3.2). The least important safeguard maintaining auditor independence is financial information showing the importance of the audit firm, such as the total turnover divided into fees from the audit of annual and consolidated accounts and fees charged for other assurance services, tax advisory services and other non-audit services (mean=2.78). A performed one way ANOVA indicates a significant difference in the assessment of importance for the seven listed safeguards ($F=24.75$, $p=0.0001$).

In research question nine I asked which of the reported safeguards contribute significantly to the assessments of expected maintenance of auditor independence. To address the research question, I analyzed the association between subjects' assessment of the effectiveness of the transparency report as an overall framework to improve the audit firm's independence and the assessment of the effectiveness of the listed safeguards. Thus, I conducted the following regression model as shown in Equation 3.

$$\mathbf{AI = \beta_0 + \beta_1\, CGS + \beta_2\, IQC + \beta_3\, QA + \beta_4\, AE + \beta_5\, IPC + \beta_6\, CPE + \beta_7\, FI + u}$$

Dependent Variable

AI:	Auditor Independence

Independent Variables

CGS:	Corporate Governance Structure
IQC:	Internal Quality Control
QA:	Quality Assurance
AE:	Audited Entities
IPC:	Independence Practice and Compliance
CPE:	Continuing Professional Education
FI:	Fee Information
β:	*Beta Coefficient (Intercept or Slopes)*
u:	*Error Term (captures the effects of all omitted variables)*

Equation 3: Regression Model of the Effect of Subjects' Assessment of the Importance of the Proposed Safeguards on Perceived Auditor Independence

Table 36 shows the coefficient data of all variables. The results are highly significant with F=10.04 (p<0.0001) and R-Square of 0.46. The results indicate that the quality assurance to maintain auditor independence is significant (t=2.24, p=0.02), as well as the continuing professional education (t=2.1, p=0.04) and the internal quality control (t=1.89, p=0.06).

Model	Sum of Squares	df	Mean Square	F-statistic	p-value
Regression	61,38	7	8,77	10,04	< 0.0001
Residual	72,47	83	0,87		
Total	133,85	90			

Model		β	t-statistic	p-value
0	Intercept	0.37	0.79	0.43
1	Corporate Governance Structure	-0.009	-0.14	0.88
2	Internal Quality Control	0.19	1.89	0.06
3	Quality Assurance	0.23	2.24	0.02
4	Audited Entities	0.09	1.38	0.17
5	Independence Practice and Compliance	0.06	0.68	0.5
6	Continuing Professional Education	0.18	2.1	0.04
7	Fee Information	0.07	1.15	0.25

Table 36: Regression Results and Coefficients Data of Subjects' Assessment of the Importance of the Proposed Safeguards

The Pearson correlation co-efficient values for the dependent and independent variables are shown in Table 37. The correlations between the dependent variable and the independent variables are highly significant. However, there are also significant correlations between the independent variables, which indicate the presence of multicollinearity. Since the seven safeguards are not mutually exclusive, multicollinearity is an issue. Continuing professional education might capture the same safeguarding aspects as independence practice and compliance does (correlation 0.43). Multicollinearity only compromises the results where a regression coefficient assumes a high incremental explanatory power, but the test for significance fails. This might be the case for the regression variables audited entities (β_4=1.38 with p=0.17) and fee information (β_7=1.15 with p=0.25).

Variable Type	Name	CGS	IQC	QA	AE	IPC	CPE	FI
Dependent	AI	0.28**	0.49**	0.54**	0.41**	0.37**	0.49**	0.34**
Independent	CGS		0.41**	0.33**	0.16*	0.21**	0.32**	0.20*
	IQC			0.61**	0.24**	0.45**	0.27**	0.18*
	QA				0.34**	0.4**	0.37**	0.2*
	AE					0.10	0.41**	0.45**
	IPC						0.43**	0.08
	CPE							0.38**
	FI							

*, ** indicate significance at the 10 and 5 percent level, respectively.

Dependent Variable
AI: Auditor Independence
Independent Variables
CGS: Corporate Governance Structure
IQC: Internal Quality Control
QA: Quality Assurance
AE: Audited Entities
IPC: Independence Practice and Compliance
CPE: Continuing Professional Education
FI: Fee Information

Table 37: Pearson Correlation and Significance Levels of Subjects' Assessment of the Importance of the Proposed Safeguards

To address the multicollinearity concern, responses to the seven item questionnaire were subjected to a principal component analysis using one as prior communality estimates. The principal axis method was used to extract the components, and this was followed by a varimax (orthogonal) rotation. Only the first two components displayed eigenvalues greater than one (2.9 and 1.24), and the results of a scree test also suggested that only the first two components were retained for rotation.[47]

In interpreting the rotated factor pattern, an item was said to load on a given component if the factor loading was 0.5 or greater for that component. Using these criteria, four items were found to load on the first component, which was subsequently labeled the 'direct safeguards' component. Specifically, the items detail corporate governance, internal quality control, quality assurance and independence practice and compliance. Three items loaded on the second component, which was labeled the 'indirect safeguards' component. It includes audited entities, fee information, and continuing professional education. The resulting constructs, direct and indirect safeguards, have Cronbach's coefficient alphas of 0.72 and 0.68, respectively. Direct safeguard captures 41% of the variation and indirect safeguard captures 18%.

Table 38 shows the relevant two components as generated throughout principal component analysis.

Items	**New Components**
Corporate Governance Structure	***Direct Safeguards***
Internal Quality Control	
Quality Assurance	
Independence Practice and Compliance	
Audited Entities	***Indirect Safeguards***
Fee Information	
Continuing Professional Education	

Table 38: Items and Corresponding New Components of Subjects' Assessment of the Importance of the Proposed Safeguards

These findings indicate that two constructs are present in the transparency report. Corporate governance structure, internal quality control mechanisms, quality assurance of an outside expert and audit firm's independence and practice compliance loaded on one construct, which I refer to as the new component "direct safeguards". "Indirect safeguards" incorporate the items audited entities, fee information and continuing

47 See Appendix 10. Questionnaire items and corresponding factor loadings are presented in Appendix 11.

professional education. These two components were used to perform a regression analysis, which is presented in Equation 4.

Auditor Independence = $\beta_0 + \beta_1$ Direct Safeguards + β_2 Indirect Safeguards + u

Dependent Variable
Auditor Independence
Independent Variables
Direct Safeguards
Indirect Safeguards
β: *Beta Coefficient (Intercept or Slopes)*
u: *Error Term (captures the effects of all omitted variables)*

Equation 4: Regression Model of the Effect of Principal Components on Perceived Auditor Independence

Regression results presented in Table 39 of which the components affect the assessment of auditor independence are highly significant with F=31.85 ($p<0.0001$) and R-Square of 0.42. Coefficients data of the principal components as analyzed before, indicate the direct safeguards to affect the auditor independence assessment significantly ($t=4.72$, $p<0.0001$). Additionally, the indirect safeguards component has a major impact on how auditor independence is perceived ($t=4.00$, $p=0.0001$). As for the two constructs, both have a significant effect on the maintenance of perceived auditor independence.

	Sum of Squares	df	Mean Square	F	p
Regression	56.21	2	28.1	31.85	< 0.0001
Residual	77.64	88	0.88		
Total	133.85	90			

	Name	β	t	p value
0	Intercept	0.53	1.17	0.24
1	Direct Safeguard	0.12	4.72	< 0.0001
2	Indirect Safeguard	0.11	4	0.0001

Table 39: Regression Results and Coefficients Data of Principal Components

5. Discussion

Transparent information about an audit firm's own policies and procedures to maintain auditor independence is argued by the European Union to be an important means of aligning information asymmetry between audit firms, existing and potential clients and investors of those clients. To ensure that the report is published by all public auditing firms, the report is proposed to become law by the European Commission (2004a). The transparency report is meant to serve as a type of signaling mechanism, which might be even more effective when oversight arrangements are put in place to ensure the report's quality. This might be, whether or not the transparency report has to be reviewed.

The findings of my third experiment indicate that the assessments of experienced accounting and finance professionals of the effectiveness of such a transparency report to maintain overall auditor independence is independent of whether or not the report is mandatory or voluntary. Furthermore, oversight arrangements in form of a review were not assessed as being more effective to ensure overall auditor independence. These results put the intention of this report to be one mechanism to strengthening the principles-based European approach to some extent in question. However, the subjects of experiment three might be reason for this result, since their assessment of the effectiveness of a mandatory and reviewed transparency report to maintain auditor independence might be compromised due to moral hazard.

The discussion concerning the proposed transparency report leads to the question of whether or not the safeguards required in the report are appropriate and if there are safeguards being perceived as relatively more important than others. The information on when the last quality assurance of the audit firm took place is rated as being important for clients and investors. This finding contradicts concerns of the German Chamber of Public Accountants (2004). The value of this information is probably seen as being high since it may imply a successfully performed quality assurance. This is a signal of quality that can be used as a basis for decision making. Evidently, investors of existing clients are interested in the reliability of the audit firm that is auditing the company they have invested into or they are planning to invest into.

As expected, the most highly rated safeguard is the audit firm's independence practice, which also confirms that an internal review of independence compliance has been conducted. Related to the discussion of how audit firms can deal with independence issues, their own policies and procedures are perceived as being important to address. The fact that fee information was assessed as being relatively unimportant may be due to the fact that subjects of this research, although representing stakeholders, are accountants and auditors, who are generally well-informed about fees. Furthermore, this result might be due to a moral hazard. Subjects of the third experiment might have assessed the fee information as being relatively unimportant, because they feel themselves addressed with the requirement. Therefore, this finding might be limited to this group of stakeholders only.

The principal component analysis results indicate two constructs: labeled direct and indirect safeguards. Information about an audit firm's policies and procedures can be categorized into these different types of safeguarding mechanisms. Direct safeguards represent certain policies and procedures to be put in place, such as corporate governance mechanisms, internal quality controls, quality assurance activities and independence practice. Indirect safeguards are more likely to be information the audit firm is reporting, such as information about audited entities, fees and continuing professional education. Audit firm's can set up their own safeguards to address auditor independence issues. There are safeguards addressing the risk of impaired auditor independence more directly and there are safeguards being more descriptive and which may mitigate impaired auditor independence risk more indirectly. The findings of regression analysis with principal components indicate that both types of safeguards are assessed to be significant means to maintain auditor independence.

Chapter VIII. Conclusions and Future Research

A. Implications for European Union Regulation

This research studied the effect of regulation approach on decisions that require applying the regulation. Subjects in the first and second experiment were asked to make a decision as to whether an audit firm should perform additional non-audit services for a financial statement audit client. Subjects' decisions were compared to what was argued to be the regulations intended outcome and were interpreted as complying, as under-complying or as over-complying. Over-compliance can be inefficient, since an unintended prohibition of providing a certain service leads to unnecessary switching costs and perhaps lower quality services, because the prohibited service needs to be outsourced to a different provider. However, if a regulation is under-complied with, it does not provide an appropriate safeguard to auditor independence and therefore the risk of impaired auditor independence may be higher.

Regulation approach differs in complexity, since rules are assumed to be less complex than principles (e.g., Nelson 2003). According to task complexity theory, task performance is moderated by knowledge and task motivation (Bonner 2005). Thus, in experiment one I manipulated subjects' knowledge related to the regulation by giving either a detailed introduction into the audit firm's own policies and procedures to maintain auditor independence or not giving any information. In experiment two I studied the effect of different audit firm-client engagement characteristics as a proxy for perceived litigation risk and monetary incentives on how the regulation was applied. I also conducted a comparative analysis of the aggregated data of the first and second experiments to investigate whether education related knowledge levels (undergraduate and graduate students) affect the interpretation and application of the regulation and therefore might lead to different levels of risk of impaired auditor independence.

Furthermore I performed additional statistical regression analysis based on two post-experimental questions. Subjects were asked to assess the level of threat to auditor independence from audit, IT and tax service fees, assuming all three services are performed. The auditor independence risk assessment was regressed on these independent variables. Table 40 restates the research questions related to the first two experiments and summarizes the main findings.

	Main Research Questions	Main Findings
1	Is the approach to auditor independence regulation associated with the effectiveness of the regulation in reducing risks to auditor independence in fact?	There is a significant difference regarding subjects' decision making in whether principles- or rules-based regulation is applied only in the second experiment for the IT service ($F=7.57$, $p=0.008$). The principles-based regulation approach was under-complied. Under-compliance leads to higher risk of impaired auditor independence. There is only a weak difference regarding subjects' decision making in whether principles- or rules-based regulation is applied in the first experiment for the tax service ($F=1.65$, $p=0.2$). This weak result was also found in the second experiment for the tax service ($F=1.76$, $p=0.19$).
2	Is the effectiveness of regulation to reduce auditor independence risk dependent on the knowledge level of the person applying the regulation?	The education related knowledge level of the person applying the regulation affects subjects' decision making significantly only for the IT service ($F=5.66$, $p=0.02$), but not the knowledge manipulation. Specifically, the higher the knowledge the more likely is decision making as intended by the regulation, which leads to lower risk of impaired auditor independence. Furthermore, regulation approach and knowledge level interact significantly ($F=5.35$, $p=0.02$). Specifically, moderate knowledge leads to significantly different decision making dependent on the regulation approach ($t=3.149$, $p=0.0053$). Principles-based regulation is under-complied. Finally, rules-based regulation is applied significantly different dependent on whether low or moderate knowledge is present ($t=4.15$, $p=0.0002$). Principles are under-complied from undergraduate students.
3	Is the effectiveness of a regulation to reduce auditor independence risk dependent on the audit firm-client engagement characteristics?	Audit firm-client engagement characteristics affects subjects' decision making significantly ($F=4.77$, $p=0.03$). Furthermore there is a significant interaction between regulation approach and audit firm-client characteristics ($F=4.43$, $p=0.04$). For the low litigation risk, the IT service was not prohibited under principles-based regulation, but under rules-based regulation ($t=1.65$, $p=0.058$), which leads to higher risk of impaired auditor independence in the principles-based setting.

4	What are significant threats, represented by fees, to auditor independence in a multi service audit firm-client engagement?	The IT fees are considered a significant threat to auditor independence risk (t=2.4, p=0.02), whereas the audit and tax fees are not considered a threat (t=-0.23, p=0.81; t=0.03, p=0.97, respectively).
5	Does auditor independence regulation safeguard against significant threats?	In experiment one, both regulation approaches led to a prohibition of the IT service. At the same time, respondents considered the IT service fees to be a significant threat. Thus, both approaches to auditor independence regulation safeguard against this threat. Principles-based regulation led subjects to be unsure about the tax service. However, the tax service was not considered a significant threat by the respondents.

Table 40: Research Questions Related to Experiments 1 and 2 and Main Findings

My findings of experiment two indicate that the approach to auditor independence regulation is associated with the effectiveness of the regulation in reducing risks to auditor independence for the IT service. Overall, results show that principles-based regulation leads to subject decisions concerning non-audit services that differ more from what is intended by the regulations and thus lead to a higher risk of impaired auditor independence. Given that, in this task setting, principles are assessed as being more complex, the additional complexity evidently lowers communication accuracy and mitigates to some extent the intended safeguarding effects. In comparison, a rules-based approach leads greater consistency of subjects' decisions with what the standards intend and thus to lower independence risk.

The need for further interpretation of principles as a result of such complexity may invite unintended application of the European regulation requirements. Since all Member States must adopt the European requirements, national regulators may want to consider local refinements or clarifying improvements to avoid notable under-compliance of regulation. The European regulatory institutions should therefore consider more precise and less complex requirements to offer an adequate basis to the Member States.

Results of the first experiment show no effect of manipulated knowledge levels on decision making. However, comparative analysis shows that the effectiveness of regulation to reduce auditor independence risk is dependent on the education related knowledge levels (not manipulated, but given) of the person applying the regulation. A higher knowledge level decreases task complexity of the regulation approach. A low knowledge level evidently inhibits the application of the regulation and therefore increases the risk of impaired auditor independence.

These findings indicate that the European principles-based conceptual approach is more difficult to apply possibly due to imprecision and required additional interpretation. This result demonstrates the importance of further mechanisms, which are being proposed to support principles-based regulation. For example, the European Union should consider requiring European-wide homogeneous initial training and education for audit and assurance personnel qualification (e.g., Coenenberg, Haller and Marten 1999) and mandatory continuing professional education that addresses regulatory changes and includes interpretation guidance (European Federation of Accountants 2001).

Furthermore, the experimental results show that there is a difference in the effectiveness of a regulation to reduce auditor independence risk that is dependent on audit firm-client engagement characteristics. Engagement characteristics were manipulated by varying the level of litigation risk and monetary incentives of the audit firm. The results provide evidence on whether litigation risk or monetary incentives dominate an audit-firm's decision making.

The high litigation risk manipulation depicted a small audit firm in terms of employees, services offered and international presence, versus a large client in terms of employees, international presence, market position and management tenure. In addition, for the high monetary incentives treatment, the relative non-audit and audit fee amounts represented a greater portion of total firm revenues. This manipulation captured both a weak position for the audit firm in a potential litigation situation if the regulation was applied incorrectly, as well as an engagement where monetary incentives were strong.

In comparison, subjects in the low litigation risk and monetary incentives version were informed that the client was small and the audit firm was large. In a low litigation risk setting the audit firm's position was stronger in a potential litigation situation if the regulation was applied incorrectly. Furthermore, the fees were not as important for the audit firm. Thus monetary incentives were weaker. As for findings, the lower the audit firm's litigation risk, the more likely it is that principles-based regulation leads to under-compliance and thus to a higher risk of impaired auditor independence.

If European Union regulation is under-complied with, the risk of impaired independence increases. In such cases, a regulation intended to serve as a safeguard actually creates a threat to auditor independence, possibly due to its complexity, and creates the need for additional mechanisms.

Additional regression analysis was undertaken to investigate significant fee threats to auditor independence risk. Subjects were asked to assess the level of threat from audit, IT and tax fees to auditor independence and the level of impaired independence risk. Auditor independence risk was regressed on the three fee threats. Results of this analysis were compared to the findings of experiment one to address the question of whether the two regulations safeguard against significant fee threats.

Findings show a significant perceived fee threat to impaired auditor independence in a multi service audit firm-client engagement to be the IT fee. With respect to this finding, both regulation approaches include requirements intended to safeguard against this perceived threat, which led to a prohibition of this service in experiment one. Thus, with respect to the IT service, both regulation approaches safeguard against the significant IT fee threat.

However, the tax service fee is not perceived to be a significant threat as results of regression analysis showed, but subjects were unsure whether to prohibited this service in the European regulation setting in experiment one. The complex principles-based regulation is possibly over-complied in experiment one, which would imply that subjects perceived the tax service to be a threat. When subjects directly assessed the level of threat due to the tax fees, they did not assess the tax service to be a significant threat to independence. Thus, with respect to the tax service, the European Union regulation might safeguard against an insignificant threat. This outcome is not as dramatic as under-compliance of regulation, which leads to a higher risk of lack of auditor independence. However, over-compliance can be inefficient, since additional non-audit services need to be performed by a different provider. Thus, European Union regulators should consider identifying relevant threats carefully to ensure that significant threats are regulated by certain requirements, but should also ensure that restrictions are clear, not leading to uncertainty, where threats are not assessed as being significant.

The previous discussion showed possible deficiencies of the proposed European Union requirements, which in experiment two and in comparative analysis led to under-compliance of the regulation. Based on the audit firm's decision whether to perform additional non-audit services for a financial statement audit client stakeholders assess the level of auditor independence risk. One important source of information for outside stakeholders is the information provided by the client itself and the client's audit firm. This limited information leads to an asymmetric information structure. Thus, the information gap between auditors and other client's stakeholders may lead auditor independence in appearance to differ between stakeholders (Mock et al. 2005). As for auditors, assuming the auditor is most likely able to assess her or his level of independence in fact more precisely; this may also lead independence in appearance and fact to differ.

Greater transparency of audit firm's policies and procedures to maintain auditor independence might help to align stakeholders' perceived assessments about auditors' independence to informed auditors' independence assessments (Backhaus, Meffert, Bongartz and Eschweiler 2003). Along this line, the European Union recently proposed a transparency report (European Commission 2004a) as a means to decrease information asymmetries related to impaired independence, between auditors and other stakeholders.

The proposed transparency report is seen differently throughout the European Union. For example, the German Chamber of Public Accountants (2004) is generally supportive towards more transparency, but questions the level of detail proposed. This leads to the question whether only the disclosure of the most effective safeguards should be mandatory, whereas reporting on additional information should be voluntary. The European Federation of Accountants (2003: 17) believes that a transparency report provides a meaningful mechanism only if appropriate oversight is arranged. Therefore, appropriate oversight, such as a detailed review process might be necessary to ensure the effectiveness of the reported safeguards (Houghton and Trotman 2003).

Experiment three was designed to test the perceived effectiveness of the transparency report proposed by the European Union. Subjects of the experiment were 91 accountants, auditors and financial analysts attending a conference on current regulatory developments organized by the University of Southern California. For this experiment I am interested in the stakeholders' assessment of the effectiveness of the transparency report. Two independent variables were manipulated in a 2 x 2 between subjects design. The first variable was whether the transparency report is mandatory or voluntary and the second variable was whether the transparency report was reviewed or not. Participants were randomly assigned to each version and were asked to assess the effectiveness of a transparency report as an overall framework to improve an audit firm's independence.

This report requires audit firms to publish annually their policies and procedures as related to auditor independence. More specifically, firms are required to publish information about their corporate governance structure, the firm's internal quality controls, the performed quality assurance, the firm's independence practice and compliance, the audited entities, detailed fee information, and the firm's continuing professional education. The transparency report gives less informed stakeholders a description of the safeguards put in place to maintain auditor independence. One post experimental question addressed in experiment three asked the conference participants to indicate which of the safeguards listed in the transparency report would be more important than the others to maintain auditor independence.

In line with this discussion, Table 41 summarizes the research questions and findings obtained from the study.

	Research Questions	**Main Findings**
6	Would a mandatory rather than a voluntary transparency report better serve as an overall framework to improve an audit firm's independence?	No significant difference in subjects' assessments on whether the transparency report serves better as an overall framework to improve an audit firm's independence when the report is mandatory or voluntary (F=0.13, p=0.72).
7	Would a reviewed report better serve as an overall framework to improve an audit firm's independence?	No significant difference in subjects' assessments on whether the transparency report serves better as an overall framework to improve an audit firm's independence when it is reviewed or not reviewed (F=1.87, p=0.17).

8	Which of the proposed disclosures are viewed as being relatively more important?	Out of the seven listed safeguards the auditor's independence practice and compliance (mean= 4.84), internal quality control (mean=4.78) and quality assurance activities (mean=4.59) are assessed as being the most important (scale 0 to 6, not important to very important, respectively).
9	Which of the reported safeguards contribute significantly to the assessments of expected maintenance of auditor independence?	Quality assurance (t=2.24, p=0.02), continuing professional education, (t=2.1, p=0.04) and internal quality control significantly contribute to the maintenance of auditor independence (t=1.89, 0.06).

Table 41: Research Questions Related to Experiment 3 and Main Findings

Based on the responses of 91 stakeholders (auditors, accountants and financial analysts), findings indicate that there is no significant statistical difference in whether or not the report is mandatory or voluntary, and reviewed or not reviewed. However, these results might only be true for these generally well informed stakeholders.

Based on these findings, the European regulators might want to carefully investigate what additional mechanisms have to be set up to strengthen the European conceptual principles-based approach. Possibly the European regulator should concentrate on improving auditor independence regulation that directly serves as a safeguard to auditor independence threats instead of focusing on indirect mechanisms, such as a transparency report.

If such transparency information is required to be published, regulators should weigh carefully which of the proposed disclosures are viewed by stakeholders as being relatively more important. The study subjects (mostly experienced auditors, accountants and financial analysts) assessed important safeguards to be auditor's independence practice and compliance, internal quality control, and quality assurance activities. This ranking is based on the means of subjects' assessment of the importance of single safeguards.

Furthermore, my last research question asked, which of the reported safeguards contribute significantly to the maintenance of auditor independence, rather than only being perceived to be an important safeguard. I performed regression analysis, where subjects' assessment of the effectiveness of the transparency report to maintain auditor independence was regressed on subjects' assessment of the importance of the listed safeguards. Findings showed that the perception that quality assurance, continuing professional education and internal quality control are important is associated to a contribution to maintain auditor independence.

The comparison of these results indicates that perceived and contributing safeguards may differ. This should be considered when regulators propose requirements based only on their own assessments of what are perceived to be important safeguards. Decisions may be supported by information about theoretically sound wealth measures. However, such measures are not well defined in a world with imperfect and incomplete markets (Ballwieser 2004: 72).

To investigate principal components underlying the transparency report and to address multicolllinearity concerns, additional principal component analysis was performed for the seven safeguards. Results show two meaningful components, which imply two different safeguarding constructs underlying an audit firm's transparency report. These two components are interpreted to be direct and indirect safeguards. Direct safeguards are the corporate governance structure, internal quality control, a quality assurance and independence practice and compliance, whereas information about audited entities, fee information and continuing professional education are considered to be indirect safeguards. The assessments of the effectiveness of the transparency report to maintain auditor independence was regressed on the two components, whereas both were significant.

Audit firm's can set up their own safeguards to address auditor independence issues. There are safeguards addressing auditor independence risk more directly, such as developing and practicing a corporate governance structure, an internal quality control system, investing into quality assurance and independence practice and compliance activities (direct safeguards). Besides, other safeguards are more descriptive and mitigate auditor independence more indirectly, such as information about audited entities, fees and professional education activities (indirect safeguards). Findings of regression analysis with principal components indicate that both, direct and indirect safeguards are assessed to significant means to maintain auditor independence. Thus, audit firms should focus and regulators should rely on greater transparency about both direct and indirect safeguards.

B. Main Contributions

The aim of this research was to extend the literature by presenting experimental results regarding two competing auditor independence regulation approaches: the Sarbanes-Oxley Act and the proposal of a revised 8th Directive of the European Union. This study provides the first attempt to research auditor independence regulation approaches and to compare the results with respect to communication accuracy and safeguarding quality. The results indicate that the European Union regulation is not applied as intended under some circumstances. When there is a low risk of litigation, subjects tend to under-comply with the principles. This leads to an increased risk of auditor independence.

Another important contribution made by this thesis is the application of the task complexity model to auditor independence regulation. The findings indicate that task complexity provides a useful vehicle for understanding auditors' decision making in a way not previously considered. When regulation is based on principles, incentive-consistent interpretation of the regulation is more likely. Rules-based regulation helps to mitigates incentive-consistent interpretation. Therefore, the Sarbanes-Oxley Act tends to provide a better safeguard to auditor independence risk than the European Union regulation, possibly due to more accurate communication.

This study also contributes to prior research (e.g., Reynolds and Francis 2001, DeFond et al. 2002, Chung and Kallapur 2003) by assessing the most relevant fee threat based in the evidence collected. The performance of additional IT services is perceived to most likely impair auditor independence.

Finally, results of the transparency report in experiment three indicate no overall effect of the report being mandatory versus voluntary and reviewed versus not reviewed on perceptions of auditor independence. These results might be associated with the participating subjects in this experiment. Most likely accountants, financial analysts but particularly auditors have the information about the safeguards listed in the transparency report available. Therefore, these stakeholders might not need to be provided with a transparency report and they might not perceive a significant difference whether the report in mandatory versus voluntary and reviewed or not reviewed. Thus, these groups of stakeholders assess the transparency report's contribution to maintaining auditor independence to be essentially the same in all experimental settings.

C. Limitations and Future Research

The use of students as participants is a potential limitation for the first two experiments. Possible demand effects and low validity of responses might have caused the weak results of experiment one. Thus, I consider this experiment as being a pilot test. Furthermore, subjects of the third experiment were auditors, accountants and financial analysts, who can be characterized as being well informed stakeholder. Thus, findings of all three studies are limited to these groups of subjects and should be generalized with caution.

Since knowledge and experience have been shown in prior research to affect judgment and decision making quality, future research related to experiments one and two should be conducted with auditors to investigate to what extent the results can be generalized. In future research the comparison of current findings with findings from an experiment with auditors will be useful because auditors are more likely to have the task specific knowledge to interpret the regulations as intended.

A related issue concerns the degree to which other explanations for the interpretation of regulation not captured in this study provide a motive for compromised interpretation. For example, certain types of risk the auditor faces in a client acceptance decision where an audit engagement already exists, need to be studied. These might be risks due to the client's financial situation, familiarity concerns or audit firm capacity issues.

Furthermore, the number of characteristics of a regulation, such as task complexity, presentation format, incentives, response mode and various cognitive processes is fairly high (Bonner 2005). In this research I use the theory of task complexity to explain differences in the application of regulation. This is only one way to study regulation approaches. Other differences in the approach may be useful to study, such as the format of a regulation or the regulation's length.

Due to limitations in an experimental setting, I could only measure communication accuracy and the safeguarding effects on a small portion of the regulations (non-audit service and audit committee regulation). Future research should also consider other controversial requirements, such as the audit partner rotation or audit firm rotation (e.g., Marten 1995).

After the revised 8th Directive is adopted (which was primary expected for mid-2005), Member States have an 24 month period to implement the European Union requirements into national law. Many Member States are already taking legislative and regulatory action on the lines of the Sarbanes-Oxley Act (2002), the Commission's Recommendation (2002) and the changes proposed by the Commission (2004) and there is expected to be an increase in legislative activity after the revised 8th Directive is European law. Since the Directive serves only as a minimum set of requirements which specifies minimum standards that all Member States are obligated to follow, there is still the flexibility for each Member State to add local requirements in those areas not specifically covered by the Directive. Regarding this, there are two major research opportunities.

First, it is important to study if the minimum requirements within the 8th Directive already encompass enough safeguards to ensure auditor independence. This would mean that Member States should not add any local requirements but should keep uniform requirements Europe-wide, so that European welfare and the economy will benefit from harmonized regulations. Second, since Member States already differ significantly in local requirements, it will be important to investigate what the differences are within the national requirements, and which added requirements are more beneficial in terms of auditor independence.

Finally, I am interested in the effects of greater transparency on capital markets and the conceptual approach based on principles. Therefore, a replication of the third experiment with other stakeholders such as shareholders or financial analysts would allow a more sophisticated analysis and comparison of a broader set of perceptions of transparency effects. Furthermore, with other participating stakeholder I could most likely control for potential moral hazard effects.

List of Appendices

Appendices

Appendix 1: A Model for Assessing the Risk of Impaired Auditor Independence

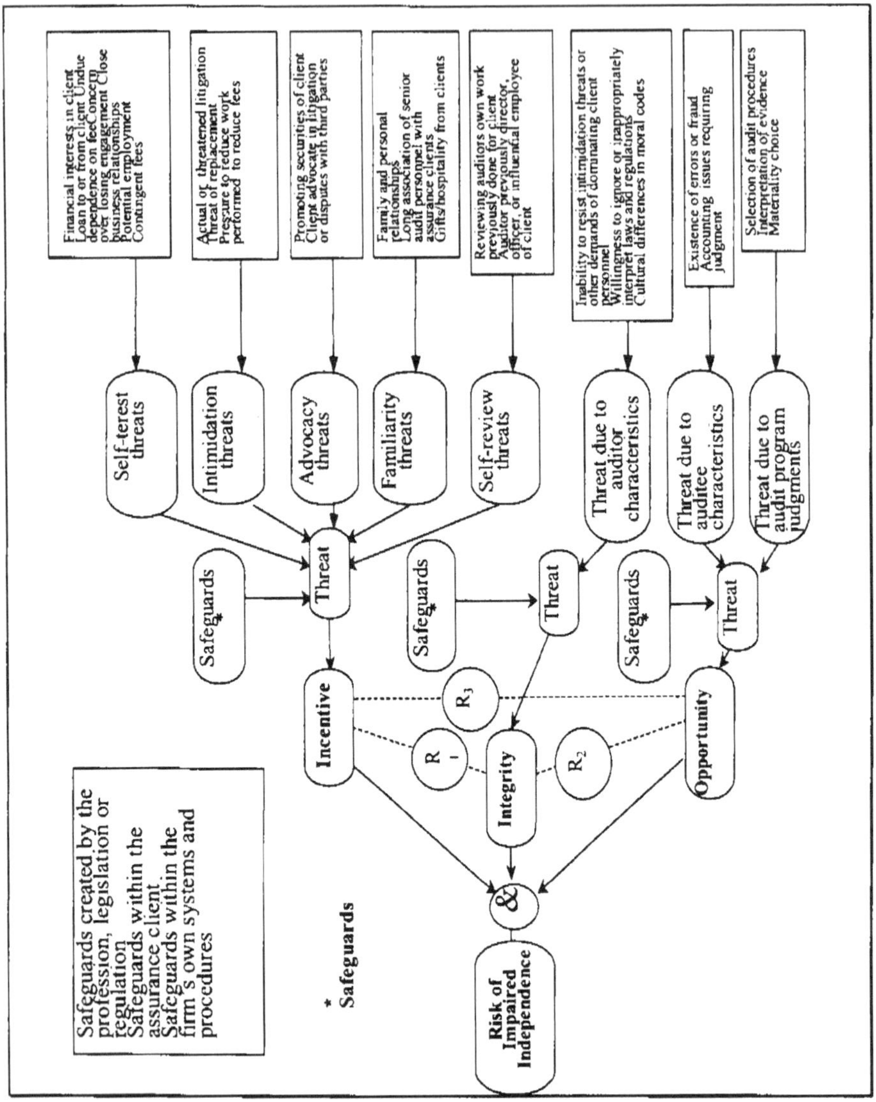

Appendix 2: Definitions of Relevant Terms

Terms	Definitions
Auditor Independence	
in Appearance	The avoidance of significant facts and circumstances that would cause a rational and informed third party to reasonably conclude that a firm's, or a member of the assurance team's, integrity, objectivity or professional skepticism had been compromised.
in Fact (Mind)	A state of mind that is unaffected by influences which compromise professional judgment and that allows an individual to act with integrity and to exercise objectivity and professional skepticism.
Auditor Independence Risk	Independence risk is the risk that threats to auditor independence, to the extent that they are not mitigated by safeguards, compromise or can reasonably be expected to compromise, an auditor's ability to make unbiased audit decisions.
Threat	Independence is potentially affected by self-interest, self-review, advocacy, familiarity (trust) and intimidation threats:
Self-interest Threats	Occur when the audit firm or a member of the audit team could benefit from a financial interest in, or other self-interest conflicts with, an audit client.
Self-review Threats	Occur when the audit firm, or an individual audit team member, is put in a position of reviewing subject matter for which the firm or individual were previously responsible, and which is significant in the context of the audit engagement.
Advocacy Threats	Occur when the audit firm, or a member of the audit team, promotes, or may be perceived to promote, an audit client's

	position or opinion to the point where objectivity may be compromised.
Familiarity (Trust) Threats	Occur when, by virtue of a close relationship with an audit client, its directors, officers or employees, an audit firm or a member of the audit team becomes too sympathetic to the client's interest.
Intimidation Threats	Occur when a member of the audit team may be deterred from acting objectively and exercising professional skepticism by threats, actual or perceived, from the directors, officers or employees of an audit client.
Safeguards	The three categories of safeguards are (1) safeguards created by the profession, legislation or regulation, (2) safeguards within the assurance client, and (3) safeguards within the audit firm's own system and procedures.
Independence	Freedom from those pressures and other factors that compromise, or can reasonably be expected to compromise, an auditor's ability to make unbiased audit decisions.

Appendix 3: Antecedents and Consequences of Independence Risk

Necessary Environmental Conditions	**What incentives create independence risk?** Direct incentives: Direct investments Contingent fees; Potential employment; Financial dependence Indirect Incentives: Interpersonal relationships; Auditing work of self or firm **What judgment-based decisions allow independence risk to affect audit quality?** Pressure on difficult accounting issues ← Pressure on materiality judgments → Pressure on audit scope and conduct
	↓
Mitigating Factors	**What factors may mitigate independence-related environmental conditions?** Corporate Governance Mechanisms: Boards of directors; Audit committees Regulatory Oversight: Standard setting; Enforcement Auditing Firm Policies: Concurring partner reviews; Peer reviews; Within-firm consultations; Auditor competence programs; Compensation plans Auditing Firm Culture and Individual Auditor Characteristics: Auditing firm emphasis on its public duty; Auditors' ethical and moral characteristics
	↓
Stakeholder Analysis	**How are stakeholders affected if mitigating factors fail?** Auditees; Shareholders and creditors; Individual auditors; Auditing profession; Regulators
	↓
Suggested Actions	**What actions should be taken by the auditing profession, auditing firms and regulators?**

Appendix 4: Archival, Interview and Survey Research on Auditor Independence

Author(s) (Year)	Method	Subjects	Dependent Variable	Results
Abbott et al. (2000)	Archival	78 firms subject to Securities and Exchange Commission Accounting and Auditing Enforcement Releases and 78 non-sanctioned firms	Fraudulent or aggressive financial statement actions	Firms with audit committees which meet minimum thresholds of both activity and independence are less likely to be sanctioned by the Securities and Exchange Commission
Ashbaugh et al. (2003)	Archival	4,959 firms from registrants' 2000 proxy statements	Auditor fees	No evidence supporting that auditors violate their independence as a result of clients purchasing relatively more non-audit services was conducted
Chung & Kallapur (2003)	Archival	Sample of 1,871 clients of Big 5 audit firms where companies revealed fees between Feb. 5 and June 30, 2001	Ratio of client fees and of non-audit fees divided by the audit firm's United States revenues or a surrogate for the audit-practice-office revenues	No evidence that auditor independence might be compromised of the extent of client opportunities and incentives to manage their earnings favorable; also no association between the fee level and client characteristics such as small-to-medium sized high-growth firms, especially firms having initial public offerings and are in specific industries are found
DeFond et al. (2002)	Archival	944 distressed firms that include audit firm disclosures for 2000, including 86 firms receiving first-time going concern audit reports	Auditor's propensity to issue going concern audit opinions	No evidence that non-audit service fees impair auditor independence

Frankel et al. (2002)	Archival	3,074 proxy statements filed with Securities and Exchange Commission between Feb. 5, 2001 to June 15, 2001	Audit fees and non-audit fees	Non-audit fees affect small earnings surprises and the magnitude of discretionary accruals positively; the opposite is shown for audit fees, as well as between non-audit fees and share values on the date the fees were disclosed
Geiger & Raghunandan (2002)	Archival	Sample entering bankruptcy during 1996 to 1998	Audit reporting failure	Indication that audit reporting failure are happen in the earlier years of the auditor-client relationship than when the auditors had served these clients for longer tenures
Jeter & Shaw (1995)	Archival	Audit report information from Compustat from 1980 to 1987; second sample just of New York and American Stock Exchange clients	Information dissemination, client-auditor alignment, and auditor independence	Auditors in the market allowing solicitation are more likely than those in the market banning solicitation to issue a nonstandard report
Kinney et al. (2004)	Archival	432 registrants announcing restatements and 512 without restatements from 1995 to 2000	Non-audit fees	No consistent evidence of positive association between audit firm fees for either financial information system design and implementation of internal audit services and restatements
Maher et al. (1992)	Archival	Fee data from 1977 to 1981	Audit fees	Decrease in real audit fees between these years: supporting claims of increasing fee competition in the market for independent audit services
Myers et al. (2003)	Archival	All Compustat firm years from 1988 to 2000	Earnings quality	Longer auditor tenure results in auditor placing greater constrains on extreme management decisions in the reporting of financial performance

Reynolds et al. (2004)	Archival	4,148 United States companies filing proxy statements with fee disclosures from Feb. 5, 2001 to May 25, 2001	Relative level of non-audit service fees	No evidence that the relative level of non-audit service fess impairs an auditor's objectivity by factoring the characteristics, like small-to-medium sized high-growth firms, especially firms having initial public offerings and in the e-commerce, biomedical, telecommunication, and pharmaceutical industries
Reynolds & Francis (2001)	Archival	Accruals of 6,747 United States companies having Big Five auditor for fiscal year 1996 as reported in *Compact Disclosure* dated October 1997	Reporting behavior of auditors	No evidence that economic dependence causes Big Five auditors to report more favorably for larger clients in their offices; larger clients also pose greater litigation risk; auditors report more conservatively for larger clients (reputation protection)
Scheiner & Kiger (1982)	Archival	Selected from *Who audits America* 500 Big Eight and 100 non Big Eight clients from 1978 to 1979	Percentage of the costs of non-audit services to audit fees	Non-audit services consist of traditional accounting services like tax services: the authors concluded that the prohibition of non-audit services would not appear to have a substantial impact on firms
Wood (1996)	Archival	Data from several data sources from 1985 to 1987	Auditing practices	Cultural and environmental factors most associated with the audit characteristics are literacy, per capita gross national product, and legal system origins; cross-cultural and environmental factors are most associated with the audit characteristics of experience requirements, examination requirements, codified ethical standards, and restrictions on auditor investments and provision of other services to clients; furthermore there is evidence, that when a country moves to a common law system auditor independence issues become more important; the same is true as population becomes literate and affluent

Beattie et al. (2004)	Interview	Audit partners and finance directors of a varied group of six major UK listed companies who had recently experienced audit interactions involving 22 significant accounting issues	Six different auditor types (seller types)	Conforming audit reports most difficult to achieve were the board's culture was less conservative, the issue was a sensitive one within the company, or the firm was disorganized; ownership and corporate culture have a major impact on attitudes to corporate governance and financial reporting
Arnold et al. (1999)	Survey	198 auditors from 16 European offices of four out of the Big Six firms	Auditor's decisions	Auditor's decisions were most influenced by stockholders' reliance on the thoroughness of the audit and the fear of loosing the client; fear of loosing the client decreased with increased country's individualism resulting in a greater likelihood of doing more work
Bartlett (1993)	Survey	300 commercial lending officers of banks and 300 Certified Public Accountants in California	Four types of consulting activities to investigate perceived independence	Most independence is assumed when only audit work is performed with no other information about the engagement given; in each of the four cases involving addition management advisory services bankers perceived significant reductions in auditor independence compared to Certified Public Accountants
Gibbins et al. (2001)	Survey	93 Audit Partners from Six International Firms	Accounting negotiation	Negotiated issues frequently arose because of unclear or non-existent generally accepted accounting principles; furthermore accounting negotiation is context dependent, which includes external conditions and constrains such as generally accepted accounting principles, generally accepted auditing standards, statutory power, accountabilities, and deadlines besides other factors

Hussey & Lan (2001)	Survey	776 named Finance Directors	Relevance of separate auditor regulation	Finance Directors concerned with the value and benefits of the audit generally and the impact on their own company support a separate regulation from the accounting profession; however, there is no relationship between regulation of external auditors and Finance Directors' own assessment of the nature of their relationship with their external auditors
Imhoff (1978)	Survey	19 offices of Big Eight Certified Public Accountants firms	Perceived auditor independence	Decrease of perceived auditor independence as time elapsed between the audit engagement and the employment
Iyer & Raghunandan (2002)	Survey	757 executives and managers of Big five firms	Ability to resolve Disagreements	Majority of the subjects believe that disagreements can be resolved more difficult if their former Certified Public Accountants firm serves as an auditor of their current employer
Shafer et al. (1999)	Survey	1,650 AICPA members who specialize in auditing	Auditors' perceptions of the effectiveness of formal sanctions as incentives for maintaining auditor independence	Litigation risk and peer-review risk were perceived as significant deterrents to aggressive reporting decisions, but the risk of disciplinary actions by professional organizations was not

Appendix 5: Experimental Research on Auditor Independence

Author(s) (Year)	Subjects	Dependent Variable	Results
Gramling (1999)	188 audit managers of one Big Five audit firm	Planned audit procedures	No evidence that auditor's initial evaluations of the quality of the internal audit department was influenced
Hackenbrack & Nelson (1996)	90 auditor of one audit firm	Reporting decision and judgment	Reporting decisions are made in favor with incentives and application of vague language in financial accounting standards consistent with selected reporting position
Haynes et al. (1998)	96 Certified Public Accountants (43 from non-national accounting firms and 53 from national accounting firms)	Client's preferred accounting treatment	Audit experience affect the tendency to support clients' treatment positively
Kadous et al. (2003)	227 auditors in the United States	Acceptance of client preferred accounting method	Auditors identify client preferred accounting method as the best method when they are committed to their own directional goals; if commitment of directional goals is likely by supporting client preferred accounting method, quality assessment is biased in favor to this
Kaplan & Whitecotton (2001)	73 audit senior of a large international accounting firm	Auditors reporting intentions	Auditors reporting intentions are stronger when personal costs of reporting are perceived to be lower or personal responsibilities for reporting is perceived to be higher
Knapp (1985)	43 senior commercial loan officers from the 150 largest commercial banks in Oklahoma	Audit firms' perceived ability to withstand pressure	Greater subjectivity in technical standards decreases audit firms' ability to withstand client pressure; pressure increases with financial health of the client

Koh & Mahatheva n (1993)	392 middle-level audit managers	Managers' perceptions of auditor independence	The shorter the time lapse between audit engagement and employment with the client, the more independence is questioned; auditor independence is questioned to a greater extent when the former auditor accepts a position as a preparer after issuing a clean audit opinion as opposed to a qualified opinion
Lowe et al. (1999)	1,000 loan officers randomly selected from a commercially prepared list; 117 usable	Financial statements users' perceptions of auditor independence and financial statement reliability	Evidence that auditor performance of management functions has a significantly negative impact on users' perceptions of auditor independence and financial statement reliability, which results in lowest percentage of loan approvals; however, when staff performing the outsourced internal audit and performing the financial statement audit is separated, perception were positive affected as well as loan approvals.
McKinley et al. (1985)	261 Bank loan officers	Loan decision, reliability of financial statements, audit firm independence	No evidence was found for management advisory service provisions affecting bank officer's loan decisions, their perceptions of financial statement reliability and their perceptions of independence
Salterio & Koonce (1997)	25 managers and 98 partners of Canadian Big Six audit firm	Auditors response to precedents	Auditors rely to a greater extent on precedents that are similar to the problem situation; available precedents are used to judge the appropriate accounting; when clients position was known and precedents were mixed, auditors tend to follow clients position

Shockley (1981)	67 Bank loan officers, 64 financial analysts and 146 Certified Public Accountants	Perception of former Big Eight audit partners, partner from local and regional Certified Public Accountants firms, commercial loan officers and financial analysts	Audit firms which provide management advisory services to audit clients are more likely to loose independence than those which do not, rotation after five or less years does not decrease the risk of impaired independence
Swanger & Chewning (2001)	250 analysts	Evaluation of auditor independence	Financial analysts' perceptions of auditor independence are negatively affected when the same audit firm performs the internal and external audits, but only if there is no separation of the two audit staffs
Teoh & Lim (1996)	100 accountants from public accounting firms and 100 from industry	Perceptions on auditor independence	Audit committees are perceived to be an important mean to enhance auditor independence, non-audit services should be disclosed separately, concerns about large audit fees and non-audit fees from a single client, rotation is perceived to be important
Trompeter (1994)	51 audit partner	Audit partner judgment	Auditors respond to client preferences when generally accepted accounting principles are ambiguous

Appendix 6: Research Instrument Experiment 1

The Assessment of Auditor Independence Risk

Dear Participant:

Thank you for participating in this study. The purpose of the study is to assess your perceptions about the risk that auditor independence may be impaired given some specific information about a particular auditor [R&P Audit and Assurance Services] and a particular client [Kelly & Co.].

You will be provided with a four page description consisting of background information on auditor independence followed by a case study. The case study does not reflect the circumstances of an actual audit firm or client. However, every effort has been made to make the case study as realistic as possible. After reading the background information and the case study, you will be asked to answer the following question on the basis of the case description: *What is your assessment of the risk that R&P's independence may be impaired, when auditing Kelly & Co's financial statement?*

In addition, several other questions ask you to rate certain factors associated with the case study. We are interested in your personal responses to the questions that are asked. Note that there are no correct or incorrect answers. The project will take around 30 minutes to complete. **The questions relate to the information presented in the following paragraphs. You may look back at any of this information as you answer the questions. However, once you have answered a particular question and have gone on to a following question, please don't change your response.**

You can be assured that your identity will remain anonymous. Individual responses will not be known to anyone other than the members of the research team. Only the aggregate results of all participants in the study will be reported.

Thank you once again for participating in this study.

BACKGROUND INFORMATION ON AUDITOR INDEPENDENCE

Recent worldwide financial scandals have emphasized that the financial statement audit is an important element in ensuring the credibility and reliability of companies' financial statements. However, significant economic damage to the capital markets and the economy has resulted from alleged impaired auditor independence. Auditor independence is impaired when audit decisions or judgements are biased in favor of the client. Independence is considered the profession's main means of demonstrating to the public and regulators that auditors and audit firms are performing their task at a level that meets established ethical principles, particularly those of integrity and objectivity.

An example of the importance of auditor independence is demonstrated by the bankruptcy of the energy giant Enron Corporation and the demise of its auditor – Arthur Andersen, LLP. As the Enron case shows, a lack of auditor independence can lead to catastrophic consequences for investors, audit firms and financial markets. The effects on audit firms of problems related to independence have not been limited to Arthur Andersen. In January 2002 another Big Four firm, KPMG, was censured because it purported to serve as an independent auditing firm for an audit client at the same time that it had made substantial financial investments in that client. Regulators found that KPMG violated the auditor independence rules by engaging in such conduct. In another case, in a ruling by an administrative-law judge, Ernst & Young was called "reckless," "highly unreasonable" and "negligent" because it formed a business venture with one of its audit clients, PeopleSoft. Ernst & Young was PeopleSoft's independent auditor and business partner from 1994 through 1999. Its audit fees during this period were $1.7 million, and revenue from its PeopleSoft partnership was $425 million. The Securities and Exchange Commission is investigating PricewaterhouseCoopers for a possible violation of auditor independence rules. In a press release announcing its quarterly results, the Royal Bank of Canada said it has received a subpoena from the U.S. securities regulator regarding PwC, which resigned as one of the bank's auditors in September 2004.

Recent changes regarding auditor independence

Policy-makers work continuously to identify and evaluate critical threats to impaired independence and to develop appropriate independence safeguards. One recent major change within the regulation of auditor independence relates to auditor regulation. The requirement can be summarized as follows:

Rules	Principles
Requirements Concerning the Regulation of Non-audit Services A public accounting firm (and any associated person of that firm) can not perform for a financial statement audit client, contemporaneously with the audit, any of the following non-audit services: 1. bookkeeping or other services related to the accounting records or financial statements of the audit client; 2. financial information systems design and implementation; 3. appraisal or valuation services, fairness opinions, or contribution-in-kind reports; 4. actuarial services; 5. internal audit outsourcing services; 6. management functions or human resources; 7. broker or dealer, investment adviser, or investment banking services; or 8. legal services and expert services unrelated to the audit. However, the public accounting firm may engage in any non-audit service, including a tax service that is not described above for an audit client, if the activity is approved in advance by the audit committee of the client.	**Requirements Concerning the Regulation of Non-audit Services** When carrying out a financial statement audit, both the auditor and the audit firm must remain independent from the client and not be in any way involved in management decisions of the client. The auditor and audit firm can not carry out a financial statement audit if there is any financial, business, employment or other relationship, including the provision of additional services, with the client that might compromise the auditor's or audit firm's independence.

In addition to the requirements of regulators, both the accounting profession and some auditing firms have created their own safeguards. For example, the AICPA requires background checks prior to issuance of the CPA certificate, such as an investigation for any possible criminal history on all applicants. Also, as part of ongoing improvement processes, audit firms may implement policies and procedures with respect to certain key aspects of its audit practice. Examples include policies and procedures with respect to conflict resolution, and the firm's own rules concerning rotation of audit staff.

CASE STUDY INFORMATION

Roberts & Partner (R&P) is a large, American registered independent public accounting firm. The firm was founded in 1963 and is headquartered in New York. Including its affiliations in Europe and Asia, R&P employs over 6,000 people. The firm is primarily involved in financial statement audit services applying US-GAAP. In addition, as a result of its expansion into Europe and Asia, the firm specializes in financial statement audit services applying international accounting standards. Furthermore, R&P also offers non-audit services in order to maintain its competitiveness in the audit market.

As part of an ongoing quality control and improvement process, R&P is proactive in keeping up with the ever-changing professional and regulative requirements. These activities include training of audit partners to satisfy additional education requirements, and developing its own audit practice improvement system. To help insure that R&P meets the profession's independence guidelines, last year R&P developed its own independence compliance system (RPICS®).

Knowledge
(Additional Information Provided)

<u>RPICS® is an online system that assists the firm in identifying and resolving potential independence issues affecting the firm. For example, the system features an investment tracking system that enables each auditor to search a database to determine if any of their investments are with current clients and thus are restricted according to SEC rules. The independence compliance system also notifies professionals when a previously unrestricted investment becomes restricted as a result of a company becoming a new audit client. In addition, R&P has a positive assurance conflict-checking database in place that provides data on all audit and non-audit services being provided to each current client. The system provides a warning message for any engagements that may violate current legal or professional requirements regarding the provision of non-audit services to audit clients. Finally RPICS® monitors each auditor's compliance with R&P risk management policies and procedures, and current</u>

legal and professional audit requirements relating to auditor independence. RPICS® also provides a monthly report of audits that require lead partner auditor rotation within the next 12 months. This enables R&P to plan for auditor rotations by assigning another partner to the audit engagement so the auditor can become familiar with the client before the actual lead partner rotation occurs. Tests of RPICS® have shown it to work properly for all the partners and managers tested.

Client Information

R&P's Boston office has performed the financial statement audit for Kelly & Co for the last seven years. After the first three years there was a change of the key audit partner (partner in charge of the audit engagement), because the former audit partner retired. Currently, the key audit partner is John Miller, who has led the audit for the last four years. The annual audit fee is currently around $3,000,000. This fee represents 6% of the average annual revenue of the Boston office of R&P and 30 % of John Miller's annual billings.

In addition, to performing the annual financial statement audit, R&P's Information Technology Department is developing new software for Kelly & Co's management information system. The new software is designed to improve strategic flexibility, to facilitate short run decision making, and to support internal operations. Senior management believes that significant efficiencies can be achieved through savings in product costs through automation, reduced data processing, more effective management of inventory and reduced raw materials waste. The new system is designed to provide more timely, relevant, and concise information to the decision making process, and improved system integration of accounting and financial reporting. Although R&P's Information Technology Department is responsible for the development and implementation of the system, Kelly & Co's management is responsible for establishing, maintaining, operating and evaluating the information system. Kelly & Co's information technology manager Clara Becker manages the development and implementation process. An R&P employee, Arthur Kellerman an IT specialist, oversees the project and its staff. Reporting lines for audits and IT projects within R&P are completely separated. It is expected that the fee for providing the system design and implementation service will be around $700,000. R&P also provides tax consultancy to Kelly & Co regarding planning and ensuring regulatory compliance. Kelly & Co's audit committee approved the tax service. The annual fee for this service is $700,000.

QUESTIONS

Based on the background information on auditor independence and the case study information, please answer the following questions by circling the appropriate number.

1. What is your assessment of the risk that R&P's independence may be impaired, when auditing Kelly & Co's financial statement?

	No Risk			Moderate Risk			High Risk
Assessment of risk of impaired independence:	0	1	2	3	4	5	6

2. Another issue of concern to the accounting and auditing profession is how the nature of regulations affects the audit. For example, some regulations are rules that are quite straightforward, some are very complex rules and some are general principles. Thinking back to the background information on auditor independence as to the stated description of the regulation non-audit services (page three), please complete the following sentence by circling the appropriate number:

	Low			Moderate			High
The complexity of the regulation regarding the performance of additional non-audit services is ...	1	2	3	4	5	6	7

3. Given the preceding regulation requirements, do you believe that
   c. R&P should be prohibited from providing the IT service to Kelly & Co?

      YES NO NOT SURE

   d. R&P should be prohibited from providing the Tax service to Kelly & Co?

      YES NO NOT SURE

4. There are a number of factors, often called threats that may increase the risk of impaired auditor independence. Please rate your perception of the significance of the listed threats on the scale below:

	Insignificant			Moderately significant			Strongly significant
The threat to audit independence from the fees for the financial statement audit service ($3,000,000).	0	1	2	3	4	5	6
The threat to audit independence from the fees for the Tax service ($700,000).	0	1	2	3	4	5	6
The threat to audit independence from the fees for the IT service ($700,000).	0	1	2	3	4	5	6

Knowledge about Auditor Independence Regulation:

( ) No prior knowledge

( ) Prior knowledge: Level of knowledge:

Some Knowledge			Medium Knowledge			Highly Knowledgeable
1	2	3	4	5	6	7

Appendix 7: Research Instrument Experiment 2

Performance of Additional Non-audit Services

Dear Participant:

Thank you for participating in this study. The purpose of the study is to obtain your recommendations regarding different services that Streich & Holz, LLP (S&H) are considering performing for their client Kelly & Co.

You will be provided with a 3 page description about an audit setting. After reading the study setting, you will be asked to answer the following question:

Do you think that S&H should perform or not perform the Information Technology and/or Tax advisory services, while the firm is auditing Kelly & Co's financial statements?

In addition, several other questions ask you to rate factors associated with the case study. We are interested in your personal responses to the questions. The project will take around 20 minutes to complete.

The questions relate to the information presented in the following paragraphs. You may look back at any of this information as you answer the questions. However, once you have answered a particular question and have gone on to a following question, please don't change your response. You can be assured that your identity will remain anonymous.

Thank you once again for participating in this study.

AUDITOR-CLIENT SETTING

Recent worldwide financial scandals have reinforced the argument that the financial statement audit is an important element in ensuring the credibility and reliability of financial statements. However, significant economic damage to the capital markets and the economy has resulted from alleged impaired auditor independence. Auditor independence is impaired when audit decisions or judgments are biased in favor of the client. Independence is considered the profession's main means of demonstrating to the public and regulators that auditors and audit firms are performing their task at a level that meets established ethical principles, particularly those of integrity and objectivity.

Audit Client

High Dependency	Low Dependency
Kelly & Co is a medium-sized corporation headquartered in Boston and listed on the New York Stock Exchange. The company was founded in 1980 and employs approximately 1,200 people in 9 offices in the United States. The Company is one of many suppliers of luxury bath equipment, such as shower heads, faucets and lamps. Customers in North America include retailers as well as direct customers.	Kelly & Co is a large corporation headquartered in Boston and listed on the New York Stock Exchange. The company was founded in 1980 and employs approximately 5,600 people in 23 offices in the United States. The Company is the leading supplier of luxury bath equipment, such as shower heads, faucets and lamps. Customers in both Europe and North America include retailers as well as direct customers. Kelly & Co has recently expanded into five additional European countries.

Management and Board of Directors

Günther Blauch has been the CEO of Kelly & Co for ten years.	Günther Blauch was recently hired as Kelly & Co's CEO.

Blauch, a CPA, earned a master's degree in accounting and has 20 years of professional experience. The Board of Directors of Kelly & Co is comprised of Blauch and two other executive members and seven non-executive members. The Audit Committee is comprised of three non-executive directors, where one Committee member holds substantial accounting and auditing qualifications. The Audit Committee is regulated by a formal written charter, which conforms to all regulation requirements and is approved by the Board of Directors. The Audit Committee reports to the Board of Directors after each meeting. The external and internal auditors have direct access to the Audit Committee.

External Auditor

The external audit firm of the parent company, Kelly & Co, is Streich & Holz (S&H). S&H is a small, American accounting and assurance services firm. The firm was founded in 1923 and is headquartered in New York. S&H employs around 1,100 people. The firm is primarily involved in financial statement audit services applying US-GAAP. Furthermore, S&H is considering performing non-audit services in order to compete in the audit market.

S&H's Boston office is performing the financial statement audit for Kelly & Co the first time. The managing partner of this audit is Wilhelm Schulz. The annual audit fee is currently $3,000,000. This fee represents 12% of the average annual revenue of the Boston office of S&H and 65 % of Wilhelm Schulz's annual billings.

The external audit firm of the parent company, Kelly & Co, is Streich & Holz (S&H). S&H is a large, American accounting and assurance services firm. The firm was founded in 1923 and is headquartered in New York. Including its affiliates in Europe and Asia, S&H employs over 6,000 people. The firm is primarily involved in financial statement audit services applying US-GAAP. In addition, as a result of its expansion into Europe and Asia, the firm conducts financial statement audits applying international accounting standards. Furthermore, S&H also performs non-audit services in order to maintain its competitiveness in the audit market.

S&H's Boston office has performed the financial statement audit for Kelly & Co since the company's inception. The managing partner of this audit is Wilhelm Schulz. The annual audit fee is currently $3,000,000. This fee represents 0.5% of the average annual revenue of the Boston office of S&H and 10% of Wilhelm Schulz's annual billings.

Additional services opportunities

In addition to performing the annual financial statement audit, S&H has the opportunity of performing two additional services for Kelly & Co. First, S&H's Information Technology Department has the opportunity of developing new software for Kelly & Co's management information system. The new system would be designed to provide more timely, relevant, and concise information to the decision making process, and to improve system integration of accounting and financial reporting. Although S&H's Information Technology Department would be responsible for the development and implementation of the system, Kelly & Co's management would be responsible for establishing, maintaining, operating and evaluating the information system. One of S&H's information technology partners, Armin Kellerman, would manage the development and implementation process. Anneliese Becker, a Kelly & Co employee and IT specialist, would oversee the project and its staff. Reporting lines for audits and IT projects within S&H are completely separated. It is expected that the fee for providing the system design and implementation service would be around $300,000.

This fee would represent 30% of Armin Kellerman's annual billings.	This fee would represent 5% of Armin Kellerman's annual billings.

The second opportunity is for Nikolaus Knubel, a tax partner, to provide tax advisory services for Kelly & Co regarding tax planning and regulatory compliance. Kelly & Co considers this service to be part of the audit, so they see no need for pre-approval by their Audit Committee. However, it is expected that Kelly & Co's audit committee would approve this service.

The expected annual fee for this service would be $150,000, which would represent 20% of Nikolaus Knubel's annual billings.	The expected annual fee for this service would be $150,000, which would represent 3% of Nikolaus Knubel's annual billings.

Regulations

S&H is aware of recently issued regulations concerning auditor independence. Therefore, an assistant was asked to find any regulations concerning the provision of IT and Tax advisory services. The assistant's findings are summarized below.

Summary of requirements prepared by the assistant:

Rules	Principles
Part A: Regulation of Non-audit Services A public accounting firm (and any associated person of that firm) can not perform for a financial statement audit client, contemporaneously with the audit, any of the following non-audit services: 1. bookkeeping or other services related to the accounting records or financial statements of the audit client; 2. financial information systems design and implementation; 3. appraisal or valuation services, fairness opinions, or contribution-in-kind reports; 4. actuarial services; 5. internal audit outsourcing services; 6. management functions or human resources; 7. broker or dealer, investment adviser, or investment banking services; or 8. legal services and expert services unrelated to the audit. However, the public accounting firm may engage in any non-audit service, including a tax service that is not described above for an audit client, if the activity is approved in advance by the audit committee of the client.	**Part A: Regulation of Non-audit Services** When carrying out a financial statement audit, both the auditor and the audit firm must remain independent from the client and not be in any way involved in management decisions of the client. The auditor and audit firm can not carry out a financial statement audit if there is any financial, business, employment or other relationship, including the provision of additional services, with the client that might compromise the auditor's or audit firm's independence. Furthermore, the auditor or audit firm shall annually disclose to and discuss with the audit committee of the audited entity threats to their independence and the safeguards applied to mitigate those threats, as well as the additional services provided. The auditor or the audit firm shall also annually confirm in writing their independence to the audit committee of the audited entity.

Part B: Audit Committee Regulation The audit committee of an issuer may delegate to 1 or more designated members of the audit committee who are independent directors of the board of directors, the authority to grant preapprovals. Furthermore, all auditing services and non-audit services provided to an issuer by the auditor of the issuer shall be preapproved by the audit committee of the issuer. This pre-approval requirement is waived with respect to the provision of non-audit services for an issuer, if 1. such services were not recognized by the issuer at the time of the engagement to be non-audit services; and 2. such services are promptly brought to the attention of the audit committee of the issuer and approved prior to the completion of the audit by the audit committee of by 1 or more of the audit committee who are members of the board of directors to whom authority to grant such approvals has been delegated by the audit committee and 3. the aggregate amount of all such non-audit services provided to the issuer constitutes not more than 5 percent of the total amount of revenues paid by the issuer to its auditor during the fiscal year in which the non-audit services were provided.	**Part B: Audit Committee Regulation** Public interest entities shall have an audit committee, composed of non-executive members of the administrative body or members of the supervisory body of the audited entity with at least one independent member with competence in accounting and/or auditing. 1. The audit committee shall among other things: a. Monitor the financial reporting process; b. Monitor the effectiveness of the company's internal control, internal audit where applicable, and risk management system; c. Oversee the financial statement audit of the annual and consolidated accounts; d. Review and monitor the independence of the auditor or audit firm and in particular the provision of additional services to the audited entity. 2. The auditor or audit firm must report to the audit committee key matters arising from the financial statement audit, in particular on material weakness in internal control in relation to the financial reporting process, and shall assist the audit committee in fulfilling its tasks.

QUESTIONS

Based on the described audit-client setting and the assistant's findings concerning applicable regulations, please answer the following questions. (Please check or circle)

1. What would you recommend that S&H performs
   (1) both the IT and TAX services, ( )
   (2) only the IT service, ( )
   (3) only the Tax service or ( )
   (4) neither of these services? ( )

2. You may be aware that regulators develop requirements, which are often called safeguards, to help maintain auditor independence. In the following set of questions, I want you to assess how effective you believe the listed safeguards are in maintaining auditor independence:

	Ineffective			Moderately effective			Very effective
Regulations concerning non-audit services as described in Part A:	1	2	3	4	5	6	7
Regulations concerning Audit Committees as described in Part B:	1	2	3	4	5	6	7

3. Please indicate the degree to which you believe the following factors influenced your recommendation as to whether S&H should perform or should not perform the additional non-audit services:

	Low influence			Moderate influence			High Influence
The likelihood that S&H's independence could be impaired assuming S&H performs the IT service:	1	2	3	4	5	6	7
The likelihood that S&H's independence could be impaired assuming S&H performs the Tax service:	1	2	3	4	5	6	7

4. Please assess the significance of the following threats to audit independence assuming S&H perform all three services:

	Low Significance			Moderate significance			High significance
The threat to audit independence from the financial statement audit fees ($3,000,000).	1	2	3	4	5	6	7
The threat to audit independence from the IT service fees ($300,000).	1	2	3	4	5	6	7
The threat to audit independence from the tax advisory service fees ($150,000).	1	2	3	4	5	6	7

5. Please indicate the level of dependency that S&H has on Kelly & Co assuming S&H perform all three services:

Low			Moderate			High
1	2	3	4	5	6	7

6. Some regulations suggest requiring pre-approval of non-audit services by the Audit Committee. At the same time, regulators have discussed the possibility of waiving the pre-approval requirement under certain circumstances. Please indicate the maximum percentage that non-audit fees could be of total fees from the client such that no pre-approval would be required.

0 5 10 15 20 25 30 35 40 45 50 55 60 65 70 75 80 85 90 95 100%

↑ 0% means you would never waive the pre-approval requirement.

↑ Total amount of fees from audit and non-audit services performed. (= 100%)

Knowledge about Auditor Independence Regulation:

( ) No prior knowledge

( ) Prior knowledge: Level of knowledge:

Some Knowledge			Medium Knowledge			Highly Knowledgeable
1	2	3	4	5	6	7

Appendix 8: Scree Test Results Experiment 2

Scree Plot of Eigenvalues

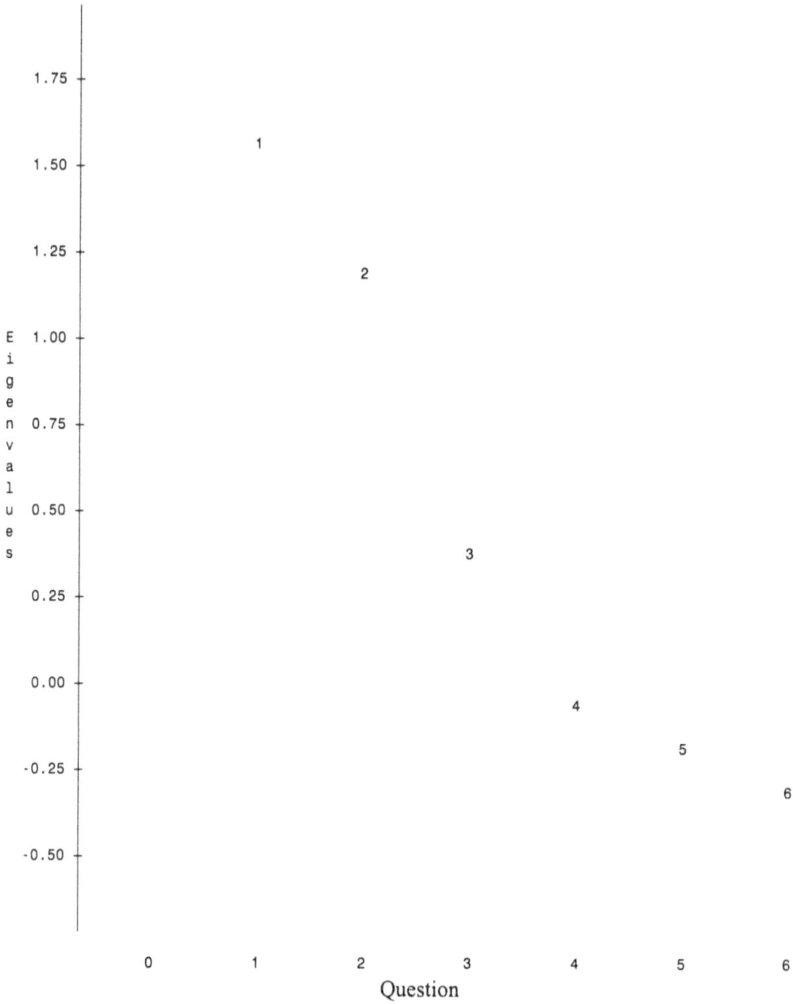

Appendix 9: Exploratory Factor Analysis Experiment 2

Factor 1			
Factor Pattern (>0.5)	**Scoring Coefficients**	**Question**	**New Factor**
0.58	0.24	What would you recommend that S&H performs (1) both the IT and TAX services, ( ) (2) only the IT service, ( ) (3) only the Tax service or ( ) (4) neither of these services? ( )	IT-Performance
0.76	0.48	The likelihood that S&H's independence could be impaired assuming S&H performs the IT service:	
0.59	0.3	The threat to audit independence from the IT service fees.	
Factor 2			
Factor Pattern (>0.5)	**Scoring Coefficients**	**Question**	**New Factor**
0.72	0.35	What would you recommend that S&H performs (1) both the IT and TAX services, ( ) (2) only the IT service, ( ) (3) only the Tax service or ( ) (4) neither of these services? ( )	Tax-Performance
0.74	0.42	The likelihood that S&H's independence could be impaired assuming S&H performs the Tax service:	
0.59	0.27	The threat to audit independence from the tax advisory service fees.	

Appendix 10: Research Instrument Experiment 3

THE IMPORTANCE OF TRANSPARENT POLICIES AND PROCEDURES

- AN INTERNATIONAL STUDY -

Dear Participant:

Thank you for participating in this study. The purpose of the study is to obtain your assessment of the importance of a transparency report that documents the policies and procedures an audit firm is carrying out to maintain auditor independence. We are especially interested in your views, so that regulators and the profession in general are informed concerning American practitioners' views on important issues such as auditor independence.

The use of such a transparency report is currently quite controversial. In the European Union one of the many discussions revolve around whether the report should be mandatory or voluntary. The discussion includes concerns over the details required and cost versus benefit implications.

With this study we want to provide evidence concerning:

1. whether a mandatory versus a voluntary transparency report would better serve as an overall framework to improve an audit firm's independence and
2. which of the proposed disclosures are viewed as being relatively more important?

We believe this study will be of interest to both the European Standard-setters and to the PCAOB. The study will only take around 5 to 10 minutes to complete.

YOUR PARTICIPATION IS VERY APPRECIATED!

Roberts & Partner

Roberts & Partner, LLP (R&P) is a large, British independent accounting firm. The firm was founded in 1923 and is headquartered in London. Including its affiliates in the USA, Europe and Asia, R&P employs over 6,000 people. The firm is primarily involved in financial statement audit services applying International Accounting Standards. Furthermore, R&P also performs non-audit services in order to maintain its competitiveness in the audit market.

As part of an ongoing quality control and improvement process, R&P is proactive in keeping up with the ever-changing *regulation* professional guidance. Assume that in the UK the *regulation* professional guidance include the *mandatory* voluntary publication of an annual transparency report on its own homepage to document the policies and procedures that R&P carries out to maintain auditor independence.

Furthermore, R&P has engaged two independent experts to review their policies and procedures. The final report of these experts is posted on R&P's homepage. R&P's transparency report contains the following:

1. a statement on the governance structure of the audit firm (Governance Structure);
2. a description of the internal quality control system of the audit firm and a statement by the administrative or management body on the effectiveness of its functioning (Internal Quality Control);
3. an indication of when the last quality assurance review took place (Quality Assurance);
4. a listing of public interest entities for which an audit has been carried out during the last year by the audit firm (Audited Entities);
5. a statement about the audit firm's independence practice which also confirms that an internal review of independence compliance has been conducted (Independence Practice and Compliance);
6. a statement on the policy followed by the audit firm concerning continuous education of auditors (Continuing Professional Education); and
7. financial information showing the importance of the audit firm such as the total turnover divided into fees from the audit of annual and consolidated accounts, and fees charged for other assurance services, tax advisory services and other non-audit services (Fee Information).

After having reviewed the policies and procedures as described in the transparency report, the two experts state the following: "Based on our review, no significant issues have come to our attention that would cause us to believe that R&P's policies and procedures to maintain auditor independence is not operating properly."

QUESTIONS

Based on the information about R&P, the *mandatory* voluntary transparency report *and the conclusion as stated by the reviewer*, please answer the following questions:

1. The policies and procedures listed in the transparency report are usually thought as being safeguards to auditor independence risk. What is your viewpoint on how these policies and procedures provide an overall framework to improve the firm's independence?

Not effective			Moderately Effective			Very effective
0	1	2	3	4	5	6

2. How important are each of the individual safeguards as related to each other? In other words, which of the safeguards might be more effective than the others? (see the prior page for complete descriptions of each safeguard):

	Not Important			Moderate important			Very important
1: Corporate Governance Structure	0	1	2	3	4	5	6
2: Internal Quality Control	0	1	2	3	4	5	6
3: Quality Assurance	0	1	2	3	4	5	6
4: Audited Entities	0	1	2	3	4	5	6

5: Independence Practice and Compliance	0	1	2	3	4	5	6
6: Continuing Professional Education	0	1	2	3	4	5	6
7: Fee Information	0	1	2	3	4	5	6

Please provide the following personal information:

Professional experience in years (auditing, accounting and/or finance):

____

Level of knowledge about Auditor Independence Regulation:

Little Knowledge (e.g. casual investor)			Moderate Knowledge			High Knowledge (e.g. CPA, Audit Committee Member)
0	1	2	3	4	5	6

Thank you again for participating in this study.

Appendix 11: Scree Test Results Experiment 3

Scree Plot of Eigenvalues

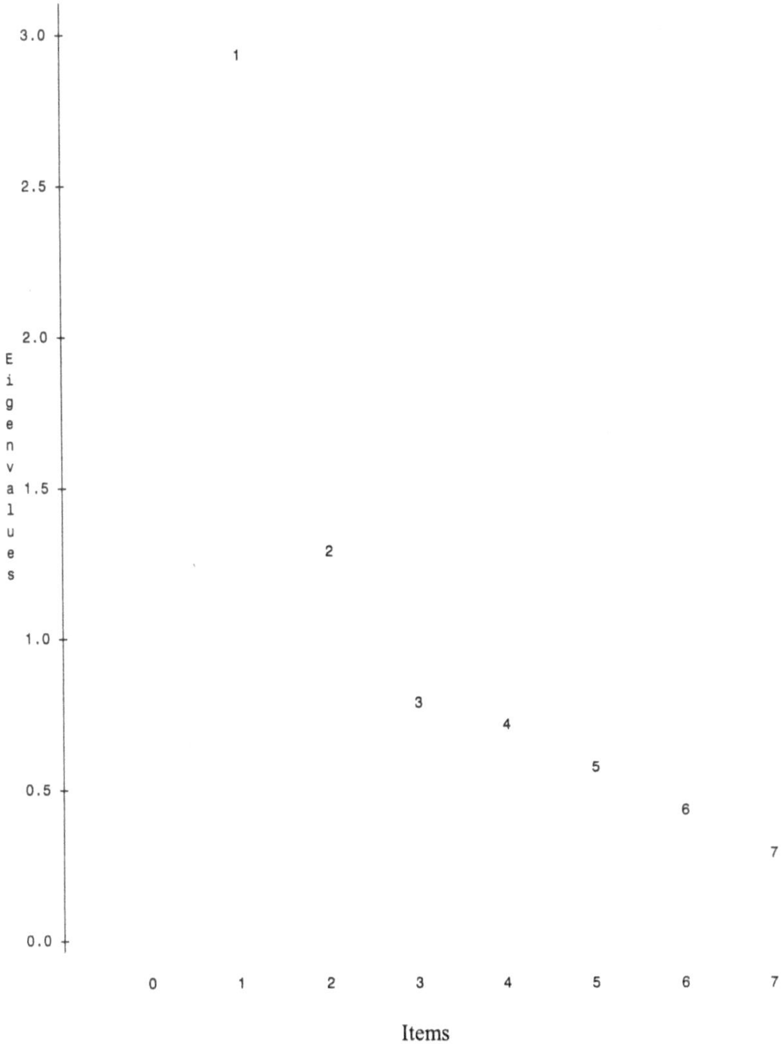

Appendix 12: Principal Component Analysis Experiment 3

Component 1			
Factor Pattern (>0.5)	**Scoring Coefficients**	**Items**	**New Component**
0.57	0.24	Corporate Governance Structure	Direct Safeguards
0.82	0.38	Internal Quality Control	
0.76	0.33	Quality Assurance	
0.74	0.37	Independence Practice and Compliance	
Component 2			
Factor Pattern (>0.5)	**Scoring Coefficients**	**Items**	**New Component**
0.81	0.5	Audited Entities	Indirect Safeguards
0.83	0.53	Fee Information	
0.59	0.28	Continuing Professional Education	

Bibliography

Abbott, L. J., Y. Park and S. Parker (2000). The Effects of Audit Committee Activity and Independence on Corporate Fraud. *Managerial Finance* 26 (11): 55-67.

Abdolmohammadi, M. J. (1999). A Comprehensive Taxonomy of Audit Task Structure, Professional Rank and Decisions Aids for Behavioral Research. *Behavioral Research in Accounting* 11: 51-92.

Abdolmohammadi, M. J. and A. Wright (1987). An Examination of the Effects of Experience and Task Complexity on Audit Judgments. *The Accounting Review* 62 (1): 1-13.

Abschlussprüferaufsichtsgesetz (2004). Gesetz zur Fortentwicklung der Berufsaufsicht über Abschlussprüfer in der Wirtschaftsprüferordnung (Abschlussprüferaufsichtsgesetz – APAG) vom 27. Dezember 2004 (BGBl. I 3846).

Ali, A. and L. Hwang (2000). Country-Specific Factors Related to Financial Reporting and the Value Relevance of Accounting Data. *Journal of Accounting Research* 38 (1): 1-21.

Anderson, J. (2000). *Cognitive Psychology and Its Implications*. 5th Edition. New York, Worth Publishers.

Antle, R. (1984). Auditor Independence. *Journal of Accounting Research* 22 (1): 1-20.

Antle, R. and B. Nalebuff (1991). Conservatism and Auditor-Client Negotiations. *Journal of Accounting Research* 29 (Supplement): 34-54.

Arnold, D. F., R. A. Bernardi and P. E. Niedermeyer (1999). The Effect of Independence on Decisions Concerning Additional Audit Work: A European Perspective. *Auditing: A Journal of Practice and Theory* 18 (Supplement): 45-67.

Ashbaugh, H., R. LaFond and B. W. Mayhew (2003). Do Nonaudit Services Compromise Auditor Independence? Further Evidence. The Accounting Review 78 (3): 611-639.

Association Française des Entreprises Privées (2002). Paris. Available at www.ecgi.org/codes/code.

Backhaus, K., H. Meffert, M. Bongartz and M. Eschweiler (2003). Selbst- und Fremdbild der Wirtschaftsprüfer - Empirische Befunde zur Positionierung des Wirtschaftsprüfers in der Öffentlichkeit. *Die Wirtschaftsprüfung* 56 (12): 625-637.

Baetge, J. and M. Lutter (2003). *Abschlussprüfung und Corporate Governance. Bericht des Arbeitskreises Abschlussprüfung und Corporate Governance.* Frankfurt am Main, Dr. Otto Schmidt.

Baker, C. R. and R. Quick (1996). A Comparison of Auditor's Legal Liability in the USA and Selected European Countries. *European Business Review* 96 (3): 36-44.

Baker, C. R., A. Mikol and R. Quick (2001). Regulation of the Statutory Auditor in the European Union: A Comparative Survey of the United Kingdom, France and Germany. *The European Accounting Review* 10 (4): 763-786.

Ball, R. (2001). Infrastructure Requirements for an Economically Efficient System of Public Financial Reporting and Disclosure. *Brooking-Wharton Papers on Financial Services*: 127-169.

Ballwieser, W. (2004). The Limitations of Financial Reporting. In *The Economics and Politics of Accounting*. Edited by C. Leuz, D. Pfaff and A. Hopwood. Oxford, Oxford University Press.

Bartlett, R. W. (1993). A Scale of Perceived Independence: New Evidence on an Old Concept. *Accounting, Auditing & Accountability Journal* 6 (2): 52-67.

Beattie, V., S. Fearnley and R. Brandt (1999). Perceptions of Auditor Independence: UK Evidence. *Journal of International Accounting, Auditing and Taxation* 8 (2): 67-107.

Beattie, V., S. Fearnley and R. Brandt (2004). A Grounded Theory Model of Auditor-Client Negotiations. *International Journal of Auditing* 8: 1-19.

Bender, C. and H. Vater (2003). Überlegungen zur Konzeption von Audit Committees in deutschen Unternehmen. *Kapitalmarktorientierte Rechnungslegung* 5 (11): 490-495.

Bilanzkontrollgesetz (2004). Gesetz zur Kontrolle von Unternehmensabschlüssen (Bilanzkontrollgesetz – BilKoG) vom 15. Dezember 2004 (BGBl. I 3408).

Bilanzrechtsreformgesetz (2004). Gesetz zur Einführung internationaler Rechnungslegungsstandards und zur Sicherung der Qualität der Abschlussprüfung (Bilanzrechtsreformgesetz – BilReG) vom 4. Dezember 2004 (BGBl. I 3166).

Black, B. (2000). The Core Institutions that Support Strong Securities Markets. *Business Lawyer* 55 (4): 1565-1607.

Bolkestein, F. (2003). Memorandum to the Commission on the Proposal for a Directive of the European Parliament and the Council on Statutory Audit in the EU. COM (2003) 284 final. Brussels. Available at www.europa.eu.int/comm/internal_market/auditing /docs/com-2004-177/com2004-177-memo_en.pdf.

Bonner, S. E. (1990). Experience Effects in Auditing: The Role of Task-Specific Knowledge. *The Accounting Review* 65 (1): 72-92.

Bonner, S. E. (1994). A Model of the Effects of Audit Task Complexity. *Accounting, Organizations and Society*: 213-234.

Bonner, S. E. (2005). *Judgment and Decision-Making in Accounting*. Upper Saddle River, Prentice Hall.

Bonner, S. E. and B. L. Lewis (1990). Determinants of Auditor Expertise. *Journal of Accounting Research* 28 (Supplement): 1-20.

Bonner, S. E. and P. L. Walker (1994). The Effects of Instruction and Experience on the Acquisition of Auditing Knowledge. *The Accounting Review* 69 (1): 157-178.

Boritz, J. E. (1986). The Effect of Research Method on Audit Planning and Review Judgments. *Journal of Accounting Research* 24 (2): 335-348.

Bormann, M. (2002). Unabhängigkeit des Abschlussprüfers: Aufgabe und Chance für den Berufsstand. *Betriebs-Berater* 57 (4): 190-197.

Brehmer, B. (1987). Note on Subjects' Hypotheses in Multiple-Cue Probability Learning. *Organizational Behavior and Human Decision Processes* 40 (3): 323-330.

Brewster, M. (2003). *How the Accounting Profession Forfeited a Public Trust.* Hoboken, Wiley.

Briloff, A. J. (1966). Old Myths and New Realities in Accountancy. *The Accounting Review* 41 (3): 484-495.

Bumiller, E. (2002). Bush Signs Bill Aimed at Fraud in Corporations. *New York Times*, 31 July: A 1

Burke, W. (1997). Auditor Independence: An Organizational Psychology Perspective. A Report Prepared on Behalf of the AICPA for Presentation to the Independence Standards Board of "Serving the Public Interest: A New Conceptual Framework for Auditor Independence." Available at www.aicpa.org/members/div/secps/isb/white .htm.

Bushman, R. M. and A. J. Smith (2001). Financial Accounting Information and Corporate Governance. *Journal of Accounting and Economics* 32: 237-333.

Campbell, D. J. (1988). Task Complexity: A Review and Analysis. *Academy of Management Review* 13 (1): 40-52.

Campbell, D. J. and D. M. Furrer (1995). Goal Setting and Competition as Determinants of Task Performance. *Journal of Organizational Behavior* 16 (4): 377-389.

Campbell, D. J. and K .F. Gingrich (1986). The Interactive Effects of Task Complexity and Participation on Task Performance: A Field Experiment. *Organizational Behavior and Human Decision Processes* 38 (2): 62-80.

Chang, C. J., J. L. Y. Ho and W. M. Liao (1997). The Effects of Justification and Experience / Training on Problem-Solving Performance. *Behavioral Research in Accounting* 9 (Supplement): 98-116.

Chung, H. and S. Kallapur (2003). Client Importance, Nonaudit Services, and Abnormal Accruals. *The Accounting Review* 78 (4): 931-955.

Coenenberg, A. G. and K.-U. Marten (1993). Der Wechsel des Abschlussprüfers. *Der Betrieb* 46 (3): 101-110.

Coenenberg, A. G., A. Haller and K.-U. Marten (1999). Accounting Education for Professionals in Germany – Current State and New Challenges. *Journal of Accounting Education* 17 (4): 367-390.

Coordinating Group on Audit and Accounting Issues (2003). Final Report to the Secretary of State for Trade and Industry and the Chancellor of the Exchequer. URN 03/567. London, Department of Trade and Industry.

Council of Economic and Finance Ministers (2005). Charlie McCreevy, Commissioner for Internal Market and Services, Welcomes the Agreement Reached in Council on the 8th Company Law Directive on Statutory Audit. IP/05/1249. Brussels, 11 October 2005. Available at www.europa.eu.int

Council of the European Communities (1978). Fourth Council Directive of 25 July 1978 on the Annual Accounts. Official Journal of the European Communities. 78/660/EEC. Brussels.

Council of the European Communities (1983). Seventh Council Directive of June 1983 on Consolidated Accounts. Official Journal of the European Communities. 83/349/EEC. Brussels.

Council of the European Communities (1984). Eight Council Directive of 10 April 1984 on the Approval of Persons Responsible for Carrying Out the Statutory Audits of Accounting Documents. Official Journal of the European Communities. 84/253/EEC. Brussels.

Craig, P. P. and C. DeBurca (2002). *EU Law*. Oxford, Oxford University Press.

Cuccia, A. D., K. Hackenbrack and M. W. Nelson (1995). The Ability of Professional Standards to Mitigate Aggressive Reporting. *The Accounting Review* 70 (2): 227-248.

Davis, L. R. and D. T. Simon (1992) Research Notes: The Impact of SEC Disciplinary Actions on Audit Fees. *Auditing: A Journal of Practice and Theory* 11 (1): 58-68

DeAngelo, L. (1981a). Auditor Independence, Low-Balling, and Disclosure Regulation. *Journal of Accounting and Economics* 3: 113-127.

DeAngelo, L. (1981b). Auditor Size and Audit Quality. *Journal of Accounting and Economics* 3: 183-199.

DeFond, M. L., K. Raghunandan and K. R. Subramanyan. (2002). Do Non-audit Service Fees Impair Auditor Independence? Evidence from Going Concern Opinions. *Journal of Accounting Research* 40 (4): 1247-1274.

Dopuch, N., R. King and R. Schwartz (2001). An Experimental Investigation of Retention and Rotation Requirements. *Journal of Accounting Research* 39 (1): 93-117.

Emerson, R. M. (1962). Power-Dependence Relations. *American Sociological Review* 27 (1): 31-41.

Emmerich, G. and W. Schaum (2003). Auswirkungen des Sarbanes-Oxley Act auf deutsche Abschlussprüfer - Berufsaufsicht, Registrierung, Unabhängigkeit. *Die Wirtschaftsprüfung* 56 (13): 677-691

European Commission (1995). Communication to the Council and the European Parliament on "Accounting Harmonization: a New Strategy vis-à-vis International Harmonization. COM 95 (508). Brussels. Available at www.europa.eu.in/comm/ internal_market/en.

European Commission (1996). Green Paper - The Role, the Position and the Liability of the Statutory Auditor within the European Union. COM (96) 338. Brussels. Available at www.europa.eu.int.

European Commission (2002). Commission Recommendation of 16 May 2002. Statutory Auditors' Independence in the EU: A Set of Fundamental Principles. 2002/590/EC. Brussels. Available at www.europa.eu.int.

European Commission (2004a). Proposal for a Directive of the European Parliament and of the Council on Statutory Audit of Annual Accountants and Consolidated Accounts and Amending Council Directives 78/660/EEC and 83/349/EEC. Brussels. Available at www.europa.eu.int.

European Commission (2004b). European Commission Proposal for a Directive on Statutory Audit: Frequently Asked Questions. Memo/04/60. Brussels. Available at www.europa.eu.int/rapid.

European Federation of Accountants (2001). The Conceptual Approach to Protecting Auditor Independence. Brussels. Available at www.fee.be/publications/main.htm.

European Federation of Accountants (2003). Discussion Paper European Co-ordination of Public Oversight. Brussels. Available at www.fee.be/publications/main.htm.

European Federation of Accountants (2004). FEE Position on the Proposed Audit Directive. Brussels. Available at www.fee.be/secretariat/Positionpaper.htm.

European Parliament (2005). 8th Company Law Directive on Statutory Audit - Vote in EP Plenary. 28 September 2005. Brussels. Available at www.europa.eu.int.

Ewert, R. (1989). Bilanzielle Publizität im Lichte der Theorie vom gesellschaftlichen Wert öffentlich verfügbarer Information. *Betriebswirtschaftliche Forschung und Praxis* 41 (3): 245-263.

Ewert, R. (1999). Abschlussprüfung, Dritthaftung und Prüfungsgrundsätze - Ergebnisse einer ökonomischen Analyse. *Betriebswirtschaftliche Forschung und Praxis* 51 (1): 94-108.

Ewert, R. (2004). Audit Regulation, Audit Quality, and Audit Research in the Post-Enron Era: An Analysis of Nonaudit Services. In *The Economics and Politics of Accounting*. Edited by C. Leuz, D. Pfaff and A. Hopwood. Oxford, University Press.

Farmer, T. A., L. E. Rittenberg and G. M. Trompeter (1987). An Investigation of the Impact of Economic and Organizational Factors on Auditor Independence. *Auditing: A Journal of Practice and Theory* 7 (1): 1-14.

Fearnley, S. and V. Beattie (2004). The Reform of the UK's Auditor Independence Framework after the Enron Collapse: An Example of Evidence-Based Policy Making. *International Journal of Auditing* 8: 117-138

Ferlings, J. and G. Lanfermann (2002). Unabhängigkeit von deutschen Abschlussprüfern nach Verabschiedung des Sarbanes-Oxley Acts. *Der Betrieb* 55 (41): 2117-2122.

Firth, M. (1980). Perceptions of Auditor Independence and Official Ethical Guidelines. *The Accounting Review* 55 (3): 451-466.

Frankel, R. M., M. F. Johnson and K. K. Nelson (2002). The Relation between Auditors' Fees for Nonaudit Services and Earnings Management. *The Accounting Review* 77 (Supplement): 71-105.

Frederick, D. and R. Libby (1986). Expertise and Auditors' Judgments of Conjunctive Events. *Journal of Accounting Research* 24 (2): 270-290.

French Commercial Code (1807). Commercial Code of September 15, 1807 Including Law Number. 2003-706 of 1 August 2003 Article 104 (II) Official Gazette of 2 August 2003. Le Journal Officiel: 13220. Also available at www.legifrance.gouv.fr.

French Conseil d'analyse économique (Council of Economic Analysis) (2003). Les Normes Comptables et le Monde Post-Enron. Paris, La Documentation française.

Gagne, R. M. (1964). Human Tasks and the Classification of Behavior. Paper Read at 10th Annual Seminar Series. Psychology in Management. Lafayette, Purdue University.

Geiger, M. A. and K. Raghunandan (2002). Auditor Tenure and Audit Reporting Failures. *Auditing: A Journal of Practice and Theory* 21 (1): 67-78.

German Chamber of Public Accountants (2004). Position of the German Chamber of Public Accountants to European Commission's Proposed 8th Directive. Berlin. Available at www.wpk.de/magazin/2-s004/.

German Corporate Governance Code (2002). Düsseldorf. Available at www.corporate-governance-code.de/#1.

Gibbins, M., S. Salterio and A. Webb (2001). Evidence about Auditor-Client Management Negotiation Concerning Client's Financial Reporting. *Journal of Accounting Research* 39 (3): 535-563.

Goldman, A. and B. Barlev (1974). The Auditor-Firm Conflict of Interests: Its Implications for Independence. *The Accounting Review* 49 (4): 707-718.

Gramling, A. A. (1999). External Auditors' Reliance on Work Performed by Internal Auditors: The Influence of Fee Pressure on this Reliance Decision. *Auditing: A Journal of Practice and Theory* 18 (Supplement): 117-135.

Grant Thornton (2004). Accounts and Transparency Report (June 2004). Available at www.grant-thornton.co.uk/pages/publications_and_events-publicationsaccounts-_and_transparency_report/$FILE/accounts+and+transparency+report.pdf.

Grant Thornton (2005). Transparency Report (May 2005). Available at www.gti.org/documents/GTIntTranspReviewFinal26May05.pdf.

Gul, F. (1989). Bankers' Perceptions of Factors Affecting Auditor Independence. *Accounting, Auditing & Accountability Journal* 2 (2): 40-51.

Hackenbrack, K. and M. W. Nelson (1996). Auditors' Incentives and Their Application of Financial Accounting Standards. *The Accounting Review* 71 (1): 43-59.

Hackman, J. R. (1969). Toward Understanding the Role of Tasks in Behavioral Research. *Acta Psychologica* 31: 97-128.

Hagemeister, C. (2002). Neue Anforderungen an die Unabhängigkeit durch IFAC und Europäische Kommission. *Der Betrieb* 55 (7): 333-340.

Handelsgesetzbuch (1897). In der Fassung der Bekanntmachung vom 10. Mai 1897 (RGBl. 219). Zulätzt geändert durch Artikel 1 G vom 3. August 2005 (BGBl. III 2267).

Hartley, R. and T. Ross (1972). MAS and Audit Independence: An Image Problem. *The Journal of Accountancy* 134 (5): 42-51.

Haynes, C. M., J. G. Jenkins and S. R. Nutt (1998). The Relationship between Client Advocacy and Audit Experience: An Exploratory Analysis. *Auditing: A Journal of Practice and Theory* 17 (2): 88-104.

Heininger, K. and K. Bertram (2004). Neue Anforderungen an Berufsaufsicht und Qualitätskontrolle durch das Abschlussprüferaufsichtsgesetz (APAG). *Der Betrieb* 57 (33): 1737-1741.

Helm, R., A. Mark and L.-J. Fischer (2003). Externe Qualitätskontrolle und Qualitätssignale in der Wirtschaftsprüfung - Eine empirische Evaluierung des Nutzens für Mandanten. *Die Wirtschaftsprüfung* 56 (23): 1301-1309.

Heppe, H. (2003a). Nach dem Vertrauensverlust - Ist es an der Zeit, die Dritthaftung deutscher Abschlussprüfer zu verschärfen? Teil (Part) I. *Zeitschrift für Wirtschafts- und Bankrecht* 57 (15): 714-724.

Heppe, H. (2003b). Nach dem Vertrauensverlust - Ist es an der Zeit, die Dritthaftung deutscher Abschlussprüfer zu verschärfen? Teil (Part) II. *Zeitschrift für Wirtschafts- und Bankrecht* 57 (16): 753-761

Herzig, N. and C. Watrin (1995). Obligatorische Rotation des Wirtschaftsprüfers - ein Weg zur Verbesserung der externen Unternehmenskontrolle? *Zeitschrift für betriebswirtschaftliche Forschung* 47 (8): 775-804.

Hilber, M. and J. Hartung (2003). Auswirkungen des Sarbanes-Oxley Act auf deutsche WP-Gesellschaften: Konflikte mit der Verschwiegenheitspflicht der Wirtschaftsprüfer und dem Datenschutzrecht. *Betriebs-Berater* 58 (20): 1054-1060.

Ho, J. L. and W. Rodgers (1993). A Review of Accounting Research on Cognitive Characteristics. *Journal of Accounting Literature* 12: 101-130.

Houghton, K. and K. Trotman (2003). *Review of KPMG Australia's Processed and Policies in Respect of Independence, Conflict Resolution and Quality Controls.* Available at www.kpmg.com.au/Portals/0/houghton_trotman_2003-11.pdf

Hussey, R. and G. Lan (2001). An Examination of Auditor Independence Issues from the Perspectives of UK Finance Directors. *Journal of Business Ethics* 32 (2): 169-178.

Imhoff, Jr., E. A. (1978). Employment Effects on Auditor Independence. *The Accounting Review* 53 (4): 869-881.

Independence Standards Board (2000a). Statement of Independence Concepts: A Conceptual Framework for Auditor Independence. Independence Standards Board. New York. Available at www.cpaindependence.org.

Independence Standards Board (2000b). Discussion Memorandum (DM 00-1) – A Conceptual Framework for Auditor Independence. New York. Available at www.cpaindependence.org

Institute of Certified Public Accountants in Germany and German Chamber of Public Accountants (2002). Stellungnahme zu dem Papier der EU Kommission 'Sarbanes-Oxley Act Overview and a Preliminary Analysis of Issues Applicable to Foreign Companies and Foreign Accounting Firms'. Available at www.idw.de.

Institute of Chartered Accountants in England and Wales (2003). Reviewing Auditor Independence. London. Available at www.ifac.org.

International Federation of Accountants (2001). IFAC Code of Ethics for Professional Accountants. New York, IFAC.

International Federation of Accountants (2004). Handbook of International Auditing, Assurance, and Ethics Pronouncements. New York, IFAC.

Iyer, V. M. and K. Raghunandan (2002). Auditors' Employment with Clients and Interaction with their Former CPA Firm. *Journal of Managerial Issues* 14 (4): 486-499.

Jamal, K., M. Maier and S. Sunder (2003). Evolution versus General Acceptance: A Comparative Study of E-commerce Privacy Disclosure in the US and the UK. *Working Paper*. University of Alberta, Iowa and Yale University.

Jensen, M. C. and W. H. Meckling (1976). Theory of the Firm: Managerial Behavior, Agency Costs and Ownership Structure. *Journal of Financial Economics* 3 (4): 305-306.

Jeter, D. C. and P. E. Shaw (1995). Solicitation and Auditor Reporting Decisions. *The Accounting Review* 70 (2): 293-315.

Johnstone K., M. Sutton and T. Warfield (2001). Antecedents and Consequences of Independence Risk: Framework for Analysis. *Accounting Horizons* 15 (1): 1-18.

Kadous, K., S. J. Kennedy and M. E. Peecher (2003). The Effect of Quality Assessment and Directional Goal Commitment on Auditors' Accpetance of Client-Preferred Accounting Methods. *The Accounting Review* 78 (3): 759-778.

Kaplan, S. E. and S. M. Whitecotton (2001). An Examination of Auditors' Reporting Intentions when another Auditor Is Offered Client Employment. *Auditing: A Journal of Practice and Theory* 20: 45-63.

Kerlinger, F. N. and H. B. Lee (2000). *Foundations of Behavioral Research*. 4th Edition. Orlando, Harcourt College Publishers.

Khurana, I. K. and K. K. Raman (2004). Litigation Risk and the Financial Reporting Credibility of Big 4 versus Non-Big 4 Audits: Evidence from Anglo American Countries. *The Accounting Review* 79 (2): 473-495.

Kinney, W. R., Z.-V. Palmrose, S. Scholz (2004). Auditor Independence, Non-Audit Services, and Restatements: Was the U.S. Government right? *Journal of Accounting Research* 42 (3): 561-588.

Klatzky, R. (1980). *Human Memory*. 2nd Edition. New York, W. H. Freeman and Company.

Klein, K.-G., W. Schaum and S. Tielmann (2003). Abschlussprüfung und Corporate Governance: Aktuelle Diskussionspapiere der FEE. *Die Wirtschaftsprüfung* 56 (20): 1100-1107.

Knapp, M. C. (1985). Audit Conflict: An Empirical Study of the Perceived Ability of Auditors to Resist Management Pressure. *The Accounting Review* 60 (2): 202-211.

Knapp, M. C. (1987). An Empirical Study of Audit Committee Support for Auditors Involved in Technical Disputes with Client Management. *The Accounting Review* 62 (3): 578-588.

Koh, H. C. and P. Mahathevan (1993). The Effects of Client Employment on Auditor Independence. *The British Accounting Review* 25 (3): 227-242.

Köhler, A. G. (2005). Audit Committees in Germany – Theoretical Reasoning and Empirical Evidence. *Schmalchenbach Business Review* 57 (3): 229-252.

KPMG (2005). KPMG's Transparency Report (March 2005). Available at www.us.kpmg.com/microsite/attachments/212-025-KPMG-International-Transparency-Report-5.pdf.

Krawczyk, K. (1994). The Influence of Tax Law Requirements and Organization of Client Facts on Professional Judgment. *Behavioral Reserach in Accounting* 6 (Supplement): 97-120.

La Porta, R., F. Lopez-de-Silanes, A. Shleifer and R. Vishny (2000). Investor Protection and Corporate Governance. *Journal of Financial Economics* 58: 3-27.

Lanfermann, G. and S. Maul (2003). Registrierung von deutschen Abschlussprüfern bei der neuen US-Berufsaufsicht PCAOB. *Der Betrieb* 56 (23): 1237-1239.

Lavin, D. (1976). Perceptions of the Independence Auditor. *The Accounting Review* 51 (1): 41-50.

Lenz , H. (2002). Sarbanes-Oxley Act of 2002 - Abschied von der Selbstregulierung der Wirtschaftsprüfer in den USA. *Betriebs-Berater* 57 (44): 2270-2275.

Libby, R. (1985). Availability and the Generation of Hypotheses in Analytical Review. *Journal of Accounting Research* 23 (2): 648-667.

Libby, R. and W. R. Kinney (2000). Does Mandated Audit Communication Reduce Opportunistic Corrections to Manage Earnings to Forecast? *The Accounting Review* 75 (4): 383-404.

Lord, A. T, N. Dopuch and M. Gibbins. (1992). Pressure: A Methodological Consideration for Behavioral Research in Auditing. *Auditing: A Journal of Practice and Theory* 11 (2): 89-108.

Love, I. (2000). Financial Development and Financing Constraints: International Evidence from a Structural Investment Model. *The Review of Financial Studies* 16 (3): 765-791.

Lowe, D. J., M. A. Geiger and K. Pany (1999). The Effects of Internal Audit Outsourcing on Preceived External Auditor Independence. *Auditing: A Journal of Practice and Theory* 18 (Supplement): 7-26.

Ludewig, R. (2003). Zur Berufsethik der Wirtschaftsprüfer. *Die Wirtschaftsprüfung* 56 (20): 1093-1099.

Magee, R. and M. Tseng (1990). Audit Pricing and Independence. *The Accounting Review* 65 (2): 315-336.

Maher, M. W., P. Tiessen, R. Colson and A. J. Broman (1992). Competition and Audit Fees. *The Accounting Review* 67 (1): 199-211.

Mandler, U. (2003). Enforcement und Unabhängigkeit des Abschlussprüfers: Ergebnisse einer Professorenbefragung. *Kapitalmarktorientierte Rechnungslegung* 5 (7/8): 343-349.

Markman, A. (1999). *Knowledge Representation*. Mahwah, Lawrence Erlbaum Associates.

Marten, K.-U. (1995). Empirische Analyse des Prüferwechsels im Kontext der Agency- und Signalling-Theorie. *Zeitschrift für Betriebswirtschaft* 65 (7): 703-727.

Marten, K.-U. , A. G. Köhler and S. Meyer (2003). Umbruch im Peer-Review-System - Deutscher Status Quo und der Sarbanes-Oxley Act of 2002. *Die Wirtschaftsprüfung* 56 (1/2): 10-17

Marten. K.-U. (1999). Externe Qualitätskontrolle im Berufsstand der Wirtschaftsprüfer. *Der Betrieb* 52 (21): 1073-1076.

McKinley, S., K. Pany and P. M. J. Reckers (1985). An Examination of the Influence of CPA Firm Type, Size, and MAS Provision on Loan Officer Decisions and Perceptions. *Journal of Accounting Research* 23 (2): 52-57.

Messier, W. F., Jr. (1983). The Effect of Experience and Firm Type on Materiality/Disclosure Judgments. *Journal of Accounting Research* 21 (2): 611-618.

Miller, R. B. (1962). Task Description and Analysis. In *Psychological Principles in System Development*. Edited by R. M. Gagne. New York, Holt.

Milliron, V. C. (1995). A Behavioral Study of the Meaning and Influence of Tax Complexity. *Journal of Accounting Research* 23 (2): 794-816.

Mock, T. J., R. P. Srivastava and J. L. Turner (2005). A Model for Assessing the Risk of Impaired Auditor Independence. *Working Paper*. University of Southern California.

Myers, J. N., L. A. Myers and T. C. Omer (2003). Exploring the Term of the Auditor-Client Relationship and the Quality of Earnings: A Case for Mandatory Auditor Rotation? *The Accounting Review* 78 (3): 779-799.

Nelson, M. W. (2003). Behavioral Evidence on the Effects of Principles- and Rules-Based Standards. *Accounting Horizons* 17 (1): 91-104.

Nelson, M. W., J. A. Elliott and R. L. Tarpley (2002). Evidence from Auditors about Managers' and Auditors' Earnings Management Decisions. *The Accounting Review* 77 (Supplement): 175-202.

Newman, D. P., E. R. Patterson and J. R. Smith (2005). The Role of Auditing in Investor Protection. *The Accounting Review* 80 (1): 289-313.

Niehus, R. (2003). Turnusmäßiger Wechsel des Abschlussprüfers. *Der Betrieb* 56 (31): 1637-1643.

Oser, P., C. Orth and D. Wader (2003). Die Umsetzung des Deutschen Corporate Governance Kodex in der Praxis. *Der Betrieb* 56 (25): 1337-1341.

Palmrose, Z. V. (1986). The Effect of Nonaudit Services on the Pricing of Audit Services: Further Evidence. *Journal of Accounting Research* 24 (2): 405-411.

Pany, K. and P. M. J. Reckers (1980). The Effect of Gifts, Discounts and Client Size on Perceived Auditor Independence. *The Accounting Review* 55 (1): 50-61.

Pany, K. and P. M. J. Reckers (1983). Auditor Independence and Nonaudit Services. *Journal of Accounting and Public Policy* 2 (1): 43-62.

Payne, J. W., J. R. Bettman, E. J. Johnson (1990). The Adaptive Decision Maker: Effort and Accuracy in Choice. In *Insights in Decision Making*. Edited by R. Holgarth. Chicagi, University of Chicago Press.

Pearson, M. A. and J. K. Ryan (1982). Perception of an Auditor-Management Conflict. *Review of Business and Economic Research* 17 (2): 1-10.

Pellens, B., K. Detert, U. Nölte and T. Sellhorn (2004). Enforcement von Rechnungslegung. *Kapitalmarktorientierte Rechnungslegung* 6 (1): 1-4

Piot, C. (2005). Auditor Reputation and Model of Governance: A Comparison of France, Germany and Canada. *International Journal of Auditing* 9: 21-44.

Plumlee, M. A. (2003). The Effect of Information Complexity on Analysts' Use of that Information. *The Accounting Review* 78 (1): 275-296.

Pratt, J. and J. D. Stive (1994). The Effects of Client Characteristics on Auditor Litigation Risk Judgments, Required Audit Evidence and Recommended Audit Fees. *The Accounting Review* 69 (4): 639-656.

Prawitt, D. F. (1995). Staffing Assignments for Judgment-oriented Audit Tasks: The Effects of Structured Audit Technology and Environment. *The Accounting Review* 70 (3): 443-465.

Rajan, R. and L. Zingales (1998). Financial Dependence and Growth. *American Economic Review* 88 (3): 559-586.

Regelin, F. P. and R. Fisher (2003). Zum Stand der Umsetzung des Sarbanes-Oxley Act aus deutscher Sicht. *Internationales Steuerrecht* 12 (8): 276-288.

Reynolds, J. K. and J. R. Francis (2001). Does Size matter? The Influence of Accounting and Economics on Office-Level Auditor Reporting Decisions. *Journal of Accounting and Economics* 30 (3): 375-400.

Reynolds, J. K., D. R. Deis and J. R. Francis (2004). Professional Service Fees and Auditor Objectivity. *Auditing: A Journal of Practice and Theory* 23 (1): 29-52.

Roby, T. B. and J. T. Lanzetta (1958). Considerations in the Analysis of Group Tasks. *Psychological Bulletin* 55 (1): 88-101.

Salterio, S. and L. Koonce (1997). The Persuasiveness of Audit Evidence: The Case of Accounting Policy Decisions. *Accounting, Orgnizations and Society* 22 (6): 573-587.

Sarbanes-Oxley Act (2002). One Hundred Seventh Congress of the United States of America. Second Session. Available at http://news.findlaw.com/hdocs/docs/gwbush-/sarbanesoxley072302.pdf.

Satzung der Wirtschaftsprüferkammer (1996). Satzung der Wirtschaftsprüferkammer über die Rechte und Pflichten bei der Ausübung der Berufe des Wirtschaftsprüfers und des vereidigten Buchprüfers vom 11. Juni 1996 (BAnz. 7509). Zuletzt geändert am 2. März 2005 (BAnz. 5).

Scheiner, J. H. and J. E. Kiger (1982). An Empirical Investigation of Auditor Involvement in Non-Audit Services. *Journal of Accounting Research* 20 (2): 482-496.

Schmidt, S. (2003). Neue Anforderungen an die Unabhängigkeit des Abschlussprüfers: SEC-Verordnungen im Vergleich mit den Empfehlungen des EU-Kommission und den Plänen der Bundesregierung. *Betriebs-Berater* 58 (15): 779-786.

Schultz, J. and S. Gustavson (1978). Actuaries' Perceptions of Variables Affecting the Independent Auditor's Legal Liability. *The Accounting Review* 53 (3): 626-641.

Schwartz, R. (1997). Legal Regimes, Audit Quality and Investment. *The Accounting Review* 72 (3): 385-406.

Schwarz, G. C. and B. Holland (2002). Enron, WorldCom ... und die Corporate-Governance-Diskussion. *Zeitschrift für Wirtschaftsrecht* 23 (37): 1661-1672.

Securities and Exchange Commission (1934). Securities Exchange Act of 1934. Washington. Available at www.sec.gov/divisions/corpfin/34act/index1934.shtml.

Securities and Exchange Commission (2001). Final Rule: Revision on the Commission's Auditor Independence Requirements. 17 CFR Parts 210 and 240. File No. S7-13-00. Washington, Government Printing Office.

Shafer, W. E., R. E. Morris and A. A. Ketchand (1999). The Effect of Formal Sanctions on Auditor Independence. *Auditing: A Journal of Practice and Theory* 18 (Supplement): 85-95.

Shockley, R. A. (1981). Perceptions of Auditors' Independence: An Empirical Analysis. *The Accounting Review* 56 (4): 785-800.

Simnett, R. and K. Trotman (1989). Auditor versus Model: Information Choice and Information Processing. *Accounting Review* 64 (3): 514-528.

Simunic, D. A. (1980). The Pricing of Audit Services: Theory and Evidence. *Journal of Accounting Research* 18 (1): 161-190.

Simunic, D. A. and M. T. Stein (1996). The Impact of Litigation Risk on Audit Pricing: A Review of Economics and the Evidence. *Auditing: A Journal of Practice and Theory* 15 (Supplement): 119-134.

Smith Report (2003). Report on Audit Committees. London. Available at www.asb.org.uk.

Smith, G. F. (1988). Towards a Heuristics Theory of Problem Structuring. *Management Science* 34 (12): 1489-1506.

St. Pierre, K. and J. Anderson (1984). An Analysis of Factors Associated with Lawsuit Against Public Accountants. *The Accounting Review* 59 (2): 242-263.

Swanger, S. L. and E. G. Chewning (2001). The Effect of Internal Audit Outsourcing on Financial Analysts' Perceptions of External Auditor Independence. *Auditing: A Journal of Practice and Theory* 20 (2): 115-129.

Tan, H.-T., T. B.-P Ng and B. W.-Y. Mak (2002). The Effects of Task Complexity on Auditors' Performance: The Impact of Accountability and Knowledge. *Auditing: A Journal of Practice and Theory* 21 (2): 81-95.

Teoh, H. Y. and C. C. Lim (1996). An Empirical Study of the Effects of Audit Committees, Disclosure of Nonaudit Fees, and Other Issues on Audit Independence: Malaysian Evidence. *Journal of International Accounting, Auditing and Taxation* 5 (2): 231-248.

Trompeter, G. (1994). The Effect of Partner Compensation Schemes and Generally Accepted Accounting Principles on Auditor Judgment. *Auditing: A Journal of Practice and Theory* 13 (2): 56-68.

United Kingdom Department of Trade and Industry (2005). UK Government Response to the Consultation Process and Updated Regulatory Impact Assessment. London. Available at www.dti.gov.uk/consultations/files/publication-1453.pdf.

Universita Bocconi (2002). The Impact of Manadatory Audit Rotation on Audit Quality and on Audit Pricing: The Case of Italy. SDA Universita Bocconi. Corporate Finance and Real Estate Department and Administration and Control Department. Milano. Available at https://www.uni-bocconi.it.

Veltins, M. A. (2004). Verschärfte Unabhängigkeitsanforderungen an Abschluss-prüfer. *Der Betrieb* 57 (9): 445-452

Wallman, S. M. H. (1996). The Future of Accounting, Part III: Realibility and Auditor Independence. *Accounting Horizons* 10 (1): 76-97.

Watrin, C. (2001). *Internationale Rechnungslegung und Regulierungstheorie.* Wiesbaden, Deutscher Universitäts-Verlag.

Watrin, C., E. Sievert and C. Strohm (2004). Reform der Konzernbesteuerung in Deutschland und Europa. *Finanzrundschau* 87 (1): 1-12.

Wertpapierhandelsgesetz (1998). In der Fassung der Bekanntmachung vom 9. Spetember 1998 (BGBl I 2708). Zuletzt geändert durch Artikel 10a des Gesetzes vom 22. Mai 2005 (BGBl I 1373).

Wilken-Braun, K. (2001) The Disposition of Audit Detected Misstatements: An Examination of Risk and Reward Factors and Aggregation Effects. *Contemporary Accounting Research* 18 (1): 71-99.

Wirtschaftsprüferordnung (1961). Gesetz über eine Berufsordnung der Wirtschaftsprüfer vom 24. Juli 1961 (BGBl. I 1049). Zuletzt geändert durch das Gesetz zur Fortentwicklung der Berufsaufsicht über Abschlussprüfer in der Wirtschaftsprüfer-ordnung vom 27. Dezember 2004 (BGBl. I 3846).

Wood, R. E. (1986). Task Complexity: Definition of the Construct. *Organizational Behavior and Human Decision Process* 37: 59-82.

Wood, R. E. (1996). Global Audit Characteristics Across Cultures and Environment: An Empirical Examination. *Journal of International Accounting, Auditing and Taxation* 5 (2): 215-229.

Wright, A. and S. Wright (1997). An Examination of Factors Affecting the Decision to Waive Audit Adjustments. *Journal of Accounting, Auditing and Finance* 12 (1): 15-36.

Wüstemann, J. (2001). Mängel bei der Abschlussprüfung: Tatsachenberichte und Analysen aus betriebswirtschaftlicher Sicht. In *Der Wirtschaftsprüfer als Element der Corporate Governance*. Edited by M. Lutter. Düsseldorf, IDW Verlag.

Zeff, S. A. (2003a). How the U.S. Accounting Profession Got Where It Is Today: Part I. *Accounting Horizons* 17 (3): 189-205.

Zeff, S. A. (2003b). How the U.S. Accounting Profession Got Where It Is Today: Part II. *Accounting Horizons* 17 (4): 267-286.

FSC
www.fsc.org
MIX
Papier | Fördert gute Waldnutzung
FSC® C083411

Kolibri 360 GmbH
Ferdinand-Jühlke-Straße 7
99095 Erfurt, Deutschland
produktsicherheit@kolibri360.de